JOURNAL FOR THE STUDY OF THE NEW TESTAMENT SUPPLEMENT SERIES
156

Sheffield Academic Press

The Metaphor of Slavery in the Writings of the Early Church

From the New Testament to the Beginning of the Fifth Century

I.A.H. Combes

Journal for the Study of the New Testament
Supplement Series 156

To Christopher

Copyright © 1998 Sheffield Academic Press

Published by
Sheffield Academic Press Ltd
Mansion House
19 Kingfield Road
Sheffield S11 9AS
England

Typeset by Sheffield Academic Press
and
Printed on acid-free paper in Great Britain
by Bookcraft Ltd
Midsomer Norton, Bath

British Library Cataloguing in Publication Data

A catalogue record for this book is available
from the British Library

ISBN 1-85075-846-8

CONTENTS

ACKNOWLEDGMENTS

This book is a revised and updated version of my doctoral dissertation which was accepted by the University of Cambridge in 1991.

During my time as a graduate student, I was supervised by Dr Lionel Wickham, Dr Catherine Osborne, Dr Andrew Lenox-Conyngham and the late Dr Caroline Bammel. I am grateful to them all, but especially to Dr Caroline Bammel who gave me such vital help in drawing the work together.

Professor Peter Garnsey kindly read the dissertation prior to its revision and gave me much valuable advice. Professor Stanley E. Porter read the chapter on Paul and I am very grateful for his insights and assistance.

Lastly I would like to thank Dr Petà Dunstan and Professor James Lesher for so many years of friendship and encouragement.

ABBREVIATIONS

AC	*L'Antiquité Classique*
AJOS	*American Journal of Oriental Studies*
AJP	*American Journal of Philology*
ARS	*Annual Review of Sociology*
Bib	*Biblica*
BPat	*Biblia Patristica*
BQ	*Baptist Quarterly*
BZ	*Biblische Zeitschrift*
CA	Classical Antiquity
CBQ	*Catholic Biblical Quarterly*
CCL	*Corpus Christianorum Series Latina*
CIG	*Corpus inscriptionum graecarum*
CJ	*Codex Justinianus*
CRINT	Compendia rerum iudaicarum ad Novum Testamentum
CTh	*Codex Theodosianus*
GCS	Griechische christliche Schriftsteller
HeyJ	*Heythrop Journal*
HPT	*History of Political Thought*
HR	*History of Religions*
HTR	*Harvard Theological Review*
IPCQ	*Interchange: Papers and Current Questions*
IS	*International Sociology*
JBL	*Journal of Biblical Literature*
JBR	*Journal of Biblical Research*
JECS	*Journal of Early Christian Studies*
JHI	*Journal for the History of Ideas*
JJP	*Journal of Juristic Papyrology*
JNES	*Journal of Near Eastern Studies*
JR	*Journal of Religion*
JRH	*Journal of Religious History*
JRS	*Journal of Roman Studies*
JSNTSup	*Journal for the Study of the New Testament*, Supplement Series
JTS	*Journal of Theological Studies*
KTR	*King's Theology Review*
LCL	Loeb Classical Library

MS	*Milltown Studies*
NTS	*New Testament Studies*
PG	J.-P. Migne (ed.), *Patrologia cursus completa... Series graeca* (166 vols.; Paris; Petit-Montrouge, 1857–83)
PL	J.-P. Migne (ed.), *Patrologia cursus completus... Series prima [latina]* {221 vols.; Paris: J.-P. Migne, 1844–65)
ResQ	*Restoration Quarterly*
RIDA	*Revue Internationale des droits de l'antiquité*
RQ	*Römische Quartalschrift für christliche Alterturnskunde und Kirchengeschichte*
SBL	Society of Biblical Literature
SBLDS	SBL Dissertation Series
SBLTT	SBL Texts and Translations
SC	Sources chrétiennes
SCH	*Studies in Church History*
SecCent	*Second Century*
SJT	*Scottish Journal of Theology*
SNTSMS	Society for New Testament Studies Monograph Series
SS	*Science and Society*
StudLit	*Studia Liturgica*
StudPat	*Studia Patristica*
SVF	*Stoicorum Veterum Fragmenta*, ed. J. von Arnim
TDNT	Gerhard Kittel and Gerhard Friedrich (eds.), *Theological Dictionary of the New Testament* (trans. Geoffrey W. Bromiley; 10 vols.; Grand Rapids: Eerdmans, 1964–)
TQ	*Theologische Quartalschrift*
TS	*Theological Studies*
TU	Texte und Untersuchungen
WBC	Word Biblical Commentary
ZNW	*Zeitschrift für die neutestamentliche Wissenschaft*
ZRG	*Zeitschrift der Savigny-Stiftung für Rechtgeschichte (Romanische Abteilung)*

INTRODUCTION

1. *The Problem of Religious Metaphor*

Metaphors are dangerous things. In the language of ideology and religion they are indispensable, providing the vehicle whereby the inexpressible, the incomprehensible and the intangible may be grasped and made visible. Without them the preacher and the politician would be equally tongue-tied. However, not only does their great emotional potential make them susceptible to abuse, but their very nature means that they are all too easily misunderstood and misapplied. More than almost any other form of language, they require interpretation by the receiver, and in the space, chronological, physical or psychological, that intervenes between the original user and the receiver of the metaphor, there can arise almost infinite opportunity for misunderstanding.[1]

This is especially so in the context of religious language, where metaphors designed to convey convictions about principles of the faith are handed down across time and culture, and, because of this, run the risk of ceasing to bear the same relevance, or indeed any relevance at all, to the cultural context in which they are used. In some cases they may even lose their obvious identity as metaphors, and become confused with literal truths. There are times when the confusion may become so great that the user loses all sight of the fact that he or she is speaking in metaphors, and draws conclusions—some of them central to his or her perception of the world—based on words which were never meant to be more than approximate, or whose implications have changed since the metaphor was first used.

The area in which this problem probably causes the most consternation today is that of the use of 'social relationship' terms in speaking of God. Many of the names which have been used for this purpose—

---

1.   'Understanding a metaphor is as much a creative endeavor as making a metaphor and as little guided by rules', D. Davidson, 'What Metaphors Mean', in A.P. Martinich (ed.), *The Philosophy of Language* (Oxford: Oxford University Press, 1985), pp. 438-49.

Father, Master, Mother, Judge, Bridegroom and so on—involve the imposition of a human social structure onto the believer's perception of the divine. Since such names, therefore, have their roots in a certain cultural context, what, we must ask, becomes of them when this context is altered, and such relationships change or simply become obsolete? In other words, does religion speak of the divine in the language of its time, or do its metaphors develop a life of their own such that they stand apart from the shifting sands of time and society—unaffected by the change or death of the institutions from which they arose? Much ink is spilled these days over the problems of calling God 'Father' in a society that rebels against male domination, 'Master' in a non slave-owning society, or 'King' or 'Lord' in a democratic one. This is a problem, let it be stressed, not only in the transmission of traditional religious literature and liturgy, but also in the production of the new. Put simply, is it acceptable to go on using apparently obsolete metaphors in these cases, or must religious language be expected to adapt itself to the changing structure of its time?

On one level this is a philosophical and theological question, best left to those whose expertise is in these areas.[2] Nevertheless, there is also a place here for the historian. Before one can decide upon appropriate methodologies for the adaptation or preservation of religious language, it is useful to have an idea of how such language has developed in the past and of the forces which have impelled it to do so.

In his *Deity and Domination*, D. Nicholls argues that 'concepts and images of God' have often 'to some degree echoed, or at times heralded, changes in the social structure and dynamics (in the economic, political and cultural life) of given communities' and asserts that 'a people's image of God affects political behaviour and conceptions of civil authority influence religious behaviour'.[3] But does language used of God always bear such a clearly definable relationship with the social dynamics of its time? I would argue that this cannot always be taken for granted, either when considering the nature and history of religious

---

2.   See, for example, N. Lash, *Theology on the Way to Emmaus* (London: SCM Press, 1986) or D.E. Nineham, *The Use and Abuse of the Bible: A Study of the Bible in an Age of Rapid Cultural Change* (London: Macmillan, 1976), esp. 'Introduction: Cultural Change and Cultural Relativism', pp. 1-39.

3.   D. Nicholls, *Deity and Domination: Images of God and the State in the Nineteenth and Twentieth Centuries* (London: Routledge & Kegan Paul, 1989), p. 2.

metaphor or when planning its future. The plan of the following work is, therefore, to look at a part of the history of a particular metaphor over a specific time in order to discover the forces and conditions that shaped it.

The metaphor addressed is that of slavery—the idea of a human being as the slave of God. The period of its history which will be taken is that between the New Testament and the beginning of the fifth century. The metaphor of slavery is a social metaphor, one that describes a particular relationship between one person and another, a relationship which was, for the most part, taken for granted in antiquity. The transference of this relationship to the spiritual plane, to the idea of an individual as a slave of (a) god is almost as old as the institution of slavery itself, and metaphors based on this have been used with a variety of implications and most frequently in the cultures of the ancient Near East and in the writings of the Old Testament. The metaphor found its way into the New Testament where it was joined by the variation *slave of Christ*, and it is at this point that I shall take up its history.

It is no longer generally accepted that early Christianity was exclusively, or even predominantly, the religion of slaves and the very poor. On the contrary, it numbered within its congregations members from many ranks of society.[4] Nevertheless it is also the case that a substantial number of Christians came from the slave and freedman classes.[5] In such circumstances, the use of the language of slavery and of

4.   'Closer analysis of the available material shows that even from the earliest stages...converts included—indeed depended on—people of substance', A. Cameron, *Christianity and the Rhetoric of Empire* (Berkeley: University of California Press, 1991), p. 37. See also A.J. Malherbe, *Social Aspects of Early Christianity* (Baton Rouge: Louisiana State University Press, 1977), pp. 29-59; W.A. Meeks, *The First Urban Christians: The Social World of the Apostle Paul* (Newhaven: Yale University Press, 1990), pp. 51-73, and G. Theissen, *The Social Setting of Pauline Christianity* (ed. and trans. J.H. Schutz; Edinburgh: T. & T. Clark, 1982), pp. 69-120, on the social makeup of early Christian communities. There are those, however, who still maintain that Christianity was originally the faith of what Evans-Grubbs calls 'the socially insignificant' although, as Evans-Grubbs goes on to say, it very soon became 'predominantly a religion of the urban "upwardly mobile" middle and lower middle classes' (J. Evans-Grubbs, *Law and the Family in Late Antiquity: The Emperor Constantine's Marriage Legislation* [Oxford: Clarendon Press, 1995], p. 8).

5.   K. Aland, *A History of Christianity* (2 vols.; trans. J.L. Schaff; Philadelphia: Fortress Press, 1985), I, pp. 7-8. See also pp. 56-57.

apparently self-abasing terminology seems unsurprising given the slave origins of some Christians, the emphasis on solidarity between the rich and poor, the threat of persecution and the fact that Christianity began life as an obscure rural cult following a messiah who had died the death of a slave. Within only a few centuries, however, this cult had become the recognized creed of state and emperor, with vast funds and congregations at its disposal, and while it continued to draw a very large proportion of its membership from the lower classes, it was represented in literature and letters by cultured, educated and, in some cases, politically powerful and influential men. The same period, moreover, saw many changes in the nature of slavery and, in rural areas, the beginning of its evolution into serfdom. In such a climate, it is an altogether different thing to go on using such language. If the use of such metaphors is dictated by the social environment of the user, some change or loss of this language correlating to these changes would be expected. In fact little superficial change of this kind can be found. To explain this, one must seek to understand the meaning and dynamics of this kind of language.

In order to do so, I will begin by looking at the background of the metaphor of slavery, first at slavery as an institution in the ancient world and within the Early Church, and secondly at the early uses of metaphors of slavery in a religious and philosophical context. From here I will go on to look at the history of the metaphor of slavery within the Christian Church, from the New Testament onwards, considering the various forms into which it evolved and the different contexts into which it was fitted.

Such an examination will show that although there is in this case an obvious influence that proceeds from the social sphere—for the social structure of the time provides the images of which the metaphor is made—it should by no means be taken for granted that this also dictates the terms in which the relationship to God is perceived. Although the earlier texts speak of humans as the slaves of God, it is clear that there is more to such language in the Christian context than a simple perception of the relationship between the individual and God as identical, or even similar, to the relationship between a master and slave. The image of God presented by Christian teaching has in this context, as I shall argue, less to do with images of secular and political authority than with the direction of Christian theology, that is, with the issues that are at the centre of the Christian consciousness at the time when such language is employed. As Christian theology develops and grows in understanding of or interest in particular areas of faith, so also its language and imagery must adapt in order to remain a useful vehicle of explanation. Because the metaphor pivots therefore not on the nature of secular authority but on the nature of the Christian kerygma, it is changes in the latter more than changes in the former that dictate the lifespan and nature of the metaphor. Thus, while the metaphor proceeds from, and works against, the background of the realities of secular slavery, the theology which makes sense of the use of such a metaphor creates its own dynamic which results in this metaphor unfolding at a completely different pace from any discernible change in the relevant culture.

If this is so, then no one theory is sufficient to provide a proper understanding of the nature of religious metaphor, and each term will have to be taken on its own merits to discover the internal and external forces that moulded it.

2. *Method and Limitations*

This study will, as mentioned above, begin with the institution that gave rise to the metaphor, and examine the role of slavery itself as a social phenomenon. While an in-depth study of the daily realities of ancient slavery would be both impractical and, given the quantity and quality of research which already exists on the subject, superfluous, I will examine some of the more important aspects of slavery in the Graeco-Roman and Old Testament worlds. I will then go on to examine the use of metaphors relating to slavery in the religious and philosophical thought of that time, considering the history and nature of this metaphor outside the context of Christianity.

As the third part of this background study, I shall turn to the situation of slaves in the Early Church. In this context, I shall be considering not only the participation of slaves within the Christian congregations, but also the treatment of slavery as a secular institution by the early Christians and their view of its origins and morality.

I shall begin the examination of the metaphor in the Christian context by discussing the use of the metaphor in its various forms in the New Testament, distinguishing between the use of the metaphor in the Synoptic Gospels, the Gospel of John and the Pauline Epistles and going on to focus especially on the very extensive and complex use of the metaphor in the Pauline writings and the important part which, I believe, this plays in the expression of Pauline theology. From this I shall go on to the use of this metaphor in the patristic period, dividing the evidence, for the sake of clarity, into three broad categories: *Doctrine*, which will cover the patristic use of the metaphor as a theological tool, that is, to describe the relationship of various individuals to God, or to clarify details about conversion and the Christian life; *Liturgy*, which will concern the use of the metaphor as a liturgical tool, in the context of prayer and the ceremonies of baptism, and *Exegesis*, which will cover some examples of the approach taken by patristic writers when confronted with uses of the metaphor in the New Testament. By means of this I shall show that the use of the metaphor in this period tends to take a number of different forms which can be used for different purposes and in a variety of contexts. This will be demonstrated further by an examination of various texts chosen to illustrate the various trends in the development of the metaphor. Finally I shall consider the changes in the metaphor which this study shows, the reasons for them and their implications.

With the vast corpus of patristic literature that is available to modern research, the first great problem in a study such as this is where to begin, and the second is where to draw the line—for if we are to consider the relationship between the Christian metaphor of slavery and the theology and society of its time it is not only the patristic literature that must be surveyed in this context, but also secular literature both prior to and contemporary with the Early Church, and the evidence concerning the realities of slavery in both the secular and the Christian environment. I have therefore dealt with the material in the following way: I begin with the obvious step of a detailed examination of slavery, as a practical reality and as a metaphor, in the Septuagint[6] and New Testament, looking at (with, in the case of the Septuagint, the guidance of computer indices) the occurrences of the words δοῦλος and παῖς in their various forms and in the various forms of the related verbs (where they are related to the concept of slavery to God or Christ), and considering their function and importance in their various contexts. I follow this by examining a number of patristic texts that deal with the subject of slavery, making use again of the available indices. To collect evidence for other uses of the metaphor, in addition to an examination of the more important patristic texts of this period, and of those writers

---

6.   As it is mainly the Greek phrase δοῦλος Θεοῦ which is under consideration, the Septuagint will be used rather than the Hebrew Old Testament.

whose surviving corpus is of a manageable length, I have made a search of the *Thesaurus Linguae Graecae* on CD-ROM and have compiled indices for selected writers of the full declensions of the following variations of the metaphor:

δοῦλος Θεοῦ	δοῦλος τοῦ Θεοῦ	Θεοῦ δοῦλος
δοῦλος Χριστοῦ	δοῦλος τοῦ Χριστοῦ	Χριστοῦ δοῦλος
δοῦλος Ἰησοῦ	δοῦλος τοῦ Ἰησοῦ	Ἰησοῦ δοῦλος
δοῦλος Κυριοῦ	δοῦλος τοῦ Κυριοῦ	Κυριοῦ δοῦλος

The limitations of what can be done in this way are obvious. There are a wide variety of possible forms for the title, the genitive may be widely separated from the noun in the text or the formula may be expressed indirectly through the verb forms of δοῦλος. While it is possible to be less specific in some texts—using, for example, simply the letters δουλ, and examining every incidence separately—this is not practicable in most cases due to the scale of the literature available. Nevertheless, this system provides a beginning, indicating the more important cases of the use of slavery language. As I have described above, I also have sought a greater understanding of the use of the metaphor by considering its use within a number of specific contexts. For the final discussion of the relationship between the use of the metaphor and individual writers, I then examine in detail a number of works of selected patristic writers. To get a view of the use of the Christian form of the metaphor outside the confines of theological debate, I also consider apocryphal Christian writings and the evidence for the use of the metaphor in the Christian funerary inscriptions.

It is necessary to set some limits for this work. I have not considered Augustine except in the briefest way, mainly in the area of the practical situation and treatment of slaves, because of the vast size of his output and the fact that both his understanding of slavery and his use of metaphors related to it have already been so extensively considered by others.[7] Although Latin texts are used to an extent in this study, the main focus is on the Greek Fathers. I have also, for the most part, limited this work to the metaphor of slavery as an expression of the relationship between the human and the divine, and have therefore not entered into the thorny problems of Christ as the Suffering Servant, a

---

7. See, for example, R. Klein, *Die Sklaverei in der Sicht der Bischöfe Ambrosius und Augustinus* (Stuttgart: F. Steiner, 1988), or P. Garnsey, *Ideas of Slavery from Aristotle to Augustine* (Cambridge: Cambridge University Press, 1996), esp. pp. 206-35.

subject which, again, has been so thoroughly examined already by others. I have, however, considered the use of the metaphor of slavery in relation to the kenosis of Christ, and in relation to controversies concerning the creation and subordination of Christ and the Holy Spirit, as its use in these contexts bears so intimately on the writers' perception of the status of the human race and of creation.

It would be an ambitious project indeed to attempt to say anything new about the institution of slavery in the Church and the ancient world, considering the enormous quantity of critical analysis on the subject in the last few decades. I therefore confine the treatment of this subject to introductory background, making use of the research that has already been done in this field, the details of which will be discussed shortly.

3. The Place of Metaphor in Religious Language

The attempt to define the nature and function of metaphor goes back at least as far as Aristotle's famous discussion of the subject[8] and continues today. For the purposes of the present study, however, since I shall confine it to the practical evidence of the behaviour of a metaphor, I shall leave aside the more theoretical considerations of metaphorical language in favour of a simple and practical understanding. In its most basic sense, religious metaphor is a reflection of a basic human tendency to draw on the mundane day to day cycle of human activities and relationships to create pictures of the unknown and unintelligible, creating gods and demons in the shape of people, animals or familiar objects, circumscribing them in the patterns created by human physical and emotional relationships—the parent and child, the judge and the judged, the king and the subject, the ravener and the prey—and giving, thereby, a degree of concreteness to the unknown. These we find throughout human history, and in all places. They range from the reassuringly familiar images of gods as the anthropomorphic councils of the Greeks to the disturbing plumed serpents and skull-headed chimeras of the Aztecs. The structures drawn, to a greater or lesser extent, from human relationships make it possible to define the terms under which the physical and spiritual worlds interrelate and provide assurance to the believer of his or her place in the order of things, specifying to a degree the behaviour expected from the believer and giving that

8.   Aristotle, *Ars Poetica* 21.

individual the means to placate and influence the supernatural world.

One must, however, go further than this and establish what is meant when one says that something is a metaphor in the religious context. The extreme view—that all words for God, including 'God' itself, must of necessity be metaphorical as they cannot be anything but approximate images to describe the indescribable—has been argued by such as D. Cupitt;[9] but whatever the merits of such a view from the standpoint of theological argumentation, it is not of much value for the present purpose. For the purposes of this study it will be sufficient to specify which sorts of 'relationship descriptions' shall be defined as religious metaphors. There are three kinds that are the most obvious in the texts question:

1. It is occasionally clear that when using a certain 'relationship description', the user intends to be understood literally. That is to say, within his or her world view there exists a real situation in which the individual is in precisely the same relationship with the deity as he or she would be with the human equivalent—the individual may, for example, be owned by, begotten by, or about to be consumed by the deity.

2. In other cases it is clear that the user is employing a metaphor. The metaphor in question expresses details of the relationship between the human and the divine but does not define it, and may be easily replaced by another, completely different, metaphor when the situation demands. Thus, God may be a father, a king or a shepherd.

3. Lastly there is an illustrative use of a metaphor, where the metaphor becomes a simple image, only describing an aspect of the divine. The receiver is not expected to explore all the implications of the metaphor, indeed it would be ridiculous to do so. In this case, God might be a flower, an eagle or the wind. The various botanical, zoological or meteorological details would hold no relevance to the meaning of such metaphors.

All three forms of religious metaphor are found in the Christian texts, and it will be useful to keep this distinction in mind when we turn to the consideration of the metaphor of slavery in the ancient world.

9. D. Cupitt, *The Long Legged Fly* (London: SCM Press, 1987).

Chapter 1

SLAVERY AND METAPHOR

1. *The Institution of Slavery*

a. *Problems of Definition*

A definition of slavery, both as an absolute concept and specifically in the context of its role in the ancient world, would seem *prima facie* to be fundamental to any discussion of the metaphors relating to it. What it is that defines one person as being in a state of slavery to another and what aspect of the relationship can be called the distinguishing feature of slavery are problems which have occupied thinkers since antiquity, and few have ever been able to propose any adequate definition of slavery which successfully differentiates it from other forms of subordination and exploitation.

J.A. Harrill, in his detailed survey of the debate on the meaning of the term, distinguishes two approaches to the definition of slavery: the 'chattel hermeneutic' of such as M.I. Finley, who sees the essential nature of slavery as lying in the status of slaves as property; and the 'social death hermeneutic', most clearly espoused by O. Patterson, who sees slavery as a destruction of all meaningful elements of an individual's life and connection with society.[1]

Most definitions of slavery fall within the 'chattel hermeneutic',[2] as, for example, Article I(i) of the Slavery Convention of 1926 which describes slavery as 'the status or condition of a person over whom any or all of the powers attaching to the right of ownership are exercised'.[3]

---

1. J.A. Harrill, *The Manumission of Slaves in Early Christianity* (Tübingen: J.C.B. Mohr [Paul Siebeck], 1995), p. 17.

2. Grant, too, appeals to this kind of definition and claims that the 'essential feature' of slavery 'is that slaves have no independence or rights or legal personalities of their own, but are the property of their masters' (M. Grant, *Greeks and Romans: A Social History* [London: Weidenfeld & Nicolson, 1992], p. 920).

3. Cited by C.W.W. Greenidge, *Slavery* (London: Allen & Unwin, 1958), pp. 224-27.

The definition of slavery as property is, as we shall see, consistent with much of the understanding of slavery in the ancient world and is a useful guard against any inappropriate romanticization of the relationship between master and slaves. The status of the slave as property ultimately leaves the owner in possession of virtually unlimited rights of exploitation and the slave with only the flimsiest, and even then possibly only theoretical,[4] guard against abuse. However, this definition of slavery is not in itself entirely satisfactory. As the elaboration of the definition of slavery in the 1956 Convention shows, the powers of ownership may be exercised over a far wider range of relationships than those commonly understood as slavery.[5]

The second approach to the definition of slavery, the 'social death hermeneutic', argues that the essential feature of slavery in any culture is not the legal status of the slave, but his or her position as a 'socially dead' outsider. The slave is one who has figuratively died at the hands of his or her master, but continues to exist, for the benefit of the master alone, in a state of social death. To become a slave is to die; to be set free is to be reborn into society.[6] The common feature of all slaves is thus that, regardless of the cruelty or kindness with which they may be treated, they are permanently rootless and alienated within the culture in which they function. Such a definition of slavery has the advantage that it clearly distinguishes slavery from other relationships where 'the rights of ownership' may be held over another person. The child or wife, for example, may be dominated by the *paterfamilias* by virtue of his or her position within the structure of the family and the part he or

---

4.   Even where laws exist that claim to protect slaves, such laws are more likely to represent an ideal than a reality—especially in the ancient world we have no way of knowing to what extent such ideals impinged on the reality of day to day existence for slaves. As Harrill, *The Manumission of Slaves*, p. 14 (see also p. 15 n. 7) points out, 'Reading law codes as descriptive rather than prescriptive overlooks the course of juridical decisions in the practice of law (jurisprudence)'.

5.   Article I of the 1956 Supplementary Convention (cited by Greenidge, *Slavery*, pp. 228-32) includes under the aforementioned heading: debt bondage, serfdom, the giving of women, without right to refuse, in marriage in exchange for payment, or transference for payment or inheritance of such a woman, and the handing over of minors for the exploitation of the person or labour of said minor.

6.   O. Patterson, *Slavery and Social Death: A Comparative Study* (Harvard: Harvard University Pres, 1982), pp. 1-70. See also his development of this argument in O. Patterson, *Freedom*. I. *Freedom in the Making of Western Culture* (London: I.B. Tauris & Co., 1991).

she plays in the kinship structure. Slaves, on the other hand, are under domination by virtue of their very lack of these things. The slave is the outsider—no matter how vital that slave might be to the household itself—and lacks any true identity except that which is found through the master. It is significant, therefore, that slavery in its original form and thereafter either in theory or in fact, rests on the fact of the slave being a foreigner (indeed the earliest Sumerian term for slave is, translated, simply 'foreigner')[7]. The first generation slave is therefore someone who has been, often traumatically through war or kidnap, uprooted from the original family and society. In many cases, the slave is even deprived of his or her name and given a new one. However well treated they may be, slaves are therefore those who come from outside and bear no relationship to anyone in their new vicinity. The second generation, houseborn, slave is a different matter, and indeed, may even have been sired by one of the males of the master's family. The alienation in this case is more an external one. While the slave's relationship with the master may be a good one, the slave still fails to be fully a part of the larger society. This is illustrated most vividly by the fact that the slave cannot be a citizen and hence has no real rights or duties in the society, cannot enter any legal agreement on his or her own behalf and cannot usually create a legally recognized family.[8] For this reason, emancipation in the ancient world was often associated with some form of assimilation into a family or society—slaves might be freed for the purpose of marriage or adoption into the family or to fight in the army, and in the Roman world, this would mean, in most cases, a right to Roman citizenship. Where the definition, taken on its own, falls short is

7. 'Male of a foreign country' or 'female of a foreign country' (*nita* + *kur* and *munus* + *kur* respectively), *IDB*, IV, p. 383. See also I. Mendelsohn, *Slavery in the Ancient Near East: A Comparative Study of Slavery in Babylonian Assyria and Palestine from the Middle of the Third Millennium to the End of the First Millennium* (New York: Oxford University Press, 1949), p. 1.

8. Slave marriage in the Roman world was never recognized by law as being anything more than *contubernium* (although in individual cases, masters and slaves might choose to regard it as a proper marriage). See W.W. Buckland, *The Roman Law of Slavery: The Condition of the Slave in Private Law from Augustus to Justinian* (Cambridge: Cambridge University Press, 1970), p. 76, who cites in this context, *Ulpian Regulae* 9.9, *Pauli Sententiae* 2.19.6 and *Codex Justinianus* 9.9.23.*pr*. Slave marriages seem to have been more respected in the cultures of the Near East, although they tended to be ignored when it came to the selling and purchasing of slaves. See Mendelsohn, *Slavery in the Ancient Near East*, p. 40.

that it relies too readily on the assumption of a certain understanding of slavery on the part of both the slave and the master. While this under-standing of slavery, as has already been pointed out, finds echoes in various aspects of slavery in antiquity, there is also little evidence in the surviving literature of any overt understanding of slavery as a social death.

The most useful definition of slavery is one that combines both approaches, taking the simple reality of the slave as an item of property in conjunction with the psychological burden of the slave as an out-sider.[9] This alienation might in some cases seem moderated or blurred, but it holds over slaves the unalterable fact that no relationship or per-sonal dignity of theirs could ever have the same security and social assurance as that of a free person.

b. *Slavery in the Ancient World*[10]
An investigation into the specific nature of slavery in the ancient world is hampered in a number of ways. In the first place, there is no such thing as the 'ancient world' as such. Although it is a useful label to indicate a general area to consider, it is, of course, not a unity in itself,

---

9.   W.D. Phillips, for example (*Slavery from Roman Times to the Early Trans-atlantic Trade* [Manchester: Manchester University Press, 1985], p. 6), makes such a combination. He proposes three distinguishing features of slavery. These are: 'The slave's position as property', 'the unlimited rights the master had over him or her' and 'that, barring a few exception...he slave was an outsider'. See also Garn-sey, *Ideas of Slavery*, p. 1, who lists three 'basic components': the slave as prop-erty; the absolute power of the master; and the fact that the slave is 'stripped of his or her old social identity and denied the capacity to forge new bonds of kinship'.
10.   For a review of such scholarship on ancient slavery over the last century, see M.I. Finley,'Ancient Slavery and Modern Ideology', in M.I. Finley (ed.), *Ancient Slavery and Modern Ideology* (London: Chatto & Windus, 1980), pp. 11-66; O. Patterson, 'Slavery', *Annual Review of Sociology* 3 (1977), pp. 407-49; J. Vogt, *Ancient Slavery and the Ideal of Man* (trans T. Wiedemann; Oxford: Basil Blackwell, 1974), pp. 180-87; *idem* (ed.), *Bibliographie zur Antiken Sklaverei* (Akademie der Wissenschaften und der Literatur, Mainz; Bochum: N. Brockmeyer, 1971); Y. Garlan, *Slavery in Ancient Greece* (trans. J. Lloyd; Ithaca, NY: Cornell University Press, rev. and expanded edn, 1988), pp. 1-14; and N. Brockmeyer, *Antike Sklaverei* (Etrage de Forschung, 2; Darmstadt: Wissenschaftliche Buchs-gesellschaft, 1979), pp. 16-70, are useful. To do more than point out some of the more important aspects of ancient slavery would only be to repeat the work of others. See, for example, Harrill, whose *The Manumission of Slaves*, pp. 11-66, gives a most detailed account of the background to first-century slavery.

but extends over an enormous period and a myriad of different societies so that one must ever steer clear of the error of assuming that what was the case in one place and at one time held true in another. Even within the 'Greek world', the structures of interaction differ vastly from area to area and from age to age. Secondly, although practical evidence is abundant enough, we are severely handicapped by the absence of any useful subjective evidence, from the point of view of the slave[11] such as are available for the more recent slave cultures—there can be no ancient historian's equivalent, therefore to E.D. Genovese's work, *Roll, Jordan, Roll*, which so effectively describes the experience of slavery from the point of view of the enslaved, drawing on the recollections of black American slaves and ex-slaves.

The other major problem we encounter is the sheer variety, not only of the states and conditions that have come under the name of 'slavery',[12] but of the different possible means of enslavement. While it seems that in its most original form, slavery had its roots in war and the

11. We have, of course, a number of texts which were, or were claimed to be, written by slaves (*The Shepherd of Hermas*, for example, and Epictetus's *Discourses*, although these were written down by Arrian). These are of no great use in understanding the point of view of slaves, however, as the individuals who composed them were so exceptional. The anonymous *Life of Aesop* claims to be the biography of the slave Aesop, but the character of Aesop amounts to little more than a caricature: 'The fabulist Aesop, the great benefactor of mankind, was by chance a slave but by origin a Phrygian of Phrygia, of loathsome aspect, worthless as a servant, potbellied, misshapen of head, snub nosed, swarthy, dwarfish, bandy legged, short-armed, squint eyed, liver-lipped ...' (trans. L.W. Daly, *Aesop without Morals* [New York: Thomas Yoseloff, 1961], p. 31). For the *Life of Aesop* see Daly, *Aesop without Morals*, pp. 31-90.

12. 'The word for slave has been applied to captives held for ceremonial sacrifice; to household servants who were part of a *familia* and under the domination of a *paterfamilias*; to the concubines and eunuchs of a harem; to children held as pawns for their parents' debts; to female children sold as brides; and by analogy to subject or conquered populations, to the industrial proletariat; to victims of racial or political tyranny and to men and women supposedly dominated by drugs, alcohol, sexual passion, mental disease or sin. And, of course, there are many examples of monetary payment being given for the economic, sexual or social dominion of nominally free persons, especially women. Thousands of nominally free workers have been transported across the seas to labour in mines or on plantations; they have been subjected to systematic debasement, dishonour, racial discrimination and corporal punishment', D.B. Davis, *Slavery and Human Progress* (Oxford: Oxford University Press, 1986 [1984]), p. 10.

enslavement of prisoners,[13] there have been, especially in the society of the ancient world, many paths into slavery. While one might become a slave through the fortunes of war or through kidnap, one could also enter it as a result of economic disaster leading to debt bondage, a state that in many parts of the ancient world, and perhaps most commonly in the ancient Near East, presented an ever present threat to all but the most financially secure;[14] or through the actions of one's parents (a child might be sold by its parents or might have been abandoned and then found and raised as a slave); through crime and subsequent penal servitude; or through accident of birth. Bondage could be a temporary state or a lifetime sentence: one might come to it in one's earliest days or at the end of life. It was sometimes thinly disguised as another relationship, with girls being sold as wives and concubines and children being 'adopted' to provide a lifetime of service to their adopters.

In the ancient world in particular, another form of slavery involved the conditional slavery of young girls. A girl, for example, might be sold to be her mistress's slave and her master's concubine.[15] The

13. Augustine, indeed, goes so far as to find in this the origin of the Latin *servus*: '...quod hi qui iure belli possent occidi, a victoribus cum servabantur servi fiebant, a servando appellati' ('Those who, by the law of war could be killed were, when sowed by the victors, known as servi'), *City of God* 19.15.

14. This is as might be expected in a society where the interest rate on corn could be anything up to 100 per cent and where the right of the creditor to enslave not only the debtor himself but also his immediate family was generally recognized. The disastrous depletion of the free population that such practices might cause in difficult years in an agricultural economy often led to legislation limiting the duration of such bondage (three years in Babylonian legislation [Code of Hammurabi, 117], six years under Hebrew law [Exod. 21.2-3, 7-11], although, in the Hebrew legislation, this limit seems only to have applied to Hebrew slaves) and, to a certain extent, preventing the sale of persons thus held (G.R. Driver and J.C. Miles, *The Babylonian Laws: Ancient Codes and Laws of the Near East*. I. *Legal Commentary* [Oxford: Clarendon Press, 1952], pp. 217-21 and 276-78).

15. Mendelsohn, *Slavery in the Ancient Near East*, pp. 10-11, and J. Finegan, *Light from the Ancient Past: The Archaeological Background of Judaism and Christianity* (Princeton, NJ: Princeton University Press, 1959), p. 67. In the world of the ancient Near East, such a sale would provide the girl with some security, because traditionally (as for example laid down in the Code of Hammurabi, 170-72), if she should bear children to her master, neither she nor her children could subsequently be sold or turned out of her master's house, and upon his death, she and her children would receive their freedom (Driver and Miles, *The Babylonian Laws*, p. 222).

restrictions placed on her resale, her possible right to freedom in the case of her master's demise and the status she might acquire as the mother of children by her master also make this state something other than what would seem to be slavery in its strict sense. Indeed there were cases, in some parts of the ancient world, where a young girl could be sold as a slave on the condition that she be given in marriage, sometimes even to her master's son, upon her attaining puberty.

A master, thus, can take different roles—the conqueror who has destroyed the captive's freedom by violence, the foundling's rescuer, the purchaser, the creditor, the lover or the future parent-in-law. The slavery may be justified in the eyes of the master, of society, and sometimes even of the slave through the claims of superior strength, the obligations of gratitude, of affection or necessity.[16]

Finally, any attempt to understand slavery from the point of view of the ancient writers is further complicated by the habit, which prevailed in much of the ancient world, of claiming the existence of such a thing as absolute slavery—a real slavery that exists independently of any social context. Thus a slave may not necessarily be a slave in the true sense, and the free person may not necessarily be free. Those who lack self-control, it is argued, or who are dominated by some external force, are the true slaves, irrespective of their actual legal or social positions. So confused do the conceptions of social and absolute slavery become, that finding a proper definition of the former in the ancient texts can become frustratingly difficult. Dio Chrysostom, for example, as mentioned earlier, begins a promising debate on the proper definition of slavery, but after rejecting each practical definition that is offered, decides to settle the problem by resorting to the realm of the psycholog-

---

16. One of the most vexing questions for any student of slavery and its implications is the role that material well-being plays in the psychological impact of slavery and, more specifically, whether slavery can ever be seen as a desirable or honourable way of life. It has often been argued that slavery, if not actually justifiable, is at least preferable to the possible alternatives of penury and misery. However, in the ancient world, at least, where society was fundamentally divided between slave and free, individual dignity was based in the first place on a person's freedom, rather than his or her economic status—rather in the same way that the penniless aristocrat in our own age enjoys a higher status than a well-to-do person of the middle classes. There is very little evidence that entry into slavery was a common career move, in spite of the opportunities that existed for the advancement of slaves, especially in the imperial household.

ical, declaring that true slavery is that of the mind.[17] Such sentiments reflect the fact that one of the most important characteristics of slavery in the ancient world was that it was perceived as a relation of domination. The main consequence of enslavement was the lack of opportunity to exercise free will and this applied as much to psychological 'slavery' as to real slavery. The other considerations of legal status, alienation and deprivation of human rights must be added to complete the definition, but in the ancient world it is the deprivation of power over one's own life and action that is the foremost characteristic of slavery.

Since the condition of slaves within the period under consideration varies so widely, from inhuman toil and misery to relative comfort and education, and since contemporary sources on the subject are so inadequate, our picture of the institution of slavery as it existed in the ancient world can never be entirely complete. The usefulness, therefore, of the comparative studies that have been carried out on this subject should not be overlooked,[18] as long as they are treated with caution and it is remembered that the slavery of the ancient world existed in a very different context and thus was of a very different nature than that which is found within any of the world's more modern slave societies. A great difficulty that the modern reader encounters in discussing the problem of slavery is that the contemporary understanding of 'slave' is in many ways shaped by the western world's most recent experience of slavery, that of the American South, and while comparisons between this experience and slavery in the ancient world may be sometimes illuminating, they are not always made with the caution they deserve. Slavery in the American South, it must be remembered, had features that made it differ in important respects from slavery in the ancient world, not least in that the American slavery was predominantly centred on race. The American slave was physically different from the master; if a slave ran away or was emancipated, he or she would still be immediately identifiable as one who was, or had been, a slave. There was no chance here, as there was in the ancient world, of a freedman melting into society and producing children who need never seem to be anything but free. The black slave was therefore permanently outside the 'host'

---

17. Dio Chrysostom, *Discourse* 14 and 15.

18. Especially the works of Davis, *Slavery and Human Progress* and *idem*, *The Problem of Slavery in Western Culture*; O. Patterson, *Slavery and Social Death* and *idem, Freedom. I. Freedom in the Making of Western Culture* (London: I.B. Tauris & Co, 1991).

society, and the social mobility of ex-slaves that characterized the world of the later Roman empire was, while not unknown, not by any means as great as that of Roman freedmen. The different function of the slave in the economy of the American South must also be kept in mind—the majority of slaves in the American South were agricultural workers, labouring in the plantation cotton fields, while the slaves we shall be considering will be primarily those of urban households.

1. *Slavery in the Graeco-Roman World*. There was, throughout the ancient world, one basic assumption about slavery, namely, that it was a necessary institution and that a slave class was an indispensable part of any well-ordered society, even where the labour of the slave might only play a negligible role in the general economy.[19] While there might be disagreement concerning the treatment and proper behaviour of slaves and, occasionally, attempts to justify the institution, there was never any serious suggestion of its wholesale abolition.

A slave in the Ancient Greek world was, in legal terms, property, and as much liable to be bought, sold and used at his or her master's pleasure as any other possession.[20] Physical punishment was considered permissible when dealing with slaves, indeed their liability to this was said by Demosthenes to be the single most important characteristic of the state of slavery.[21] In the strictest sense they could not own any property, although it might happen that they controlled property or income which, although belonging to the master in the last resort, was

19. In some circumstances slave labour may prove to be more expensive to employ than hired labour, since slaves must be housed, fed and cared for in a way that is not necessary for the employer of free labour. A slave force is also inflexible in that it cannot be paid off when there is only a limited need for labour. There are, however, other functions which the existence of a slave class may provide, since slaves are very often seen as symbols of the wealth, power and status of their owners, with the result that slaves may still play an important part in a society even where they make no substantial economic contribution.

20. 'A slave was property. The slaveowner's rights over his property were total', Garnsey, *Ideas of Slavery*, p. 1. On the 'juridical status of Athenian slavery', see, for example, Garlan, *Slavery in Ancient Greece*, pp. 40-45.

21. 'If you wished to consider what the difference between a slave and a free-man was, this most of all you would find—that in the case of slaves, their body is answerable for all their wrongdoings, while the free even in the most unlucky circumstances can protect themselves' (Demosthenes, *Against Androtion* 55). This passage is also to be found in his *Against Timocrates* 167.

informally seen as the slave's own.[22] In principle it was argued that Greeks should not enslave Greeks,[23] although in practice this frequently happened through the enslavement of rival cities conquered in war and through debt bondage. Enslavement for debt, however, was abolished by Solon,[24] making it more likely that in Attica slaves would be foreigners, or at least captives from another city.[25] They usually had no chance of ever receiving citizenship in the city to which they had come.[26]

It is unclear whether the slave in the Greek world had any personal rights at all. It may have been forbidden to kill one's slave, but no clear legislation survives on the subject.[27] Slaves were tortured as a matter of course in criminal trials as their evidence was usually inadmissible otherwise.[28]

22. J.W. Jones, *The Law and Legal Theory of the Greeks* (Oxford: Clarendon Press, 1956), pp. 282-83.

23. See, for example, Plato's discussion of this in *Republic* 469b, cited by A.R.W. Harrison, *The Law of Athens: The Family and Property* (Oxford: Clarendon Press, 1968).

24. Plutarch says that Solon forbade the practice of using the borrower himself as security for loans and set free those who were in slavery due to debt (Plutarch, *Solon* 15). See also Aristotle, *Athenian Constitutions* 2.2, 4.5, 6.1 and 9.1. Aristotle calls this one of the most important democratic features of Solon's constitution. There were, Harrison argues (*The Law of Athens*, p. 165), two exceptions to this rule: the failure of an ex-captive to pay back his ransom to his redeemer and the reduction to slavery of a freedman through his losing a δίκη ἀποστασίου. See also Garlan, *Slavery in Ancient Greece*, pp. 91-92, on possible regional exceptions to the ban on debt-bondage.

25. Harrison, *The Law of Athens*, p. 165.

26. See Jones, *The Law and Legal Theory of the Greeks*, p. 285 and Harrison, *The Law of Athens*, pp. 184-86, on manumission in the Greek world and the subsequent status of freedmen.

27. 'slaves were not entirely without a legal guard against death at their masters' hand. But the guard was at best flimsy; indeed the passage from Ant. 6 Chor. 4 which states that a master who killed his own slave must undergo purification suggests by its wording that this might be all that he did, though if he failed to do even that he would be in peril' (Harrison, *The Law of Athens*, pp. 171-72. See also D.M. MacDowell, *The Law of Classical Athens* (London: Thames & Hudson, 1978), p. 80. Further on the general rights and position of Greek, slaves see Harrison, *The Law of Athens*, pp. 163-80.

28. According to Garlan, *Slavery in Ancient Greece*, p. 42, who argues that the only exceptions to this were in cases of the denunciation of a traitor, commercial litigation, public slaves and slaves witnessing against their master's murderer. See

Even though slavery was taken by all as being an inevitable fact of life,[29] there was some debate as to its origin and the reason for its existence. Plato discusses slavery in his *Laws* and recommends, for the sake of domestic harmony, that they not be all of one race—for that would encourage revolts[30]—and that they be treated fairly but firmly, with their masters 'not being arrogant to them, and wronging them even less, if possible, than our own equals'[31] and punishing them justly, without 'making them conceited by merely admonishing them as we would free men'.[32]

The purpose of this is, however, almost entirely pragmatic and

---

also MacDowell, *The Law of Classical Athens*, pp. 245-47. The demand that slaves be handed over for torture, or the offer of slaves for the same, for evidence in criminal cases, is a repeated theme in Demosthenes' orations. See *Against Aphobus* 3.11-12, 3.25; *Against Boeotus* 2.15; *Against Pantaenetus* 27 and 40; *Against Stephans* 1.62–2.21; *Against Neaera* 120 and, for an account of the torture of a slave in such a trial, *Against Olympiodorus* 16-19.

29. The slave character is ubiquitous in the works of drama and literature and reflects a clear concept of what constitutes the behaviour of the 'good slave' and the 'bad slave'. There is the stock character of the crafty slave, as in Aristophanes' *The Frogs*, where the slave moans, complains and cheeks his master, eventually outwitting him so that the master, who out of cowardice has persuaded him to swap clothing, shares in his beating. *The Clouds* virtually begins with a joke about whipping slaves, with the master complaining that one cannot even beat one's own slaves these days (*Clouds* 7) However, it must be said that most of the characters in this play come, at some point, under the lash, and the slaves are no more abused, verbally or physically, than any other character. For a detailed description of the slave as a stock character in Greek comic theatre, see F.H. Sandbach, *The Comic Theatre of Greece and Rome* (London: Chatto & Windus, 1977). There are, however, also many romantic portrayals of the good slave to be found in the tragedies where, in the main, slaves are shown as loyal and obedient, sharing in their master's griefs and giving wise advice. In Euripides' *Medea*, for instance, the nurse asserts that good slaves suffer along with their masters in their misfortunes (*Medea* 54-55) and his *Hippolytus* shows a slave calling his master 'son' and speaking to him in a free and easy manner, offering advice on his behaviour towards the goddesses (*Hippolytus* 90ff.). Literature abounds with such idealizations of the master/ slave relationships; the theme is equally common in the novels (see J. Perkins, *The Suffering Self: Pain and Narrative Representation in the Early Christian Era* [London: Routledge, 1995], pp. 58-59).

30. Plato, *Laws* 777c–d.

31. Plato, *Laws* 777d–e.

32. Plato, *Laws* 777e.

concerned with household order,[33] and has little to do with any compassion for the slaves themselves. Indeed, Plato warns masters against being too kind and familiar with their slaves, arguing that this will make it 'harder for the master to rule and the slave to be ruled'.[34] Hand in hand with his warnings against brutality to slaves also go recommendations for their treatment which, Morrow points out,[35] are even harsher than the slave legislation that existed in Athens at the time, and which do not specify, as the Athenian laws did, any upper limit on the severity of slave punishment.

33. From these recommendations, R. Schlaifer ('Greek Theories of Slavery from Homer to Aristotle', in M.I. Finley [ed.], *Slavery in Classical Antiquity: Views and Controversies* [Cambridge: W. Heffer & Sons, 1960], pp. 93-132) has gone on to argue that, in Plato's mind, 'the slave has no 'human rights'; he is lacking in the most essentially human element of the soul.'

I think Schlaifer is going too far here, as can be seen from Plato's recommendations concerning the murderers of slaves. One of the indications of whether one sees an individual as having human rights or not, is the degree to which one thinks such a being can be abused or killed without moral guilt being incurred. Schlaifer argues that Plato does not think that moral guilt is incurred by the killing of slaves, and that 'If a man kills his own slave, it is true, he must make expiation; but since the only penalty for killing another's slave is to pay double the value, it would seem that the only reason for the former provisions was to delude the citizens into a belief that would prevent intemperance of any sort.'

In proof of this, he cites *Laws* 9.868a. However, a closer look at this passage shows that it continues with: 'If anyone of all these types of slayers does not obey the law, but rather being unpurified, defiles the market place or the gymnasium or the other sacred assemblies ... (he shall be prosecuted).'

Thus, it is clearly assumed that 'all these types of slayers' (including one who has killed another's slave) must be purified, as is confirmed by 865c–d: 'If he kill a slave he shall compensate the master fully, judging the value as if it were his own slave, secure the master against damages...and he must also employ means of purification greater and more numerous than those employed by persons who kill a man at the games... if it be a slave of his own that he has killed, he shall be set free after legal purification' (translations from Plato, *Laws*).

While this does not, of course, imply full recognition of the slave's humanity, it is clear that the slave occupies a position in Plato's thought quite distinct from that of a mere animal, and thus cannot be said so radically to be 'lacking in the most essential human element of the soul'.

34. *Laws* 778.

35. G.R. Morrow, *Plato's Law of Slavery in its Relation to Greek Law* (Illinois Studies in Language and Literature; Illinois: University of Illinois Press, 1939), pp. 194-98.

As for the origins of slavery, Plato asserted that the institution derived from the fact that there were those who, being incapable of a full use of reason, were best suited to a life under the mastership of others. In doing so, Garnsey points out,[36] Plato provided the foundations for the theory of natural slavery that is most fully developed by Aristotle, who argued that there existed certain people whose very nature, physical and intellectual, had so fitted them for a life of servitude that they could be neither happy nor useful outside such a situation, just as others were naturally masters and in need of slaves so that, freed from the drudgery of daily life they might devote themselves to the pursuit of virtue appropriate to their station:[37]

> One that can foresee with his mind is naturally master, and one that can do these things (labour) with his body is subject and naturally a slave.[38]

This is because the slave 'participates in reason so far as to apprehend it, but not to possess it'.[39]

36. Garnsey, *Ideas of Slavery*, pp. 13-14.

37. Aristotle, *Politics* 1252b. However, as Garnsey points out, 'slave theory in antiquity does not begin and end with Aristotle. Nor does the idea of natural slavery', *Ideas of Slavery*, p. 96.

38. *Politics* 1253b. 20-23. He also points out that there exists some controversy over the nature of the slave. In this case, he alludes to some who regard slavery as being contrary to the laws of natural justice and based simply on force and convention. On this, see G. Cambiano, 'Aristotle and the Anonymous Opponents of Slavery', in Finley (ed.), *Slavery in Classical Antiquity*, pp. 22-41.

39. *Politics* 1254b.22. Does this, however, indicate that slaves are rational or is Aristotle's position on this, as Robert Schlaifer ('Greek Theories of Slavery', pp. 93-132) exclaims, 'hopelessly confused'? Schlaifer thinks that such words can only be explained by assuming that Aristotle means to argue that the slave possesses that part of the soul which shares in reason (κοινωνῶν λόγου) to the extent of perceiving it (αἰσθάνεσθαι), but lacks that part of the soul which possesses reason to the extent of being able to make 'moral choice in advance of action' (a similar analysis is reached by W.W. Fortenbaugh, 'Aristotle on Slaves and Women', in J. Barnes, M. Schofield and R. Sorabji [eds.], *Articles on Aristotle. II. Ethics and Politics* [London: Gerald Duckworth, 1977], pp. 135-39). Thus, while the slave is not an entirely irrational creature (being able to perceive reason he can acknowledge that a certain decision is rational), he lacks himself the ability to use this reason for long term or organized thought and is thus incapable of coming up with such a decision himself. See also Fortenbaugh, 'Aristotle on Slaves and Women', p. 137. For a detailed discussion of Aristotle and slavery see Garnsey, *Ideas of Slavery*, pp. 107-27 and P.A. Brunt, 'Aristotle and Slavery', in *idem, Studies in Greek History and Thought* (Oxford: Clarendon Press, 1993), pp. 343-89.

The idea of natural slavery and the beneficial symbiosis of master and slave has throughout history proved to be a comforting justification for the continued existence of slavery.[40] However, a second tradition on slavery equally important in later thought was the Cynic/Stoic argument that slavery was a social institution, not a natural state, as summed up most famously in Philo's statement that 'no one is a slave by nature'.[41]

Chrysippus emphatically denies the existence of any natural basis for slavery when, according to Cicero, he defines the slave as 'a labourer hired for life'[42] and recommends that he be treated as such. The Stoic tradition emphasized the spiritual equality of all people regardless of their station in life,[43] and asserted that true slavery is more a state of mind than a physical occurrence.[44]

These sentiments were frequently accompanied by energetic denunciations of the inhuman treatment of slaves by some masters. Seneca, for one, speaks vividly and with disgust about the sufferings and humiliations that slaves endure in some households.[45] However, neither the assertion of the inner freedom of slaves, nor the condemnation of the brutality towards them leads to any explicit desire for the wholesale abolition of slavery.[46] Rather, the Stoics confine themselves to the

40. See, for example, L. Hanke, *Aristotle and the American Indians: A Study of Race Prejudice in the Modern World* (Bloomington, IN: Indiana State University Press, 1959).

41. Philo, *Spec. Leg.* 2.69: ἄνθρωπος γὰρ ἐκ φύσεως δοῦλος οὐδείς. A discussion on the source of this sentiment may be found in M.T. Griffin, *Seneca: A Philosopher in Politics* (Oxford: Clarendon Press, 1976), Appendix E2, p. 459. P.A. Brunt ('Aristotle and Slavery', pp. 343-89) thinks that this means merely that 'no man is produced by nature with the characteristics of a slave...not that it is contrary to nature that some men are slaves'.

42. Cicero, *De Officiis* 1.13.41; Seneca, *De Beneficiis* 3.22.

43. See Seneca, *Moral Epistles* 47, and Dio Chrysostom, *Discourse* 14 *On Slavery and Freedom* 1.18.

44. 'The Stoa (...) deserves the chief credit for deciding definitively the old Sophistic problem whether a slave's status was one imposed by nature or by human enactment (φύσει or θέσει) in the sense of the latter, namely that it was a condition imposed by law (νόμῳ)', W.L. Westermann, *The Slave Systems in Greek and Roman Antiquity* (Memoirs of the American Philosophical Society, 40; Philadelphia: American Philosophical Society, 1955), p. 116.

45. *Moral Epistles* 47.

46. On Seneca and his contemporaries on the subject of slavery, see also Griffin, *Seneca*, pp. 256-85.

recommendation that a master treat his slaves kindly and take an interest in their wellbeing, showing respect for their inner freedom[47] and regarding them as fellow human beings, 'humble friends' and, indeed, as fellow slaves considering the power that fortune has equally over all.[48]

Since, as they argued, such external matters as social roles made no difference to the internal well-being of the individual, the only person who really might suffer through slavery was the master himself, since having a slave encouraged his dependence on another person rather than on himself.[49] True slavery or freedom, to the Stoic, was a condition of the soul and thus, it was the wise man who was 'king and master',[50] even if he might be, in social terms, a slave, while the fool, be he master or king, was the true slave, for true slavery was the state of the uninformed or corrupt mind.

In Roman law, the distinction between the idea of natural slavery and social slavery finds concrete expression in acknowledgment by the Roman jurists that slavery represents the one clear case in Roman law where the *ius gentium* (the law common to all peoples) contradicts the *ius naturale* (the law of nature).[51] Slavery was defined as being an institution of the *ius gentium*, 'contrary to nature and resulting from war',[52] and thus, although an accepted part of all societies, a violation of the natural laws of human equality. Under the laws of property, the slave was classed as a *'res mancipi'*, a classification that placed the slave in the same category as land and cattle.[53] The slave was also held to be

47. However, it must be remembered that in general the main intention, as Brunt ('Aspects of the Social Thought of Dio Chrysostom and of the Stoics', in *idem, Studies in Greek History and Thought*, pp. 210-43) points out, is to prevent the master falling into the vices of anger and loss of self control. The well-being of the slave is in many cases simply a side effect.

48. Seneca, *Moral Epistles* 47. See also Chrysippus (SVF 3.350) and Philo (SVF 3.352) and H.C. Baldry, *The Unity of Mankind in Greek Thought* (Cambridge: Cambridge University Press, 1965), p. 164.

49. Griffin, *Seneca*, p. 262.

50. Epictetus, *Discourse* 3.22.49. See also Dio Chrysostom, *Discourse* 14, *On Slavery and Freedom* 1.18.

51. Buckland, *The Roman Law of Slavery*, p. 1.

52. *Digest* 1.5.4, *Institutes* 9; T. Wiedemann, *Greek and Roman Slavery* (London & New York: Routledge, 1994), p. 15.

53. Buckland, *The Roman Law of Slavery*, p. 10.

pro nullo at law,[54] and so was legally without rights or duties[55]—these seem to have been held by the master on his or her behalf. The slave also had no civil duties such as paying tax or performing military service (indeed, slaves were barred from the army, and when occasions of national crisis necessitated the recruitment of slaves into the army, this was almost invariably preceded by the manumission of said recruits).

As was the case among the Greeks, violent physical punishment and torture were considered appropriate for the slave.[56] Indeed, in the Roman law courts, a slave's evidence was apparently only admissible if obtained under torture.[57] A distinctive feature of the later Roman empire, in spite of the brutal treatment meted out to some slaves, is the extraordinary rank others managed to attain, mainly within the Imperial household and other high ranking families.[58] These slaves could attain

54. See, however, Garnsey, *Ideas of Slavery*, p. 260 n. 4.

55. Patterson disagrees on this point: '"The conventional legal explanation of personality", writes G.B.J. Hughes (*Jurisprudence*, p. 442), "is that a person in law is an entity which may be the bearer of rights and duties". Even if we rephrase the word "rights" and "duties" in realist terms—the *stricto sensu*, for example, of the technical terminology of Hohfield—we find that the idea of a slave without a legal personality has no basis in legal practice. It is a fiction found only in western societies, and even there it has been taken seriously more by legal philosophers than by practising lawyers. As a legal fact, there has never existed a slaveholding society, ancient or modern, that did not recognize the slave as a person in law. All we need to do to demonstrate this is to examine the legal response in slaveholding societies to the delicts of slaves: in all cases the slave is held legally and morally responsible', Patterson, *Slavery*, p. 22.

56. 'The XII Tables impose a penalty (half that applicable to a freeman) for breaking a slave's bone, and a Lex Cornelia (as early as 60 AD) which makes it a capital offence to kill a man includes slave in the term *homo*. A variety of later legislation also attacked such practices as the prostitution of slaves, their castration, or selling them for gladiatorial purposes', Buckland, *The Roman Law of Slavery*, p. 31.

57. As was so in the case of Greek slaves: 'In cases in which the evidence of slaves was admissible it was taken normally by torture; indeed it appears that it could not be received in any other form. It should be added that, while the evidence of slaves was not to be used except where proof was lacking, on the other hand recourse was not to be had to it, at least in later law, unless there was already some evidence', Buckland, *The Roman Law of Slavery*, p. 87. See, however, *Digest* 48.18, which limits the torture of slaves to cases where there is no alternative and 'as a last resort'.

58. See Seneca, *Moral Epistles* 47.9, or Juvenal, *Satires* 7.13-15, or his complaint in *Satires* 5.59-66, about the arrogance of a rich man's slaves. For an

such heights of wealth that they might own slaves of their own and demand deference from less fortunate free persons. Nevertheless, such status could never, in Roman eyes, eradicate the taint of slavery, and the resentment that the success of these slaves aroused among the free is clear.[59]

2. *Slavery in the Ancient Near East*. In the case of the Graeco-Roman culture and economy, we have been dealing with a world where slavery was regarded as an unquestionable and essential part of life.[60] The situation in the ancient Near East was, however, quite different. Here the largely agricultural economy depended on a work force for the most part made up of free labourers, and there are no signs, in this part of the world, of the existence of massive gangs of slaves such as were so prominent in the Roman mines and *latifundia*. Indeed the presence of slaves even in domestic positions was rare, save in the households of the very wealthy.

Nevertheless, slavery was sufficiently widespread to inspire a substantial quantity of legislation regulating its practice and forms. As in other parts of the ancient world, the slave in the Near East was legally regarded as a chattel, to be used at the master's pleasure, often classified with cattle and sometimes tagged or branded as such.[61] As mentioned earlier,[62] a special feature of Near Eastern slavery was the prevalence of debt bondage, on the duration of which, at least in theory, a time-limit was set. Hebrew slavery, as recorded in the Old Testament, although it had much in common with the customs of its neighbouring states, had also some distinctive features that are worth mentioning. One of the most outstanding of these is the concept of separate codes of treatment for the native and the alien slave. While it is commonplace to find prejudice in any society against the enslavement of fellow nationals, in reality this would happen frequently and it is the Hebrew

extensive study on the mobility of slaves and freedmen within the Roman imperial household, see P.R.C. Weaver, *Familia Caesaris: A Social Study of the Emperor's Freedmen and Slaves* (Cambridge: Cambridge University Press, 1972).

59. See, for example, Juvenal, *Satires* 1.100 on the arrogance of a successful freedman.

60. See M.I. Finley, 'Was Greek Civilization Based on Slave Labour?', in Finley (ed.) *Slavery in Classical Antiquity*, pp. 53-72.

61. On the tagging and marking of slaves, see Mendelsohn, *Slavery in the Ancient Near East*, pp. 42-50, esp. p. 49.

62. See above, p. 26 n. 14.

legislation that first takes account of this and seeks, instead, to mitigate its hardship with specific legislation.[63] The Hebrew slave was, by law, to be released after a set period of time, while the Gentile slave might be held in perpetuity.[64] Harsh treatment was forbidden,[65] and fugitive slaves could not be sent back to their masters.[66]

The humanity of slaves was recognized in the fact that not only were they entitled to Sabbath rest, but they were expected to participate in certain family religious observances.[67] Nevertheless, their personal rights did not equal those of a free person. A slave was entitled to freedom if mutilated by his or her own master,[68] although the master was not liable to further punishment, as he or she would be in the case of injury to a free person,[69] and the killing of a slave was punishable by law.[70] Nevertheless, in spite of attempts to humanize the condition of slaves and to encourage the master to treat the slave as a fellow human being, a degree of suspicion and resentment seems to have remained on both sides. Among the free, there is an intense horror at the thought of entering slavery. A predictably repetitive theme in the Old Testament is, of course, that of the liberation from Egypt—'You shall remember that you were a slave in Egypt'[71]—a memory that carries such weight

63. Mendelsohn, *Slavery in the Ancient Near East*, p. 90, speaks of this national distinction as 'a new element in the slave laws of the Ancient Near East'.
64. Exod. 21.1-7; Lev. 25.39-42; Deut. 15.12-18. One must wonder, though, how often these regulations were strictly observed; certainly there are records of much longer periods of debt bondage, and although we possess numerous documents recording the entry into bondage of defaulting debtors, far fewer attest to their release upon the expiration of the legal period—'The suspicion that Jewish masters neglected their religious duties and kept Jewish slaves in perpetuity was recently given dramatic support by the papyri discovery of F.M. Cross. The papyrus concerns a group of Samarian nobles massacred by Alexander's soldiers and the translation clearly indicates that the Jewish slaves received no special treatment and were being held in perpetuity', Patterson, *Slavery*, p. 275.
65. Lev. 25.43.
66. Deut. 23.15-16.
67. Exod. 22.12; Deut. 16.12, although later rabbinic commentators point out that the slave, being under the *potestas* of his master 'cannot be liable to fulfil certain ritual acts which are dependent on a specific time' (*CRINT* 1.1, p. 509, quoting *m. Baba Metzia* 1.5, *b. Hagigah* 4a).
68. Exod. 21.26-27.
69. Exod. 21.28-32.
70. Exod. 21.20-21.
71. Deut. 24.22.

that it becomes a positive duty for the Israelite to avoid permanent enslavement.[72]

3. *Emancipation.* 'Men desire above all things to be free', wrote the Stoic, Dio Chrysostom, 'and say that freedom is the greatest of all good things, while slavery is the most shameful and unfortunate state'.[73] Throughout the ancient world, one of the great motivations held out to slaves to encourage hard work was the prospect of emancipation, and it is a tribute to the depth of the human desire for personal freedom that the vast majority of slaves were willing to make great sacrifices in order to obtain this, and regarded it as one of their highest goals in life.[74]

72. It is sometimes argued that the boring of the ears of slaves described in Exod. 21.6 and Deut. 15.17 is part of this prohibition against allowing one's own permanent enslavement—i.e., if, for some reason a Hebrew slave should opt for permanent slavehood, this ritual would act as a token punishment of the ear which has failed to heed God's injunctions against allowing oneself to be enslaved. See S.S. Bartchy, *Mallon Chresai: First Century Slavery and 1 Corinthians 7:21* (SBLDS, 11; Missoula, MT: SBL, 1973), p. 53. Mendelsohn, *Slavery in the Ancient Near East*, p. 49, on the other hand, thinks that this boring was simply for the purpose of inserting a tag of some kind to denote ownership.

73. *Discourse* 14.1.

74. Manumission as a right, or a gift from the master, had three major recognized forms in the Mesopotamian world (Mendelsohn, *Slavery in the Ancient Near East*, p. 79). These consisted of (a) the termination of the fixed period of debt-bondage, (b) the freeing of a slave concubine and her children after the death of her master and (c) the unconditional release of a Babylonian slave, sold in a foreign country, upon his return to his home city. Moreover, any children born of the legitimate marriage between a free woman and a slave were free, a custom presumably stemming from the fact that offspring were regarded as part of the woman, and therefore owned by whoever owned her.

There are two further, and very common, methods of emancipation which were clearly practised in the Mesopotamian world: manumission by adoption and manumission through fictive purchase by a god (Mendelsohn, *Slavery in the Ancient Near East*, pp. 78-82. See also Patterson, *Slavery*, p. 234), although they are not mentioned in the Code of Hammurabi.

In the Greek and Roman world, apart from the case of war captives receiving freedom upon reaching their own city, there existed no circumstances under which a slave was legally entitled to manumission, although, in the later Roman empire, sick slaves who had been abandoned by their masters could not be reclaimed upon their recovery. Slaves who had been forcibly circumcised by their masters were also entitled to freedom. The actual procedures of manumission varied. The fictive sale of a slave to a god was practised widely in the Greek world (see below, pp. 85-87). In the Roman empire there was a division between formal and informal

Indeed such was the importance placed on it that Pliny can even speak of comforting slaves on their deathbeds by granting them freedom.[75]

In the Greek and Roman world, such a promise of manumission was almost entirely up to the master, and it provided a very powerful tool for motivating slaves. It might come as a gift or reward, or a slave might be required to pay a (usually inflated) price raised out of his or her own *peculium* or from loans from a third party. In its most cynical form, it might also be a way for a master to avoid the cost of maintaining slaves who were too old or disabled to continue work. As mentioned above, the Old Testament laid down that a Hebrew slave should be manumitted after a fixed term had expired, and that a slave had a right to freedom if mutilated by his or her master.

The value obviously placed on manumission by slaves is quite interesting in view of the incompleteness of the freedom actually granted to them, at least in the Greek and Roman worlds. By the last century BCE, Greek or Roman slaves manumitted in any of these ceremonies remained severely constrained by a host of obligations to their ex-master and the ex-master's family. A failure to fulfil these duties, as well as any others agreed upon as a condition of their release, could lead to punishment or re-enslavement under the charge of 'ingratitude'.[76] This is not to say, however, that the possibilities for wealth and advancement for freedmen were not sometimes very great indeed, and many held high positions in the Imperial bureaucracy.

4. *Summary*. What general idea, thus, can we have of slavery in the world in which the first Christian communities came into being? First, it can safely be said that slavery was taken to be a natural part of life, one which was questioned by few. That slavery was, and would continue to be, for better or worse, an inevitable characteristic of human society was accepted without serious question by all but the most visionary, and while writers and philosophers might dream up utopias

---

methods of manumission, the former taking place in a legal setting and usually conferring citizenship along with freedom, and the latter, which did not confer citizenship, occurring in a less formal setting.

75. Pliny, *Epistle* 8.16.

76. See Garlan, *Slavery in Ancient Greece*, pp. 77-81, and W.L. Westermann, 'The Freedmen and the Slaves of God', *Proceedings of the American Philosophical Society* 92 (1948), pp. 55-64.

or ideal pasts where such a state of affairs would be unknown,[77] none of them proposed any coherent course of action to turn such ideas into social reality.[78] Even on those few occasions when slaves themselves rose up in rebellion against their masters, they concerned themselves not with a levelling but with an inversion of power. They sought not to abolish slavery but to become masters themselves.[79]

The explanation of the nature of slavery was divided into two broad camps: those who felt that slavery had come into being as a result of the natural division of human beings into slave and free, and those who attributed its existence to human and legal coercion, the unjust but necessary result of the nature of human society. Recognition of the humanity of the slave and encouragement to masters to treat their slaves well, even if for purely pragmatic reasons, is sporadically attested in the ancient literature, but even those who argue most vociferously for the status of slaves as 'humble friends' and fellow humans make no apparent attempt to pursue this as far as any substantial challenge to the institution itself. Most societies in the ancient world had some forms of legislation attempting to restrain some of the worst extremes of brutality a slave might suffer, and law and custom together usually granted the enslaved a modicum of rights and privileges, at least to urban and household slaves. Nevertheless, the fact remained that slaves were legally chattels and their quality of life depended almost entirely on the goodwill of their master. Beyond the few rights that I have discussed above, the position and treatment of a slave in the ancient world depended very much for better or worse on the nature the master.[80] We do have records of individual slaves who were highly trusted and well treated, and sometimes even adopted as heirs to their master's estate. Again, depending on the slave's relationship with the master, a slave might enjoy varying degrees of independence from direct control. Slaves might have a *peculium*, or sum of money under their own control which, although it remained legally the possession of

77. On such utopias, see Vogt, *Ancient Slavery*, pp. 26-38.

78. The one notable exception being the Essene community (see below, p. 54 n. 20).

79. Vogt, *Ancient Slavery*, pp. 54, 61 and 89-90; also K. Hopkins, *Conquerors and Slaves* (Cambridge: Cambridge University Press, 1980), p. 120.

80. On the physical coercion of and brutality towards slaves in general, see K.R. Bradley, *Slaves and Masters in the Roman Empire: A Study in Social Control* (Collection Latomus, 185; New York: Oxford University Press, 1987), pp. 113-37, and Griffin, *Seneca*, pp. 382-83.

the master,[81] the slaves were often at liberty to use as they wished, and there were even some slaves who were able to set up businesses of their own and to live relatively independently from the direct control of their masters.

Although many slaves were well treated and might become wealthy through business interests of their own, sometimes rising to positions of power and influence, and although the urban domestic slave might have, in many cases, enjoyed a higher standard of living and education than their free counterpart, the idea of freedom never lost its power in the slave's mind and many would go to great lengths to attain it.

2. *Slavery as a Metaphor in the Ancient World*

Slavery is one of the main metaphors that has been used in the description of the relationship between the human and the divine. It is also an exceptionally adaptable one, its ambivalent force allowing it to be effectively used in two completely opposing senses. The connotations of devotion and submission, as well as of a merging of identity with and an absolute dependence on the master possessed by the term *slavery*, make it an effective metaphor for the attitude of the devoted believer or industrious philosopher before his or her god. On the other hand, its connotations of degradation and abasement, of loss of self will and of forced captivity and misery, make it a useful label for all that is mean and inadequate in human nature, and for those who are unable to be independent of physical needs and greeds.

Both of these forms of the metaphor are found in the literature of the ancient world. They usually occur in one of two forms, either as indicating a kind of literal slavery, where people are seen as being, in a very real sense, slaves of a deity, or in a more illustrative sense, where the users are clearly aware that they are using a metaphor. In the first case, individuals are seen as being the actual possessions of a deity. In spite of seeming so literal, this is, of course, still a metaphor. It clearly does not describe an empirically obvious relationship in the manner of the enslavement of one human to another. Those using this metaphor, however, clearly think, in some cases, that they are saying something empirically true. In the second case, the idea is intended only as a metaphor and is used to describe the way in which individuals relate to

---

81. Further on this, see A.H.M. Jones, *The Later Roman Empire 284–602: A Social, Economic and Administrative Survey* (London: Basil Blackwell, 1986), pp. 282-83.

a deity, to the other forces in their life or to their own shortcomings.

The understanding of God expressed in the Hebrew tradition often takes the first of these forms, and God is shown as having a special ownership of a certain people, namely the Israelites: 'For the people of Israel are slaves to me, they are my slaves whom I brought out of the land of Egypt.'[82] This is a very real slavery to God, and as such has practical implications: the Israelites are slaves of God and therefore cannot be enslaved by anyone else without their relationship with God being violated. Slavery to God is just as real as earthly slavery, and is therefore inconsistent with any other slavery. Thus:

> There came from (God) this word to Shemaiah '...My wrath shall not be poured out on Jerusalem by means of Shishak, but they shall become his slaves; then they will know the difference between serving me and serving the rulers of other countries'.[83]

Here, slavery to God is placed in apposition to slavery to an earthly master and is obviously meant to be understood with the same concreteness.

This kind of use clearly has roots in the conventions of oriental culture where concepts of ruler/subject and master/slave are so closely interwoven. The phrase 'I am your slave' and its variations were widely used in this part of the world as a polite formula of humility in day to day speech, as we see reflected in the language of the Old Testament. In the earlier part of the Septuagint, δοῦλος is not used for this, but numerous examples of παῖς, used as a token of humility, may be found.[84] δοῦλος, however, becomes more common in the later books and we find such passages as:

> ...and it happened that the king came by, and he (the prophet) cried out to the king and said ὁ δοῦλος σου ἐξῆλθεν ἐπὶ τὴν στρατιάν ('your slave went into the battle') (1 Kgs 21.39; NEB 1 Kgs 20.39)

and

> οὐχὶ σὺ κύριε μου βασιλεῦ ὤμοσας τῇ δούλῃ σου ('Did you not, my lord king, swear to your slave...') (3 Kgdms 1.13).[85]

Stemming, at least in part, from such usage, we find the same kind of formula used in addressing God in

82. Lev. 25.55.
83. 2 Chron. 12.7-9.
84. As in Gen. 32.4, 18, 20; 33.6 and 42; 10, 11.
85. See also 1 Kgs 1.26-27.

...and he wept before the Lord and said

σὺ εὐδόκησας ἐν χειρὶ δούλου σου τὴν σωτηρίαν τὴν μεγάλην ταύτην ('You have let me your slave win this great victory') (Judg. 15.18)

and in the famous words of Anna:

ἐὰν ἐπιβλέπων ἐπιβλέψῃς ἐπὶ τὴν ταπείνωσιν τῆς δούλης σου ('If you will look down upon the lowliness of your slave')[86] (1 Kgdms 1.11)

and Samuel:

λάλει ὅτι ἀκούει ὁ δοῦλος σου ('Speak because your slave hears you') (1 Kgdms 3.9).[87]

God may also be shown as referring to individuals as his slaves:

διά Δαυὶδ τὸν δοῦλόν μου ('for the sake of David my slave') (3 Kgdms 11.13).[88]

Those who worship God are, in the Hebrew mind, God's slaves, and those who worship other gods and idols are likewise slaves of these. The Hellenic tradition on the other hand shows no sign of such communal, literal slavery. In this case, literal slavery to a deity is individual and only exists in the form of temple slavery.[89] Such slavery refers to slaves of the gods who actually live and work in the temple precincts. There is, in the Greek world, another form of slavery to the god, where slaves are actually purchased from their master by the temple on behalf of the god. This purchase, however, being nothing more than a legal fiction, is only a manumission procedure and the slaves, although purchased by the god, obtain their freedom in this way and do not, in most cases, continue to be thought of as slaves of the god. This procedure of *sacral manumission* will be discussed more fully in the next chapter.

Where the use of the idea of slavery to the gods does occur, it is more clearly a metaphor and usually functions on a more specific and individual basis. Although Plato asserts that men and women are 'by nature fitted to δοῦλειν the gods',[90] and, on one occasion calls Socrates a δοῦλος of God,[91] the use of such language is rare in the Hellenic

86. Cf. Lk. 1.48.
87. See also 1 Kgs 3.7, 9 and 1 Kgs 8.23; 1 Kgs 23.10-11; 2 Sam. 7.18-29; 24.10; 1 Kgs 8.33-59; 1 Chron. 17.18, 26; Neh. 1.6; Est. 5.4.
88. Also 11.32-38. See also 2 Sam. 3.18; 1 Kgs 19.34; 21.8; 8.9; 1 Chron. 17.4, 7; 2 Chron. 6.42; Ezek. 28.25 and 37.34-35; and Hag. 2.24.
89. As in Euripides, *Ion* 132, 182, 309 and 327.
90. *Phaedo* 80a.
91. *Phaedo* 85b. See also *Laws* 6.762e.

tradition and examples are few and far between, although Epictetus is fond of it, as in:

> The cynic reviles all he meets as a father, as a brother, and as a slave (ὑπηρέτης) of Zeus the father of all.[92]

The dramatists whose work, although it dates from several centuries before the time of the New Testament, can be expected to have been part of popular culture at the time, make very little use of the kind of language we have been examining. It is entirely absent from those of Aeschylus's and Sophocles' plays that survive, and in Euripides' work, the uses of the 'slave of god' idea are in most cases in the context of a literal temple slavery. In *Orestes* we do find the sentiment 'We serve (δουλεύομεν) the gods, whatever the gods may be',[93] but even this has more to do, in its context, with despair and helplessness than with a real perception of slavehood as a constructive and meaningful relationship with the gods. Indeed in the entire corpus available to the modern reader the only use of the metaphor in the form we have been discussing is Tiresias's assertion that he is the δοῦλος of Apollo,[94] and Hippolytus's slave's reminder that only the gods can be called master.[95] It is clearly not a popular metaphor in this tradition. Although it would be going too far to call it, as some have done, 'unthinkable',[96] it is certainly not a metaphor that immediately springs to mind in this context. It is slightly more common among the Latin writers. Tacitus attributes such a notion to the Germans, who, he says, consider their nobles and priests to be slaves of the gods (*ministros deorum*).[97]

As worshippers of God were, in the Old Testament tradition, termed his slaves, so were the worshippers of other gods and idols thought of

92. Epictetus, *Discourse* 3.22.82. See also 1.8.15 and 1.8.19.
93. Euripides, *Orestes* 418.
94. Sophocles, *Oedipus the King* 410.
95. Θεοὺς γὰρ δεσπότας καλεῖν χρεών. Euripides, *Hippolytus* 88.
96. W.K. Pleket ('Religious History as the History of Mentality: The "Believer" as Servant of the Deity in the Greek World', in H.S. Versnel (ed.), *Faith, Hope and Worship: Aspects of Religious Mentality in the Ancient World* (Leiden: E.J. Brill, 1981], pp. 152-92) thinks that one could go further than this and that 'elements (of the notion of slavery to the gods) did exist in the realm of Greek religiosity already in the classical era, seldom and cursorily though they might be attested'. Certainly 'elements' existed, but I doubt that they ever played a very important role in Greek religious thought.
97. *Germania* 10.

as the slaves of these gods and idols. Thus, mirroring the slaves and priests of God, we find the slaves of Baal,[98] and concern is expressed that the people of Israel will fall away into the service of other gods:

> ...and there you will serve (δουλεύσεις) other gods[99]

and

> Then your fathers cried to the Lord for help 'We have sinned...we have served (ἐδουλεύσαμεν) Balaam and Ashtaroth. But now save us from the hands of our enemies and we will serve (δουλεύσομέν) you'.[100]

In all these cases, the misdirected slavery is a slavery to idols, a mirror image of the slavery due to God, but with the wrong master. The opposition always exists, whether explicit or implied, between slavery to God and slavery to other gods. It is a perversion of action, a conscious turning from one thing to another and is indissolubly linked with a conscious, active response, that is, worship. What we do not find here is slavery as a perversion of the individual character, the subjection of individuals by their own shortcomings or the unconscious subjection to nonpersonified externals. No use, therefore, is made of such ideas as individuals enslaved to their passions, or to physical needs, or, indeed to externals such as nature, chance or the opinion of others.

In the Hellenic tradition, in contrast, we find a very different usage. Here such slavery is not wrong in that it is misdirected; it is wrong in itself, and the writer, while condemning slavery to such things, does not suggest an alternative master. Rather his purpose is to emphasize the lack of freedom of the individual, as for example in the following:

> (Timarchos) behaved as he did because he was a slave to the most shameful pleasures:[101] to gluttony and extravagant dinner parties and flute girls and courtesans and dice and the other things by which no properly-born and free man should be mastered.[102]

This slavery has nothing to do with worship in any real sense; indeed it is, for the most part, unconscious and the writers thus take great

98. 1 Kgs 10.20, 23 and Jer. 13.10. See also Jer. 8.2; 1 Kgs 16.31, 22.54; 2 Kgs. 10.18 and 2 Chron. 33.3.
99. Deut. 28.64. See also Exod. 23.33; Judg. 10.6; 1 Sam. 26.19; 1 Kgs 9.6; 2 Kgs 17.41; 2 Chron. 7.22, 24.18, 33.23, 36; and Ps. 106.36.
100. 1 Sam. 12.10. See also 1 Sam. 8.8, and Jer. 5.19; 16.11-14; 22.9 and 25.6.
101. δουλεύων ταῖς αἰσχίσταις ἡδοναῖς.
102. Aischines, *Timarchos* 42. Translation by R. Just, 'Freedom, Slavery and the Female Psyche', *HPT* 6 (1985), pp. 1-188.

delight in emphasizing the paradox of the apparently free person who is in truth a slave, or in the impossibility, as Euripides' Hecuba points out, of anyone being truly free:

> There is no one who is free; one is a slave to money, another to chance.[103]

Indeed, even the gods themselves may fall prey to slavery, and Zeus, who rules all else is a δοῦλος of Hera.[104]

Thus, individuals may be the slave to their own needs and desires, and this kind of formula is especially dear to Seneca:

> Show me a man who isn't (a slave); one is a slave to lust, another to greed, another to ambition, and all (are slaves) to fear.[105]

The same terms may be used to describe political domination. Plato speaks of life under political tyranny as 'most bitter and unbearable slavery',[106] while Tacitus describes the subjugation of the Britons as slavery[107] and shows Calgacus comparing his people's situation to that of slaves:

> Slaves (*manicipia*) born into slavery are sold once and for all, and are cared for by their masters. Britain, however, purchases her own slavery daily.[108]

Equally, an inappropriate relationship between the sexes may be described in this way, and Tacitus speaks of the rule of the Sitones by their women as causing them to fall even beneath slavery,[109] and Juvenal speaks of marriage as a voluntary slavery.[110]

In the Graeco-Roman tradition, we begin to see an interesting breakdown of the links between the metaphor and the reality. While at one end of the spectrum we saw the relationship with the divine operating, at least in theory, on a basis identical to that between the master and slave, we now begin to see that an emphasis on the *difference* between such slavery and earthly slavery is frequently enforced by those who

103. Euripides, *Hecuba* 865-66.
104. Euripides, *The Women of Troy* 950-55.
105. Seneca, *Moral Epistles* 47.7 (see also 77.15 and 90.10).
106. Plato, *Republic* 569c.
107. *Agricola* 14 (King Cogidumnus was an *instrumenta servitutis*), 15, 21.
108. *Agricola* 31. The speech goes on to describe the world as a *familia* of fellow slaves.
109. *Germania* 45.
110. *Satires* 6.186-213.

use such language, as for instance at the end of Apuleius's *The Golden Ass*: 'Nam cum coeperis deae servire, tunc magis senties fructum tuae libertatis' ('For when you begin to serve the goddess you will more fully experience the fruit of your liberty').[111] Here emerges the idea that true freedom lies in slavery, as Epictetus asserts: 'To win true freedom you must be a slave to philosophy'.[112]

There is, moreover, a difference in context that becomes more important. These two forms of slavery exist on two different levels and do not interfere with each other. Human slavery makes no difference to the slavery or freedom that subsists in the soul alone, and the one who in the course of this world is a slave to someone else, may actually be truly free, due to the inward enlightenment of his soul,[113] whereas a king who caters to his own lusts is a slave in spite of his wealth and authority.

It is such a division between human and divine slavery that makes possible the complex use of the metaphor of slavery that we shall encounter as we turn to the New Testament.

111. Apuleius, *Metamorphoses* 11.15.
112. 'philosophiae servias oportet, ut tibi contingat vera libertas' (cited in Seneca, *Moral Epistles* 8.7).
113. Epictetus, *Discourse* 1.19.9. See also Seneca, *Moral Epistles* 3.20.1.

Chapter 2

SLAVERY AND THE CHURCH

1. *Slaves in the Congregations*

From its earliest days, the Christian message held great attraction for slaves and many of these played a very active part in the early congregations, as can be seen even in the New Testament. The existence of slaves as members of the Christian congregation is taken for granted throughout the Epistles and they are included in admonitions concerning the behaviour of Christians within their households. Slaves are instructed to obey their masters willingly and masters are to treat their slaves well.[1] Similar instructions to slaves may be found in the *Didache* (late first century CE) and in the *Epistle of Barnabas* (c. 130 CE).

Although there survives no patristic work specifically on the subject of slavery,[2] much space within other works is devoted to the subject. Chrysostom (late fourth/early fifth century CE) and Augustine (late fourth/early fifth century CE), as we shall see, take particular interest in the treatment and wellbeing of Christian slaves, and most of the Fathers mention slaves at some point, taking it for granted that there will be

1. Col. 3.22–4.1. Similar instructions are found in Eph. 6.5-8, which, although of dubious authorship, accurately reflects the reciprocity of the relationship enjoined by Paul on masters and slaves. 1 Tim. and Titus do not and are closer to 1 Peter in this sense.

2. In the 430s CE Theodoret devotes a portion of his *On Divine Providence* to a discussion of slavery, arguing that the slave gains substantial benefits from his position as a slave (*On Divine Providence* 7, 'That the division into slaves and masters is an advantage in life', PG 83.665-85). I have left this aside as it falls at the end of the period under consideration, but see Garnsey (*Ideas of Slavery*, pp. 51-52) and R. Klein ('Die Sklavenfrage bei Theodoret von Kyrrhos: "Die 7. Rede des Bischofs über die Vorsehung" ', in G. Wirth [ed.], *Romanitas-Christianitas: Untersuchungen zur Geschichte und Literatur der römischen Kaiserzeit, Johannes Straub zum 70 Geburtstag am 18 Oktober 1982 gewidmet* [Berlin: W. de Gruyter, 1982], pp. 586-633) for a fuller discussion of Theodoret's views.

members of the Church who are of such a status. As the legal structure of the Church grows, we also begin to find a number of canon laws passed on slavery, and the adoption of Christianity as a state religion sees the beginning of state-legislated Christian laws on slavery. The *Shepherd of Hermas* (c. 120 CE) is also a most interesting text in this context as it claims to have been written by a slave, or an ex-slave. This indicates the status possible in the Church for one in such a position (for even if the fact of the matter be doubtful, it nevertheless shows that it was credible that a slave should have and declare such experiences as those recorded in the text).

In the earliest Church, the equal participation of slaves in worship does not seem to have been disputed. While the demands on time and freedom imposed on a slave by a master might limit active participation, there is no explicit suggestion that any unworthiness implicit in the slave's station in life should prevent advancement in this community, and some slaves do seem to have attained positions of responsibility. Pliny the Younger, for instance, records torturing a pair of deaconesses in order to obtain information on Christianity.[3] The fact that he could order this suggests that these two women were slaves and thus legally liable to torture.

The conflict of loyalty possible when a slave became a Christian was especially apparent in the question of the ordination of slaves and their reception into monasteries. In 451, the Council of Chalcedon (Act 6) threatens with excommunication anyone who violates the decree that 'no slave shall be received into the monasteries contrary to the will of his own master, for the purpose of becoming a monk'.[4] The *Apostolic*

---

3.   Pliny, *Epistle* 10.96.

4.   J. Stevenson (ed.), *Creeds, Councils and Controversies: Documents Illustrative of the History of the Church AD 337–461* (rev. with additional documents by W.H.C. Frend; London: SPCK, 1976), p. 325. On the monasticism of slaves, *CTh* 9.45.3. This was another problem for the legislators. There is a growing tendency throughout this period to encourage slaves of both sexes to take up the ascetic life. Some writers urge their readers to give their slaves freedom that they may respond to this call: 'He that has a daughter or young woman of his race, let her come and become the bride of my Glorious One! He that has a servant set him free that he may come and serve his lord.' Ephraim (early/mid fourth century), *Hymns on the Nativity* 12.8 and Melania the younger is reported to have built a monastery for her male slaves and a convent for her female ones, emancipating vast numbers of

Canons (c. 380) forbid the ordination of slaves without the consent of the master concerned, but allow the ordination of slaves who 'appear worthy', 'as our Onesimus appeared' and have their master's permission.[5] The main anxiety is that the ordination of a slave would incur loss to the master of that asset. Such ordinations did occasionally take place—Basil (mid/late fourth century CE) seems to have caused great consternation on one occasion by ordaining a slave against his mistress's will.[6]

The ordination of slaves was forbidden, according to A.H.M. Jones, by Arcadius in 398, by Valentinian III in 452,[7] and by Zeno in 484,

slaves. Such an action was commended first as an example of personal asceticism and less as one of humanitarianism.

In consequence of the monasticism of slaves was the inevitable problem of slaves who sought monasticism without the permission of their masters. Perhaps partly to assure themselves of the blessing of the masters and to insure themselves against the reclamation of slaves, it was usually ruled that slaves should be manumitted previous to their entry into the religious life.

5.   *Apostolical Constitutions* 82.8.47.

6.   Basil, *Epistle* 115. See footnote to this in *NPNF*, VIII, which cites, on this incident, Maran, *Vit. Bas* 15, Gregory Nazianzus, *Ep.* 38. See W.H.C. Frend, *The Rise of Christianity* (Philadelphia: Fortress Press, 1989 [1984]), p. 570 and p. 588 n. 122. Jerome, too, reports that one of the charges made against him (Jerome) by John of Jerusalem was that he had allowed the ordination of a slave. But, Jerome replies that not only does his accuser have 'clergymen of the same class', but that the slave Onesimus too was made a deacon after his conversion by Paul (Jerome, *Epistle* 82.6)

7.   This, however must refer to the *Letter of Valentinian III on Episcopal Judgement and on Various Matters* 452 (LNV 35) (see P.R. Coleman-Norton), the relevant section of which reads, 'No registered cultivator, tenant slave or tenant farmer, not a guildsman of the city of Rome or of any other city at all, not a municipal senator nor a leading municipal senator, not a receiver of the gold tax, a citizen who is a sevir of a guild or a public slave should attach himself to monks or monasteries, that he may evade the bond of his obligated service. Moreover, registered cultivators or slaves, who, avoiding the bond of birth, have transferred themselves to an ecclesiastical order should return their masters' legal controls (bishops and priests excepted), if they have not completed the thirtieth year in the said office; likewise a deacon of this status should give to his master a substitute for himself, all his peculium also having been restored (if he cannot provide a substitute, he is to be recalled)', P.R. Coleman-Norton (ed. and trans.), *Roman State and Christian Church: A Collection of Legal Documents to AD 535* (London: SPCK, 1966), II, pp. 812-13. It is clear, therefore, that the prohibition against the ordination of slaves

although Justinian 'allowed slaves to be ordained with their owner's consent'. They reverted to him if they abandoned the Church and could be recalled, but only within a year.[8] Nevertheless, there was some advancement through the ranks. Callistus, the bishop of Rome, was an ex-slave.[9] Strictly, of course, this is not a case of the advancement of a slave but of a freedman, a person who enjoyed a qualitatively different status from a slave. He is, therefore, not as unusual a case as it might seem, since the rapid upward mobility of freedmen is a characteristic feature of the later Roman empire. It would seem that, in most cases there are two basic objections to the ordination of slaves, 'the incompatibility of such a state with clerical dignity, and the fact that, because of their dependence on another, they would not be able to dispose of their own time'.[10] The first of these objections appears in the complaint of Leo the Great (mid fifth century CE) that

> men are indiscriminately admitted to the Sacred Order who are recommended by neither any dignity of birth nor character: even some who have not been able to obtain liberty from their masters are admitted to the dignity of priesthood... Twofold, thus, is the offence in this matter, both that the sacred ministry is polluted by such base association, and that, in regard to the unlawful possession which is taken of them, the rights of masters are subverted.[11]

This objection is not one which is frequently appealed to, however, in forbidding the ordination of slaves. The far more important issue at stake is the fact that such a move deprives the master of his economic investment.

2. *The Perception of Slaves*

The constant theme in Christian writings, from the earliest texts onwards, is the spiritual equality of all, slave or free, before God. With God, the Pauline writings assert repeatedly, 'there is neither slave nor

---

proceeds almost entirely from a concern that the legal rights of the master not be infringed upon.

8.   A.H.M. Jones, *The Later Roman Empire*, p. 921.

9.   On the career of Callistus, see H. Gülzow, *Christentum und Sklaverei in den ersten drei Jahrhunderten* (Bonn: Rudolf Habelt, 1969), pp. 146-72.

10.   A. Garcia y Garcia, *Historia del Derecho Canonico* (Salamanca: Instituto de Historia de la Teologia Española, 1967), p. 232, my translation.

11.   Leo the Great, *Epistle* 4.3.

free', since God is the master equally of slave and lord. The *Didache* reminds masters that their slaves 'hope on the same God'.[12] This concept of spiritual equality continues to be a consistent theme throughout the patristic period. Chrysostom, for example, is only one of the many who assert that the one who is inwardly free is truly free[13] and that slavery in the flesh in no way diminishes one's status with God.[14] The slave must serve willingly rather than under compulsion.[15] In doing so, even under non-Christian masters, the slave will bring glory to God, impressing and maybe even converting his or her master.[16] In religious terms, as Chrysostom reminds the master, the slave

> ...is a brother, or rather has become a brother, he has received the same (gifts), he belongs to the same body. Indeed, he is the brother not only of his own master, but even of the son of God.[17]

One of the most interesting aspects of the New Testament discussion on slavery is the fact that terms referring to slaves or to their nature are never used in a derogatory manner. No generalizations, positive or negative, are made on the character of slaves, save the general assumption that it is only wicked slaves who fail to be obedient and faithful to their masters.

A few more negative attitudes towards slaves are found in later texts, but these are rare and are often modified by reminders that it is not their nature but their situation that makes them so. John Chrysostom may agree with his audience that slaves are a 'troublesome, audacious, impudent, incorrigible race'—a far cry from the New Testament tone—but, having said that, he does immediately admit that such characteristics arise 'not through their nature, God forbid, but from their ill

---

12. *Didache* 4.10-11.

13. Chrysostom, *Homilies on Ephesians* 12.4 (PG 62.367).

14. Indeed, Ephraim implies that, in some ways, the slave is better off spiritually: 'The son of the free man who bears thy yoke, my son (God speaking to Christ) shall have one reward; the slave that bears the yoke of two masters, of him above and of him below, there are two blessings for him and two rewards of two burdens... The free woman, my son, is thy handmaid, also she who is in bondage serves thee, in thee she is free', *Hymn on the Nativity* 12.9.

15. *Homilies on Ephesians* 22.1 (PG 62.156).

16. *Homilies on Titus* 4.2 (PG 62.685-86).

17. *Homilies on Ephesians* 12.2 (PG 62.155).

breeding and the neglect of their masters'.[18] He is willing to point out that in certain circumstances, the behaviour and character of the slave may be superior to that of the master.[19]

3. *Slavery and Church Authority*

However seriously the Church might take the theory of spiritual equality of all, the fact remained that unless it was to follow the example of the Essenes in the abolition of slavery among believers,[20] it would have in some way to come to terms with the structures of human domination that the continuation of slavery entailed. Thus, from the New Testament onwards, slaves are exhorted to be content with their lot and work with a good will. Naturally, as the Church grew in scope and stature, the spiritual equality of the slave came to be more and more of a problem and many adjustments had to be made to avoid causing chaos in the relationships between the free and servile members of the congregation. The beginning of these problems is already apparent in the writings of the earliest centuries. It cannot be expected, however, that masters, even Christian ones, would always have been pleased to see their slaves taking an active role in the Church. In the conflict of loyalty that would inevitably have arisen between a slave's religion and his or her master, the Church usually sought to support the demands of the master. Thus, the *Apostolic Tradition* directs that no slave is to be accepted for baptism without the permission and recommendation of the master—if these are not forthcoming, the slave is to be taught 'to please his master' instead.

Nevertheless, the fact that the slave was a Christian, and therefore a subject of concern for God, made it necessary for the writers to take care to point out some of the resulting obligations of the masters. They are called upon to recognize the spiritual equality of the slave, and to treat them with kindness and consideration. The *Didache* commands, 'You shall not rule your male slave (δοῦλος) or female slave (παιδίσκη) who hope on the same God, in bitterness'.[21] The slave must

18. *Homilies on Titus* 4.2 (PG 62.685).
19. See also *Homilies on Ephesians* 12.4 (PG 62.92). Conversely one may be enslaved by one's own superstition and folly.
20. See Josephus, *Ant.* 18.21 and Philo, *Omn. Prob. Lib.* 457.79.
21. *Epistle of Barnabas* 19.7 and *Didache* 4.10-11.

obey their master 'in fear and trembling'.[22] This fair and kind treatment of slaves continues to be urged by the Christian authorities, and this soon develops into an expectation that masters should take responsibility not only for the slave's material wellbeing but also for their spiritual progress. Chrysostom acknowledges no difference between the personal rights of the slave and the free, and urges masters to take their slaves to church, to teach them to be religious[23] and to talk to them about Hell (!),[24] and we find similar concerns expressed by Augustine,[25] who pleads that slaves be treated considerately and that unreasonable demands not be made on them. The best kind of masters, according to Augustine 'serve' and 'take care' of their slaves and only 'appear' to command them.[26]

4. *Rights of Slaves*

Those, moreover, who set out the canons of the Church and the legislation of the Christian state began to recognize the difficulties that Christian slaves might face in fulfilling their obligations in their servile state. For example:

> Canon VI: Slaves forced by their masters to offer incense to idols, and doing it in their master's stead, are enjoined a year's penance.

> Canon VII: The masters who forced them to it are enjoined three years' penance, as being hypocrites and forcing their slaves to sacrifice.[27]

The emperors Honorius and Theodosis, in 415, allow Jews to own Christian slaves 'on the sole condition that they permit such slaves to retain their own religion'.[28] They are forbidden by the same emperors,

22. *Didache* 4.10-11.
23. Chrysostom, *Homily on Ephesians* 22. 6 (PG 62.157-58).
24. Chrysostom, *Homily on 2 Thessalonians* 3.1 (PG 62.479).
25. Augustine, *City of God* 19.16 where he urges masters to be just as concerned about their slaves' religious wellbeing as they are about that of their own children.
26. Augustine, *City of God* 19.14.
27. *Canons of Peter of Alexandria* AD 311. 'Christians did send slaves to sacrifice on their behalf and clear the household's name. Sometimes their slaves would be pagan, but not always: if anyone risked going to hell it might as well be one of the servants', R.L. Fox, *Pagans and Christians* (New York: Viking, 1986), p. 458.
28. *CTh* 16.9.3 (415 AD).

in 423, to purchase Christian slaves.[29] Constantine in 336–337 protects the slaves from conversion or circumcision by Jewish masters,[30] and laws are enacted by 373 to prevent the forcible baptism of slaves into heretical sects.[31]

The absolute authority of the master over the slave extended into the sexual realm. This and the fragile nature of any slave union—given that most slave marriages could not be given formal legal recognition—placed the ideals of lifelong virginity or a single chaste marriage beyond the reach of most slaves. The *Apostolic Tradition* therefore allows the slave concubine to be baptized if she brings up her children and is faithful to her master,[32] and reminds his reader that slave girls who have been forced to have intercourse with their masters should not be condemned for doing so.[33]

5. *The Manumission Debate*

The debate whether such good behaviour should include either a desire for emancipation on the part of the slave or, on the part of the master, a determination to set slaves free, begins in the New Testament with the enigmatic passage 1 Cor. 7.21:[34]

> Every man should remain in the condition in which he was called. Were you a slave when you were called? Do not let that trouble you; but if a chance of freedom should come, make use of it rather (μᾶλλον χρῆσαι).

The dilemma is, of course, whether it is slavery or freedom that the slave is urged to make use of. While the majority of scholars in the past have interpreted the passage as 'make use of slavery', J.A. Harrill[35] in his recent reconsideration of the text has argued, mainly on philological

---

29. *CTh* 16.9.5 (423 AD).
30. *Sirmondian Constitutions* 4. See also *CTh* 16.8.22.
31. *CTh* 16.5.65.4 and 16.6.4.
32. *Apostolic Tradition* 2.16.2.
33. Basil, *Epistle* 199.49.
34. Further on the interpretation of this passage, see Bartchy's *Mallon Chresai*. For a detailed history of the interpretation of this passage, see also Harrill, *The Manumission of Slaves*.
35. Harrill, *The Manumission of Slaves*.

grounds, that Paul is instructing the slave to 'take freedom' and that this passage should not only be understood as permission to take freedom but as the reflection of a positive tendency on the part of the Church to emancipate slaves. The main part of his argument rests on two grounds: that the adverb μᾶλλον is adversative not to its protasis ('if you can indeed become free') but to the previous apodosis ('do not worry about it')[36]; and that ἐι καί should not be understood as 'even if' but as 'indeed' or 'the more so'. The command to slaves, argues Harrill, runs 'Were you a slave when called? Don't worry about it; but if you are able to become free then indeed make use of that' and is thus to be seen as one of the exceptions to the rule that each should remain in the position to which he or she has been called. In support of this he presents a collection of parallels in ancient literature where μᾶλλον and ἀλλ᾽ εἰ καί are to be understood in this manner.

Nevertheless, the context of the passage weighs strongly in the other direction. Paul has, indeed, already presented a number of exceptions to the rule that each should remain in the position of one's calling, but as Corcoran points out, in each of the cases where Paul allows an exception, he gives an explanation for the exception. Not so in the case of slavery. The general principle under discussion is that each should remain in the position of one's calling, and so it 'would seem self defeating to introduce an exception to the general principle being illustrated'.[37] In addition to this, none of the exceptions begin with ἀλλ᾽ εἰ καί.[38] On the contrary the link between slavery and marriage (where exceptions are permitted) is far weaker than the link between slavery and circumcision (where no exception is permitted): The passage continues:

> Was a man called with the marks of circumcision on him? Let him not remove them. Was he uncircumcised when he was called? Let him not be circumcised. Circumcision is neither here nor there; what matters is to keep God's commands. Each man should remain in the position in which he was called. Were you a slave when you were called? Do not let that

36. Harrill, *The Manumission of Slaves*, p. 118.

37. G. Corcoran, 'Slavery in the New Testament II', *MS* 6 (1980), pp. 62-83 (67).

38. See R. Klein, review of *The Manumission of Slaves in Early Christianity*, by J.A. Harrill (Tübingen: J.C.B. Mohr [Paul Siebeck], 1995), in *RQ* (1996), pp. 262-66.

trouble you; but if a chance of liberty should come μᾶλλον χρῆσαι. For the man who as a slave received the call to be a Christian is the Lord's freedman and, equally, the free man who received the call is a slave in the service of Christ. You were bought at a price; do not become the slaves of men. Thus each one, my friends, is to remain before God in the condition in which he received his call.

The assertion that each is to remain in the position to which they were called is repeated both after the example of circumcision and the example of slavery. The question of circumcision and slavery are preceded by the questions of marriage and celibacy and the exceptions allowable in each case. However, after the mention of circumcision and slavery, Paul reiterates the options concerning a change in or out of marriage, but slavery is not mentioned again, as one would expect if it were to be grouped with marriage as a condition for which there were allowable exceptions. It seems clear that he groups slavery with circumcision as a situation to which no alternatives should be chosen or even desired. Conzelmann points out that the main thrust of the passage on slavery is to comfort the slave—'let it not matter to you'—and that this implies that δουλεία must then be supplied after μᾶλλον χρῆσαι.[39]

It is possible that 'You were bought at a price; do not become the slaves of men' is intended to link circumcision and slavery by emphasizing that the believer is not to be ruled by the opinions and social values of others—one should not worry about circumcision or the lack of it, and one should not worry about slavery. There is a further link back to 1 Cor. 6.20 in the parallel between ἠγοράσθητε γὰρ τιμῆς and τιμῆς ἠγοράσθητε. In both cases, the individual is reminded that he or she belongs to Christ. There is a spiritual dimension to one's physical being, and so, by abusing 'freedom' the fornicator sins against the temple of the Holy Spirit, and through indifference to earthly freedom, the slave becomes a freedman of God. Further, in Gal. 3.28, Paul clearly locates slavery among those conditions which are unalterable but unimportant in the eyes of God: 'There is no such thing as Jew and Greek, slave and free man, male and female'.

39. D. Martin in *Slavery as Salvation: The Metaphor of Slavery in Pauline Christianity* (New Haven: Yale University Press, 1990), p. 65, makes the point that this passage also concerns the overturning of social norms in Christ, for by asserting that the free man is a slave of Christ and the slave is a freedman of Christ, Paul places the slave not on an equal footing with his or her master, but on a higher one.

A second text relevant to this question is *Philemon,* where Paul apparently sends the fugitive slave Onesimus back to his master.[40] In doing so, he requests that the master receive the slave 'no longer as a slave, but as more than a slave, a beloved brother'. It is not clear what this is supposed to entail; if Paul is requesting the emancipation of Onesimus, he certainly does not make any unequivocal statement to that effect. He is remarkably vague, even allowing for the constraints of tact and diplomacy. It is clear that he expects Philemon to take some kind of positive action, and issues the veiled threat that he will come to make sure his request is carried out: 'I write to you confident that you will meet my wishes; I know that you will in fact do better than I ask. And one thing more: have a room ready for me, for I hope that, in answer to your prayers, God will grant me to you.' (Phlm. 21–22). He even mentions that Philemon's debt to him is greater than Onesimus's debt to Philemon: 'not to mention that you owe your very self to me as well' (Phlm. 19). Nevertheless, he makes no more explicit request than that Philemon receive Onesimus back 'as more than a slave—as a dear brother' (Phlm. 16).

Barclay suggests that the reason for this ambiguity is that Paul himself was uncertain as to the proper course of action in this case:

> It would have been both awkward for Philemon and, ultimately, disastrous for his and similar housechurches if he had felt obliged to manumit his returning slave; but there was also a fundamental incongruity in their relationship between Philemon and Onesimus if they continued to be master and slave as well as brothers in Christ (in the full Pauline sense).[41]

The letter does tell us that Paul at the very least expected Philemon to receive Onesimus back without punishment and with a certain amount of good will: 'If, then, you count me as a partner in the faith, welcome him as you would welcome me' (Phlm. 17). Philemon is also expected to forgive Onesimus any wrongdoing he might have committed; Paul guarantees to repay Philemon for this, though he immediately reminds him that his own debt to Paul is immeasurably greater (Phlm. 20). It

---

40. In contravention of Deut. 23.15: 'You shall not surrender to his master a slave who has taken refuge with you'. It is not certain whether, under Roman law, Paul was obliged to return Onesimus—this may have only been the case if Philemon was a Roman citizen (Bradley, *Slaves and Masters*, p. 170).

41. J.M.G. Barclay, 'Paul, Philemon and the Dilemma of Christian Slave Ownership', *NTS* 37 (1991), pp. 161-86 (183).

might even be said that Paul hints tactfully that manumission would be appropriate: 'I know that you will in fact do better than I ask' (Phlm. 22). It would be understandable if Paul were unwilling to commit himself in writing to urging a master to manumit his slave, lest he cause a rush of other slaves expecting the same. Perhaps this hint was as far as he could go. If he is indeed requesting the manumission of Onesimus, the fact that he is so very circumspect in his request actually indicates that he does not see the general manumission of slaves as being on the Christian agenda. The very tact of his letter shows that he is anxious to sustain the authority of the master while requesting an exception in a particular and personal case. While the ultimate intent of this letter remains uncertain, there is certainly little evidence in the rest of Paul's writings to suggest that he encouraged slaves in general to expect their freedom in anything other than a spiritual sense.[42]

In his argument that early Christianity sought to encourage the manumission of slaves, Harrill also cites Ignatius of Antioch's instruction to Polycarp (early second century CE) that slaves should not 'seek to be set free ἀπὸ τοῦ κοινοῦ':

> Do not behave arrogantly towards slaves, either male or female. But let them not be puffed up. Rather let them be enslaved all the more to the glory of God, so that they may happen on a greater freedom from God. Let them not desire to be manumitted out of the common chest (ἀπὸ τοῦ κοινοῦ), so that they may not be found slaves of lust (ἵνα μὴ δοῦλοι εὑρεθῶσιν ἐπιθυμίας).[43]

This again, he argues, does not indicate a reluctance to free slaves— rather the opposite. Citing a collection of passages that appear to

---

42. However, there is much debate on this issue. Rupprecht points out that even if Onesimus was not expected to be released from slavery (and he feels there is a possibility he was), the very fact that Paul clearly expects him not to be punished was 'an unheard of thing in the ancient world', and would indicate that the Church expected 'physical as well as spiritual freedom for slaves' (A.W. Rupprecht, 'Attitudes on Slavery among the Church Fathers', in R.N. Longenecker and M.C. Tenney [eds.], *New Dimensions in New Testament Study* [Grand Rapids, MI: Zondervan, 1974], pp. 261-77). It is an interesting point—by tacitly forbidding Philemon to exercise his rights as master over his slave, Rupprecht suggests that Paul is rocking the very foundations of that relationship and making it untenable in the long run.

43. Ignatius, *Epistle to Polycarp* 4.3 (c. 108 CE). Translation adapted from Harrill, *The Manumission of Slaves*, p. 160.

encourage the purchase and liberation of slaves,[44] Harrill argues that Ignatius simply sought to curb abuses of the corporate manumission of slaves by individual churches and the threat to church order that would entail, not least through the unworthy conversion of slaves who sought baptism simply for the benefits it would bring by way of funds for manumission.[45] Harrill says, 'Ignatius does not prohibit private manumissions of Christian slaves by individual slaveholders, but seeks in particular to curb abuses of common chest (or corporate) manumissions by local house churches'.[46] It is true that the church did occasionally encourage some manumission of slaves. The *Didascalia* urges Churches to use their funds for the liberation of slaves.[47] Ambrose recommends the redemption of those who have been captured and sold into slavery as one of the greatest forms of liberality,[48] and tells of having himself broken up the sacred vessels of his church to raise funds for this purpose.[49] It is also true that the addition of ἀπὸ τοῦ κοινοῦ indicates that Ignatius is thinking primarily of manumission at the cost of the Church rather than of private manumission. It would indeed be a strange thing if Ignatius were seeking to curb individual, private manumissions when these were so common in the society at large.

The context of the passage, however, gives little grounds for supposing any encouragement of manumission, corporate or otherwise. The desire to be liberated leads to becoming a slave to lust, while remaining in slavery brings glory to God and freedom for the slave. Even if Ignatius is mainly concerned that the common funds of the Church not

44. Hermas, *Sim.* 1.8, *Mand* 8.10, *Apostolic Constitutions* 1.54-62, and Justin Martyr, *Apology* 1 are cited by Harrill, *The Manumission of Slaves*, pp. 179-80, as examples of Christian corporate manumission. However, *Sim.* 1.8 refers merely to the purchase of 'afflicted souls' and *Mand* 8.10 λυτροῦσθαι τοὺς δούλους τοῦ θεοῦ ('redeem from distress the slaves of God') which probably refers not to slaves per se, but to believers. Justin Martyr, *Apology* 1, speaks of the liberation of 'those in chains'. With the exception of the *Apostolic Constitutions* 1.54-62 (ῥυόμενοι δούλους) therefore, none of these passages refer unambiguously to the purchase for manumission of slaves—they could equally be taken to indicate the release or assistance of prisoners.

45. Harrill, *The Manumission of Slaves*, p. 166.

46. Harrill, *The Manumission of Slaves*, p. 158.

47. *Didascalia* 3.4.7.

48. *On the Duties of the Clergy* 3.15.

49. *On the Duties of the Clergy* 3.28. Acacius, Bishop of Amidia is reported to have done the same (Socrates, *Ecclesiastical History* 7.21).

be expended in the purchase for manumission of slaves, or that unworthy slaves not attach themselves to Christianity for the sake of manumission, it shows that he does not consider the liberation of slaves to be a matter of high priority either to the Church or to slaves themselves.

It is important to keep the question of manumission in perspective. Even if the Church approved or even encouraged the manumission of slaves, it would have been doing nothing humane or radical for its time. Manumission was as much a part of the institution of slavery as the chain and the whip—simply another tool at the owner's disposal to motivate the slave to good service. To encourage legal manumission may seem a kindness to individual slaves, but it also confirms the owner's right to possess the slave in the first place. In 321, the Church was given the power to carry out fully legal and complete manumissions '*in ecclesia*'.[50] Westermann takes this development as yet more evidence of the wholesale approval of 'the institution of slavery with all its mundane formulas and practices' and no more a result of concern for the welfare of slaves than the sacral manumissions in the Greek temples had been.[51] Bradley agrees that this form of manumission amounted to little more than 'a convenience for those who wished to manumit and wished to do so in the context of their religious way of life'.[52]

The more important question is whether the Church ever mounted any deliberate challenge to the institution of slavery itself. The demands of equality and love before God seem, in the modern perspective, to be fundamentally incompatible with the continuation of slavery, and yet the two managed to continue to coexist, even flourish. But is there any sign that the writers of the Early Church envisioned their teaching as leading to the eventual abolition of slavery? Klein finds in Chrysostom an agenda for the gradual withering away of slavery through the new relationship in Christ between master and slave.[53] We

50. *CTh* 4.7.1. These manumissions were equal to the civil manumissions—they provided not only freedom, but also Roman citizenship 'without the necessity of any witness or any intermediary of the law'. C. Pharr, T.S. Davidson and M.B. Pharr, *The Theodesian Code: And Novels and Sirmondian Constitutions* (Princeton, NJ: Princeton University Press, 1952), I, p. 88. For legal details of this, see Buckland, *The Roman Law of Slavery*, pp. 449-51.

51. Westermann, *The Slave Systems in Greek and Roman Antiquity*, p. 153.

52. K. Bradley, *Slavery and Society at Rome* (Cambridge: Cambridge University Press, 1994), p. 156. He does not feel that 'the rate of manumission was significantly raised by Christianity'.

53. Klein, 'Die Sklavenfrage bei Theodoret von Kyrrhos'.

shall also see that a closer examination of the texts of this period provide more examples of a disquietude with slavery than might be expected. However, there is among the writers a general failure to develop the practicalities of any challenge to the system, beyond the suggestion that one should minimize one's own slave retinue or retrain one's slaves to be self sufficient.

6. *Origins of Slavery*

There are, Klein points out, two axioms fundamental to the Early Church understanding of the origins of slavery—first, that there is no such thing as a slave by nature, and secondly, that slavery is the result of sin and of a human corruption of the original Edenic state of equality.[54] In one case it is the whole of the human race that is at fault, the emergence of sin representing a degradation of humanity from its original state of equality. In the second, the imperfection is that of the individual and the origin of slavery lies in the wise and secret ordering of the inferior under the authority of the better.[55] Chrysostom, for example, finds the origins of slavery in human sin and disobedience:

> It was greed, degradation and savagery which gave birth to slavery; since Noah had no slave, nor did Abel, nor did Seth, nor did those who came after them. Sin gave birth to this thing, (it was the result) of rebellion against parents. Let children listen to this; that whenever they are rebellious against their parents, they deserve to be slaves. Such a one strips himself of his noble birth, for he who rebels against his father is no longer a son, and if he who rebels against his father is not a son, how shall he who rebels against our Father be a son? He has left behind his noble birth, he has outraged nature. Thus wars and battles come and take prisoners. But Abraham, you will say, had slaves. Yes, but he did not treat them as slaves (ὡς οἰκέταις).[56]

The ultimate cause lies, then, in sin, which creates the environment for the more direct causes of slavery: the fortunes of war and the imposition of slavery by parents on their children. These secondary causes are even more clearly enumerated by Basil:

> people are brought under the yoke of slavery either through being captured in battle, or through poverty as the Egyptians were to Pharaoh, or

54. Klein, 'Die Sklavenfrage bei Theodoret von Kyrrhos'.
55. Basil, *On the Holy Spirit* 20.
56. *Homily on Ephesians* 22.6 (PG 62.157).

through a wise and secret providence by which inferior children are commanded by their father to serve their more noble and wise siblings.[57]

A rather more sophisticated form of this, and one that is most often appealed to as a fully thought out philosophy of the nature and origin of slavery is that of Augustine. He argues, again, that slavery is not a part of the originally created order, but has come into being through human sin. Much of this sin involves 'the lust for domination'. He points out that slavery is not mentioned in the Scriptures until the occasion of the sin of Ham, where he is cursed by Noah, with slavery as a punishment for his misdeed. It is sin, therefore, which is the original root of human slavery. Sin remains the cause of slavery, even on those occasions when slavery has come about through war, for in these cases, he asserts, the slavery has been justly imposed as either a punishment or a corrective for sin, and he points, as an example, to the enslavement of the Israelites in Babylon.[58]

Slavery, thus, although not natural, is necessary for the maintenance of the fabric of society owing to the shortcomings of the human race.[59] Moreover, although there is no such thing as the 'natural' slave, there are those who, in this fallen world, are benefited by becoming slaves to another, for this may save them from a worse enslavement, since 'It is better to be a slave to a human being than (a slave) to lust'.[60]

7. Summary

Thus, then, the situation stood—a compromise between the idealism of spiritual equality and the practical difficulties of this ideal within a slave-owning society. We have seen that the Church chose the course of acquiescing in the existence of the institution of slavery. While involving slaves in the congregations, the Church also supported the legal rights of the master, and did so more and more explicitly as time went on. Moreover we also find a number of Christian writers eventually (this does not occur in the very early writings) expressing some of

57. *On the Holy Spirit* 20.
58. Augustine, *City of God* 19.15.
59. See G. Corcoran, *Saint Augustine on Slavery* (Rome: Institutum Patristicum Augustinianum, 1985), pp. 70-71 (for another detailed discussion, see R.A. Markus, *SAECULUM: History and Society in the Theology of St Augustine* [Cambridge: Cambridge University Press, 1970], pp. 92-94, 197-201).
60. *City of God* 19.15.

the popular prejudice and hostility towards slaves in general.

Acquiescence in the continued existence of slavery laid upon Christian thinkers the necessity of explaining and justifying the existence of an institution which many of them recognized as being in many ways an evil institution. It must thus be, they concluded, a result of the fallen nature of humanity, both historically through the various falls recorded in the Old Testament (the original fall from Eden, the sin of Ham, the conflict between Jacob and Esau), and spiritually in terms of human greed, foolishness and desire for domination. All these made the existence of slavery inevitable. Given this, however, it was nevertheless thought to have potential for good and to have been used by God as a positive tool, whereby the foolish might be placed under the practical and moral care of the wise, and sinful persons or races might be punished or corrected.

However, it must also not be forgotten that here and there voices were raised in protest against the institution itself. Chrysostom tells his readers that the earliest Christians were not slaveowners, setting free those slaves that they had, and he condemns those who are surrounded by a large retinue of slaves. It is best to do without slaves altogether, he argues; if absolutely necessary one should have only one slave or at the most two, and even those should be taught a trade and then set free.[61]

Gregory of Nyssa, moreover, roundly condemns the whole idea of slavery:

> Who can buy a man, who can sell him, when he is made in the likeness of God, when he is ruler over the whole earth, when he has been given as his inheritance by God authority over all that is in the earth? Such power belongs to God alone, or rather it does not even belong to God himself. For as Scripture says 'The gifts of God are unrevocable'. Of his own free will God called us into freedom when we were slaves to sin. In that case he would hardly reduce human beings to slavery. But if God does not enslave what is free, who dares to put his own authority higher than God's?[62]

Is this a genuine condemnation of slavery? G. Corcoran thinks not:

> It seems, in fact, that he is not speaking about the actual institution of slavery but the vain attempt of a proud man to become master of

61. Chrysostom, *Homilies on 1 Corinthians* 40.6.
62. Gregory of Nyssa, *In Ecclesiasten*, IV (trans. T.J. Dennis, 'The Relationship between Gregory of Nyssa's Attack on Slavery in his Fourth Homily on Ecclesiastes and his Treatise *De Hominis Opificio*', StudPat 17.3 [1982], 1065-72).

another's soul...man is made in the image of God and so cannot be enslaved—according to him not even God can do it. So the type of slavery he is condemning is in fact impossible.[63]

Even if this is probably too cynical a reading, it cannot be denied that neither these protests nor any of the others seem to have had any discernable consequences in the social sphere in terms of an amelioration of or a decline in slavery, even among Christians themselves.

It is difficult, in short, to find any definite indication that early Christianity made any attempt to undermine the institution of slavery as such. It is not even clear if the participation of slaves in the Christian communities and the notion of the equality of all before Christ did anything much to ameliorate the condition of the enslaved.[64] It is even possible that by emphasizing the idea of 'spiritual freedom', the Church made emancipation more, not less, difficult for the slave. By locating the origins of slavery in human sin and in the divine ordering of the wise over the foolish, the Church provided a justification of enslavement in the very will of God. To yearn after freedom from one's master was not the proper behaviour of the Christian slave. Perhaps there were some who realized the inconsistency between Christian love and the enslavement of one's spiritual brother or sister, but we hear little from them in the surviving literature and find no trace of a social implementation of such an idea.

One must, however, follow Finley's warning and avoid the 'teleological fallacy' of 'assuming the existence from the beginning of time of the writer's values—in this instance the moral rejection of slavery as an evil—and in then examining all other thought and practice as if they were, or ought to have been, on the road to this realization; as if men in other periods were asking the same questions and facing the same problems as those of the historian and his world'.[65] Without entirely abdicating the right to make moral judgments on the past behaviour of the Church, we should also remember to consider such

---

63. G. Corcoran, 'The Christian Attitudes to Slavery in the Early Church', *MS* 13 (1984), pp. 1-16.

64. 'If we ask, in summary, whether life was on the whole easier for slaves in Christian times than in pagan, the answer is probably no', R. MacMullen, 'What Difference did Christianity Make?', *Historia: Zeitschrift für Alte Geschichte* 35 (1986), pp. 322-437 (325). See also Brunt, 'Aristotle and Slavery', pp. 343-89 (385).

65. Finley, *Ancient Slavery and Modern Ideology*, p. 17.

subjects in their own historical context.[66] Not all the same questions as ours were asked by the patristic writers, but to assert that Christians of the early centuries never felt a qualm about their position in the system would be to commit a grave injustice. The truth of the situation most probably lies, as it usually does, somewhere between the two extremes—at that point where, by compromise on both sides, reality and idealism finally meet.

66. 'It is a serious anachronism to marvel at the ancient church's lack of interest in the abolition of slavery or the lateness of its interest in promoting manumission', Patterson, *Freedom*, p. 321.

Chapter 3

THE METAPHOR OF SLAVERY IN THE NEW TESTAMENT

1. *Introduction*

The early Church came into being in a society where slavery was an everyday commonplace. It is hardly surprising, therefore, that the metaphor of slavery should play a central and vital role in the structure of New Testament theology.[1] Language related to slavery, as I shall be seeking to demonstrate, appears in the New Testament as a theme implicit in the unfolding of the understanding of the nature of Christian conversion and its implications for the believer, and of the authority of the Apostle to act as the agent of God. It is used by Paul, in particular, to express his understanding of the new status of the believer, of his own role as leader, and of the conduct required in the context of the new life to which he and all believers are called. Paul's use of this metaphor, however, is by no means simple to analyse, and on closer examination a number of apparent illogicalities and contradictions may immediately be seen.

One case of this may be found in the use of the phrase δοῦλος Θεοῦ or δοῦλος Χριστοῦ, which I shall discuss in more detail later in this chapter. The word δοῦλος, if taken seriously in this context, poses difficulties since it is a term which may easily describe two very different

---

1.   'The most cursory examination of "the three terms which are the keywords" (according to J.G. Davies) immediately reveal the extraordinary role of the slave experience as a metaphoric source. These key words are redemption, justification and reconciliation. Redemption quite literally means release from enslavement... Justification means that the believer has been judged and found not guilty, in much the same manner as the slave who has received the most perfect of manumissions, the restoration of his natality with the legal fiction that he had been wrongfully enslaved. "Reconciliation or Atonement means the bringing together of those who have been separated" in much the same way that the manumitted slave is reborn as a member of the community' (Patterson, *Slavery*, p. 70).

situations. In one sense, the reader is encouraged by the addition of Θεοῦ or Χριστοῦ to understand the phrase as describing the state of the individual who devotedly submits himself to a greater power, a picture which, however humbly expressed, may be seen as conferring a certain nobility, even importance, when used in the religious context. Paul's claim, for example, to be δοῦλος Χριστοῦ has thus, as we shall see, frequently been taken as an appropriation of a title of honour, one that sets him over and above his fellow men as a special, chosen instrument of God. On the other hand, in its social context, δοῦλος is an expression of absolute humility which refers to the lowest rung on the social ladder,[2] and to a state where the potential (even if this is not always put into practice) of suffering dehumanization and legalized brutality at the hands of another individual and by the state is at its highest.

Unhesitatingly to see the first of these two interpretations as being a sufficient and entire description of the implications of the word δοῦλος or any of its associated concepts within the New Testament, is to reason backwards. It is to fail to take into account the initial impact of the use of such language on one approaching Christianity from within a context where slavery is the daily reality, and to whom the use of images relating to this state must seem startling if not entirely distasteful. Moreover, although the slave of the ancient world might, and many did, obtain freedom from (and even adoption by) their masters, one could hardly be in both states at once.[3] Yet the New Testament writings sometimes seem to assert precisely this, and the description of the believer as freed from slavery and as a son/daughter of God is all but simultaneous with the assertion that the proper status of the individual is as the slave of God.

There are inherent contradictions, therefore, in the use of slavery as a metaphor for the state of the believer. The assertion of the desirability of becoming a slave of God is at odds with the reader's experience of the physical and psychological implications of slavery in the secular world; the description of salvation as an entry into freedom contradicts the idea of conversion as an entry into slavery to God; and, lastly there

---

2.   For even though there might be individual slaves who had high flying and powerful careers, these were the exception rather than the rule.

3.   At least not if the sonship is as full and personal as that described in the New Testament. It is true that in many cases (especially in the case of the Delphic *paramone* contracts) the fiction of adoption might seem not far removed from slavery. But even in these cases manumission must precede the adoption.

is the confusion that arises from the inevitable blurring of the boundaries between metaphor and reality, a blurring that is most clearly exemplified when, for instance, Paul must speak of the Christian who is himself a slave or master while maintaining that all are equally slaves of God and that we all have one 'master in Heaven'.[4]

2. *The Metaphor of Slavery in the Synoptic Gospels*

Before turning to Paul in detail, however, we should begin by looking at the use of the metaphor in the Gospels. In its most obvious form, it plays an important role in the parables where accounts of the master and the good or wicked slave are used to represent the relationship between man and God. In addition we come across a few occasions on which individuals use δοῦλος of themselves with respect to God. Mary, for instance, in Lk. 1.38 refers to herself as δούλη.[5] The δοῦλος formula also appears in Lk. 2.29 ('now master you let your slave depart', νῦν ἀπολύεις τὸν δουλόν σου, δέσποτα). The Baptist, moreover, in all four Gospels, declares himself to be unworthy even to untie the shoes of the one who comes after him.[6] The individual believer is also urged to behave as a slave both of God, and of others:[7] 'And whoever would be first among you shall be your δοῦλος'.[8] In the performance of the slavish task of washing the feet of the disciples, Jesus provides a pattern for this ideal of mutual service.[9]

A large proportion of the parables concern the relationship between a master and a slave. In Mt. 24.5, for instance, the believer is compared to the faithful slave who is ready for his master's return.[10] A similar parable, that of the slaves and their talents, occurs in Mt. 25.14-30. This is interesting because at first glance it seems to refer to the institution of

4.   Col. 4.1.

5.   The words that follow shortly after (Lk. 1.48) are not only an expression of humility, but a direct quotation of 1 Sam. 1.11: εαν ἐπιβλέπων ἐπιβλέψῃς ἐπὶ τὴν ταπείνωσιν τῆς δούλης σου.

6.   Mt. 3.2. Here, of course, although he is using a servile image to express the degree to which the Messiah is superior to him, he is not necessarily referring to himself as a slave. Here it is the elevation of the Messiah which is emphasized, rather than the idea of obedience and submission.

7.   See also Lk. 16.13.

8.   Mt. 20.27. See also Mk 10.44 and Lk. 12.37-48 (διάκονος).

9.   Jn 13.2-17.

10.   See also Mk 13.34-37 and Lk. 12.37-48.

the slave's *peculium*—the custom of allowing slaves a certain amount of money with which they might trade. However, as this generally remained the possession of the slave (although in law it belonged to the master), the master's anger at the unprofitable slave is rather out of place. It is more likely that the giving of the money to the slaves is here more in the tradition of the capacity of the slave to conduct business on behalf of the master. This interpretation is probably confirmed by the form this parable takes in Lk. 19.12-26 where the slaves are explicitly commanded to trade with the money they have been given. These are the more important parables for our purpose, because in these the identity of the slave *as a slave* is crucial to the sense of the story.

Another example of this occurs in Lk. 17.7-10 where the listeners are told to think of what is demanded of their own slaves, and to compare this to how in fulfilling what is commanded of them they should not regard this as being any special virtue: 'Even so you also, when you have done all the things that are commanded you, say, we are unprofitable δοῦλοι; we have done that which was our duty to do'.

Slaves also occur as minor figures in many other parables, illustrating the extent to which they were a part of daily life in the ancient world. They carry messages and invitations, acting as the representatives of their masters,[11] and they execute their masters' orders.[12] The regular use of the image of the master and slave shows the degree to which the institution of slavery is taken for granted. The focal aspect of the metaphor in this context is the faithfulness and devotion of good slaves who exert themselves on their master's behalf, go beyond the call of duty with no expectation of reward and can be expected to behave themselves when their master is away. Conversely, the master in the parables illustrates the absolute and unquestioned power of God over his people. Liberation from slavery plays no part in these metaphors— on the contrary the slave in the parable is never offered manumission as a reward but, as Beavis points out 'more trust and responsibility' as a slave.[13]

11. Mt. 22.1-4; Lk. 14.16-24; Mt. 21.33-45; Mk 12.1-2; Lk. 20.9-19.
12. Mt. 13.24-30; Lk. 15.11-32.
13. M.A. Beavis, 'Ancient Slavery as an Interpretative Context for the New Testament Servant Parables with Special Reference to the Unjust Steward, Luke 16.1-8', *JBL* 111 (1992), pp. 37-54.

3. *The Metaphor of Slavery in the Gospel of John*

Examples of the metaphor of slavery in the Gospel of John are rare, but where they do occur, they present considerable interest, for they appear in forms quite distinct from those found elsewhere in the New Testament. The first of these occurs in the following passage, Jn 8.30-35:

> 'If you dwell within the revelation I have brought, you are indeed my disciples; you shall know the truth and the truth will set you free.' They replied, 'We are Abraham's descendants; we have never been in slavery to any man. What do you mean by saying "You will become free men"?', 'In very truth I tell you' said Jesus 'that everyone who commits sin is a slave. The slave has no permanent standing in the household, but the son belongs to it forever. If then the Son sets you free, you will indeed be free.'

'Everyone who commits sin is a slave': this particular translation of the passage, found in the New English Bible, omits some words that many witnesses include. Nestle-Aland[14] gives this passage as:

πᾶς ὁ ποιῶν τὴν ἁμαρτίαν δοῦλός ἐστιν τῆς ἁμαρτίας.

τῆς ἁμαρτίας is omitted in D, b, Sy(s) and Clement of Alexandria,[15] making it possible that this is in fact a later addition to the text, as C.K. Barrett argues.[16] If the gloss is omitted, the passage acquires an importance that sets it apart from all other uses of the metaphor in the New Testament, for while the idea that the sinner is a *slave to sin* is a common New Testament sentiment, the idea that a sinner, because of his or her sin, is a slave is one that we find nowhere else in the New Testament. It echoes the Stoic concept of the freedom of the wise man and

---

14. *Novum Testamentum Graece.*

15. *Novum Testamentum Graece*, p. 276.

16. C.K. Barrett, *The Gospel According to St John* (London: SPCK, 1978), p. 346: 'They (the words τῆς ἁμαρτίας) may be an editorial supplement (rightly) giving the sense of the passage, provided that sin is understood not simply in moral terms but as a barrier between man and God'. C.H. Dodd (*The Interpretation of the Fourth Gospel* [Cambridge: Cambridge University Press, 1953], p. 177) holds a similar view. R. Bultmann (*The Gospel of John: A Commentary* [trans. G.R. Beasley-Murray; Oxford: Basil Blackwell, 1971], p. 438), however, differs on this: 'τῆς ἁμαρτίας is an interpretative gloss, which admittedly is not false factually, but it destroys the point, since it depends on the definition of the concept of slave ("a slave is one who does sin, and is thus a slave of sin")'.

the slavery of the fool, using the word 'slave' as a derogatory term for mental and spiritual inferiority—a concept which in the New Testament is most remarkable by its absence. Is this, however, the intention of this passage? Bultmann, for example, argues that it is not, and that the slavery referred to is not the Hellenistic 'slavish nature' but a real bondage to sin.[17]

However, if we look back to the beginning of the passage quoted earlier, we find the words, 'You shall know the truth and the truth will set you free', a statement which again brings to mind the idea asserted so often in the philosophy of the Greek world, namely, that the only truly free man is the one who possesses knowledge. Taken against this background of philosophical tradition, it casts further doubt on the v. 34 gloss since this would destroy the possible balance of 'he who knows the truth is free' as opposed to 'he who sins is a slave'.

However, we must consider what is meant by 'truth' and 'freedom' in this context. The first question that must be asked concerns the relation this need for ἐλευθερία (freedom) bears to the Greek quest after ἀλήθεια (truth). Some are quick to point out the parallel, and claim that 'It is now clear that what is here promised to the disciples of Christ is liberty through knowledge of divine reality'.[18] However, Barrett warns us that:

> The Rabbis and the Stoics, however, did not think of 'truth' and 'freedom' in the same way, and it must not be assumed that John's thought was either Stoic or Rabbinic. ἐλεύθερος, ἐλευθεροῦν occur in this context (vv. 32f., 36) only in John, and it is clear (v. 34) that by them John means to express primarily the Christian liberation from sin, that is, being made free is nothing other than a synonym for salvation (cf. 17.3 where knowing God is the ground of eternal life). Again, knowledge does not stand over against faith as purely rational analysis (Bultmann, p. 435) but involves a relation of man to God.[19]

And of this 'truth', Bultmann argues:

> It is self evident that the ἀλήθεια here is not the 'truth' generally, the disclosure of all that exists in the sense of the Greek quest after ἀλήθεια. It is not a rational knowledge that is promised to the believer... Rather the question after ἀλήθεια is oriented on the question after ἀλήθεια as

17. '(The statement) that he who does sin is a bondsman is intended to affirm that the sinner is enslaved exactly to sin', Bultmann, *The Gospel of John*, p. 439.
18. Dodd, *The Interpretation of the Fourth Gospel*, p. 177.
19. Barrett, *The Gospel According to St John*, p. 345.

the authentic being of the man who is concerned about his life, to whom
the question is proposed because he is a creature. God's ἀλήθεια is thus
God's reality.[20]

Thus, however tempting it might be to read into this passage a philosophical balance of the free nature of the wise man as against the slavish nature of the sinner, this evidence on its own is insufficient to
justify such a claim. However, there is one more point that must be
taken into account when weighing the merits of the gloss in v. 34, and
this is the statement that immediately follows:

> everyone who commits sin is a slave (to sin). The slave has no perma-
> nent standing in the household, but the son belongs to it forever. If then
> the Son sets you free you will be free indeed.

But which house is it in which the slave will not abide for ever? If the
gloss is correct, and the slave is a slave to sin then it is the 'house of
sin' that the slave inhabits. If so, there is no point in the threat that the
slave will not abide there for ever and neither can the son, if equated
with the Son of God, be said to abide there at all. The passage becomes
nonsensical, and can only be retrieved in this form by either asserting
that there is an abrupt change of metaphor between v. 34 and v. 35, or
by taking Odeberg's line that

> The hearers who, according to the sequel, by their acts acknowledge the
> devil as their father, are only slaves not sons and freemen, in the world
> with which they have identified themselves, the world of darkness and
> essential falsehood. Therefore they do not even in their own world (the
> house οἰκεῖος) possess any abiding power. Only the member of the
> spiritual world is a son, who *qua* son abides 'for ever'.[21]

By far the simplest reading, however, may be obtained through omitting the v. 34 gloss and understanding the passage thus: He who
commits sin is by nature a slave and, thus, can only relate to God as a
slave. So long as he remains in this slavish state he has no 'security of
tenure' in the house over which God presides as master unless he be set
free by the Son, who does have a permanent place in the house and
through whom the individual comes to relate to God not as a slave to a
master but as a free son to a father. Such a metaphor of the change of
the relationship between the individual and God with the individual
moving from a state where he relates to God in a slave/master context

20. Bultmann, *The Gospel of John*, p. 434.
21. H. Odeberg, *The Fourth Gospel* (Stockholm: Uppsala, 1929), part 1, p. 301.

to one where he is in a son/father relationship is, as has been pointed out earlier, not an image that appears often in the New Testament, but which does become more popular in later thought. This part of the passage may, thus, suggest that the v. 34 gloss may not be as justified as might first appear.

Such a reading is further strengthened by a reappearance, further on, of this same image in 15.14-15:

> I call you slaves no longer, for a slave does not know what his master is doing. I have called you friends because I have disclosed to you everything that I have heard from my Father.

There is, therefore, a case for omitting the v. 34 gloss, and if this is so, then we have, in 8.30-35, an example of the idea that an individual is a slave in the spiritual sense *because* of his sin, rather than a slave *to* sin. He relates to God only within a slave/master structure, but is given the opportunity to move on to a son/father relationship. This form of the metaphor is subtly different from that used by Paul, and while it is rarely explicitly used in the New Testament, it is one that, as we shall see, becomes more important in later Christian literature.

4. *The Non-Pauline Epistles, Acts and Revelation*

Slavery also appears in other texts of the New Testament. 1 Peter urges its readers to 'Live as free men; not however as though your freedom were there to provide a screen for wrongdoing, but as slaves in God's service'[22] and evokes the image of a slave redeemed: 'you know that it was no perishable stuff, like gold or silver, that bought your freedom from the empty folly of your traditional ways'.[23]

In Acts, Jesus continues to be referred to as the παῖς of God, as does David.[24] The apostles, on the other hand, are referred to as, and call themselves, δοῦλοι.[25] Paul speaks of serving in humility and of being in the bonds of the Spirit.[26] However, there is no expression here of the metaphors of liberation or enslavement that we see later. We see merely

22. 1 Pet. 2.16.
23. 1 Pet. 1.18.
24. Acts 3.13, 26; 4.25, 26, 30.
25. Acts 4.29. The apostles are also recognized by demons as being slaves of God, see Acts 16.17: 'She followed Paul and the rest of us shouting, "οἱ ἄνθρωποι δοῦλοι τοῦ Θεοῦ τοῦ ὑψίστου εἰσίν"'.
26. Acts 20.22.

the idea of the individual as the slave of God, but its implications are not here explored.

Similarly, in Revelation, the writer refers to himself and his fellow Christians as δοῦλοι and σύνδουλοι.[27] The prophets, for the first time in the New Testament, are referred to as δοῦλοι θεοῦ. Even Moses is referred to as such.[28] God is referred to as δεσπότῃ in Rev. 6.9 and the idea of purchase by the blood of Christ plays a part here, too.[29] Without wishing to venture too far into the complex symbolism of Revelation, it is worth pointing out that the sealing of the slaves of God on the forehead,[30] as well as the mark of the beast on others, is reminiscent of the possible Near Eastern and Babylonian practice of placing a slave mark or *abbuttum* on the forehead of the slave.[31]

27. Rev. 1.1; 2.20; 6.11; 19.2; 22.3, 6.
28. Rev. 15.3.
29. Rev. 5.9; 14.3.
30. Rev. 7.3.
31. See B.A. Brooks, 'The Babylonian Practice of Marking Slaves', *AJOS* 42 (1922), pp. 80-90. The nature of this slave mark is something of a mystery today. It is not clear whether all slaves bore this mark in a literal sense (although they all did at least in a figurative sense, hence the 'cleansing' aspect of emancipation, see Mendelsohn, *Slavery in the Ancient Near East*, pp. 45-46) since it is sometimes spoken of as being the punishment of runaway slaves, arrogant maids, and even disobedient children. It may simply have been for the purpose of the identification of ownership, or inflicted on the lowest slaves, possibly as a sign of disgrace (Driver and Miles, *The Babylonian Laws*, p. 222), or on those particularly prone to running away (Mendelsohn, *Slavery in the Ancient Near East*, p. 49).

The nature if the mark is also unclear. It may have involved anything from an incision or brand on the face to a metal or clay tag—possibly in the ear, which would in part explain the boring of the ear of the Jewish slave (see above, p. 38 n. 72)—such as those worn by cattle, or a combination of these. Sometimes it is spoken of as having been broken, at other times its removal or defacement called for the services of a barber or surgeon. There are also references to the tattooing of one or both of the slave's wrists (Mendelsohn, *Slavery in the Ancient Near East*, pp. 44-46).

Certainly it must not be taken for granted that an obvious marking of slaves would have been commonplace in the first-century world, indeed contemporary sources actually bemoan the fact that slaves did not tend to be readily recognizable as such and some even suggested a special uniform for slaves—although this proposal was said to have been rejected as having risks of its own: 'Once in the Senate a proposal was made to have slaves wear a distinctive dress: then it became clear what great danger would threaten us if our slaves should start to count us', Seneca, *De Clementia* 1.24.1. There is no real reason to suspect that Paul's assertion that he

5. *Paul and the Metaphor of Slavery*

The most important aspect of the metaphor of slavery in the New Testament is the use to which it is put in the writings of Paul as a pattern of faith for all believers. Several interwoven strands may be found in this—the apostolic claim upon the title δοῦλος Χριστοῦ, the enslavement of Paul to his followers and the enslavement of all believers to each other and to God through their liberation from their previous slavery. Paul's own enslavement is presented as an example to those who follow him and is modelled on the kenosis of Christ himself. It is thus both a claim on leadership and a challenge to the popular notions of status and authority within his own world.

a. *Paul, the δοῦλος Χριστοῦ*
The very first words of Romans give Paul the title Παῦλος δοῦλος Χριστοῦ. The apostle who was forever justifying his right to speak with the authority of the apostles of Christ addresses his readers not, as one might expect, with an obvious assertion of authority but with a phrase which, to Gentile eyes, would have seemed all but repugnant.[32] This apparent discrepancy between the role of Paul and his choice of metaphor to describe himself has puzzled many commentators from the patristic period onwards.[33] Modern scholars tend to take one of two approaches to this problem and assert either that (a) Paul is making use of the traditional Old Testament motif of the chosen servant of God, or that (b) Paul is appealing to the career structures of his time and claiming the status of high-ranking slaves sharing in the authority and honour of their master.

1. *Paul as Old Testament Prophet.* The first way in which the seeming discrepancy between apostolic authority and servile language might be reconciled is to seek a parallel in the Old Testament tradition that might

bears 'the mark of Christ' has anything to do with a slave mark.

32. 'When Paul describes himself and Timothy as slaves of Christ, he is using language which would sound strange and even shocking to Greek ears. Cynics and Stoics would indeed hold that the slave was a man and a brother and that the wise man is truly free whatever his status, but not even among the philosophers did any Greek speak of his own relation to the divine power which he served as that of a slave.' C.K. Barrett, *A Commentary on the First Epistle to the Corinthians* (London: A. & C. Black, 2nd edn, 1971), p. 50.

33. See below, pp. 122-28.

indicate that Paul's intention is to place himself in the position of the Old Testament patriarchs and prophets—the devoted mouthpiece of his God.[34]

In the Hebrew Old Testament, the term *ebed Yahweh*, or servant/ slave of God, is a title of honour and distinction and it may be argued that this point of view was carried over to the New Testament. Barrett believes that it is the Greek Old Testament that introduces the motif of slavery:

> ...nor did the Hebrew think of himself as a 'slave' of his God. It is strange, therefore to find that the Greek Old Testament freely employs doulos (slave) and its concepts to express the relationship of the true Israelite to his God. Paul is clearly making use of a vocabulary created by the Septuagint when he speaks of Christian life as slavery.[35]

However, the title δοῦλος Θεοῦ is actually rare in the Greek Old Testament. Although the phrases 'the prophets the slaves of God (οἱ δοῦλοι τοῦ Θεοῦ)' are relatively common and various individuals are shown as being addressed as δοῦλος μου by God,[36] the title δοῦλος Θεοῦ as an explicit personal title rarely occurs in the Septuagint. Although Isaiah does use δοῦλος on a few occasions to describe an individual's relationship with God, παῖς[37] is far more common vis à vis the chosen men of God,[38] as for example in the classic expression of vocation:

34. E.g. 'This use of δοῦλος reflects not only the OT custom of the pious call-ing themselves "slaves" in the sight of Yahweh (Pss. 27.9, 31.16, 89.50) but espe-cially its OT use to describe the great figures who served Yahweh in salvation his-tory (Moses: 2 Kgs 18.12, Joshua: Judg. 2.8, Abraham: Ps. 105). Paul as the slave of Christ, belongs to the same line.' Jerome, *Biblical Commentary* 53.15 (p. 294). Also E. Käsemann, *Commentary on Romans* (trans. and ed. G.W. Bromiley; London: SCM Press, 1980), p. 5. Cf. also P. Trümmer, 'Die Chance der Freiheit: Zur Interpretation des mallon Chresthai in 1 Kor 7.21', *Bib* 56 (1975), pp. 344-68 (365), and also Sass, 'Zur bedeutung von δοῦλος bei Paulus', *ZNW* 40 (1941), pp. 24-32.

35. Barrett, *Commentary on the First Epistle to the Corinthians*, p. 50. How-ever, Barrett believes that this does not explain Paul's use of the title: 'Something more is involved when the Apostle uses the phrase slave of Christ Jesus...by it Paul acknowledges his total submission to the will of Christ, his duty of implied obedience'.

36. See above, p. 44, and p. 44 n. 87.

37. Isaiah: Isa. 20.3; Eliakim: Isa. 22.20; David: Isa. 37.35; Jacob: Isa. 42.41, for example.

38. Isa. 42.19.

Καὶ εἰπέ μοι, μέγα σοι ἐστὶ τοῦ κληθῆναί σε παῖδά μου.[39] ('And he said to me "it is a great thing for you to be called my servant"')

It is also more usual to see Moses, especially in the Hexapla, given the title of θεράπων, οἰκέτης or παῖς. Even in the rest of the Septuagint he is rarely referred to as δοῦλος in any form. Although this term is on many occasions used for David, and while his slave relation to God is thereby implied, he is, again, never given the explicit title of δοῦλος Θεοῦ. δοῦλος κυρίου is somewhat more widespread, but even so, it hardly plays a major role.

Furthermore, to trace the Pauline title to the Old Testament *ebed Yahweh* is to neglect the fact that nowhere Paul does call himself δοῦλος Θεοῦ.[40] The title that Paul claims is δοῦλος Χριστοῦ. It is an inaccurate reflection of his theology to think that he could simply have substituted Χριστοῦ for Θεοῦ. One certainly cannot find any traces of Old Testament antecedents for the metaphor within his own work—he never refers to any patriarch or prophet as δοῦλος Θεοῦ. The nearest one can get to any possible parallel is that the author of Hebrews calls Moses by his Septuagint title of θεράπων.

2. *Paul as Manager Slave.* Another possible means of explaining Paul's claim has been put forward by Dale Martin, who in his *Slavery as Salvation: The Metaphor of Slavery in Pauline Christianity*,[41] seeks the answer in an analysis of the 'sociohistorical context' of the writings. Paul's self designation as the slave of Christ emerges,[42] Martin argues, from the traditions of the household where slaves occupy various social levels and where all share, to differing degrees, in the status of the master. Paul is thus appropriating for himself the role of the manager slave who shares in the status of his master and wields power over the other slaves in the household. By calling himself a slave of Christ, Paul is using terminology which would have been deeply offensive to the upper-class Christians but not, in Martin's view, to those of the lower classes. To those in the upper classes, slavery would have represented the worst possible fate, but Martin draws on numerous examples of

39. Isa. 49.6.
40. Tit. 1.1 is deutero-Pauline. The closest Paul comes is to number himself as διάκονοι Θεοῦ in 2 Cor. 6.4.
41. Martin, *Slavery as Salvation*, p. ix.
42. 'It is clear that Paul's claim to act unwillingly and under compulsion would have been heard as an admission of slavery', Martin, *Slavery as Salvation*, p. 76.

slave-sponsored inscriptions to show that such a designation would have excited a positive response among the lower classes. Those who were slaves themselves and those whose low estate compelled them to defer to the slaves of powerful families would see slavery not as a disgrace but as an opportunity for social mobility and reflected glory. Hence, Paul's role as slave of Christ would have confirmed him in their eyes as one who held great power and authority in virtue of his relationship with Christ and his position as 'manager slave' within the hierarchy of the ecclesiastical household. This self-designation is intended to appeal to the aspirations of those classes who, unlike those from more privileged backgrounds, would have seen slavery as an honourable and desirable career.

By Martin's own admission, however, the effectiveness of such a metaphor depends crucially on the thesis that members of the lower classes would not have participated in the social prejudices of their superiors.[43] But as Harrill points out in his review of *Slavery as Salvation*, 'it is questionable whether the humble freeborn population felt class or even order solidarity with the servile masses. Lower status people often share if not exaggerate the values and prejudices of their social betters.'[44] We are hampered, of course, by the lack of evidence shaped by the attitudes of the lower classes and Martin's use of funerary inscriptions to make up this deficiency is admirable. But such ritualized sentiments as those found in such a context cannot be regarded as complete evidence of an entirely different mindset from the enormous resentment that so often arose against the power of favoured slaves.

In further support of his argument that Paul's slavishness was specifically intended to appeal to the lower classes, Harrill also cites 1 Cor. 9.16-18: 'Even if I preached the Gospel, I can claim no credit for

---

43. 'There is no reason to suppose that language was heard by lower-class persons in the same way as by upper-class persons', Martin, *Slavery as Salvation*, p. 148.

44. Harrill, review of *Slavery as Salvation* by D.B. Martin, pp. 426-27. See also Garnsey, *Ideas of Slavery*, p. 186, who points out that 'Slavery for most slaves was highly undesirable and anything but an avenue of upward mobility'. K. Bradley (*Slavery and Society*, p. 72) also argues that there was no 'sense of common identity' among slaves and points out the high degree of antagonism between low and high status slaves that was conventional in the literature of the time. It must also be remembered that slaves of all rank were liable to humiliation and degradation. See Bradley, *Slavery and Society*, p. 152.

it; I cannot help myself; it would be misery for me not to preach. If I did it of my own choice, I should be earning my pay; but since I do it apart from my own choice, I am simply discharging a trust.' According to Martin, this compulsion would have been shameful to those of the upper classes but to the lower class reader it would be replete with all the implications of high status domestic slavery. However, this idea that 'acting under compulsion' would invariably be seen as debasing and a sign of slavery[45] is also not entirely convincing. As Harrill[46] points out, Socrates' claim to act under compulsion to Apollo and a personal daimonion[47] was surely not seen as shameful.[48]

It must also be noted that Paul clearly has at his disposal the vocabulary to express specifically the authority of the agent or manager. When he argues with his opponents in 2 Cor. 11.23, it is over the title διάκονος Χριστοῦ. In Colossians, when he speaks of the task assigned to him by God, he calls himself a διάκονος.[49] In 2 Cor. 5.20-21, he comes as an ambassador—παρακαλοῦντος. He claims that the authorities are instruments of God, and yet the term he uses is not δοῦλοι, but διάκονοι.

Another problem with the theory that Paul uses δοῦλος Χριστοῦ as a title of honour, either in virtue of its apparent Old Testament precedents or the Graeco-Roman career structure parallels, is that Paul clearly thinks of other Christians as also being slaves of Christ and uses the

45. As Martin, *Slavery as Salvation*, p. 76, asserts.
46. J.A. Harrill, Review of *Slavery as Salvation*, by D.B. Martin, *JR* 72 (1992), pp. 426-27.
47. Plato, *Apology* 2b-c, 3c-d.
48. Socrates' words in 31b are also relevant as they show a remarkably similar rejection of personal interests: 'If you doubt whether I am really the sort of person who would have been sent to this city as a gift from God, you can convince yourselves by looking at it in this way. Does it seem natural that I should have neglected my own affairs and endured the humiliation of allowing my family to be neglected for all these years, while I busied myself all the time on your behalf, going like a father or an elder brother to see each one of you privately and urging you to set your thoughts on goodness? If I had got any enjoyment from it, or if I had been paid for my good advice there would have been some explanation for my conduct; (...) The witness that I can offer to prove the truth of my statement is, I think, a convincing one—my poverty.' Translation by H. Tredennick, *The Last Days of Socrates* (Harmondsworth: Penguin Books, 1969).
49. Col. 1.25.

same title for them.[50] More than that, his entire understanding of the position of the believer vis-à-vis his or her relationship with Christ is bound up in the metaphor of slavery. It is, thus, impossible to look at the title δοῦλος Θεοῦ in isolation. A closer look at his other uses of the idea of slavery will help give a clearer insight into Paul's concept of slavery to Christ.

b. *The Believer as δοῦλος Θεοῦ*
1. *Negative Slavery.* All Christians are called to be slaves of Christ, but first they must escape the slavery to which they are presently bound. The slavery to be avoided may be slavery to the body and its appetites, or to sin:

> I am unspiritual, the purchased slave of sin (Rom. 7.14).

> When you were slaves of sin you were free from the control of righteousness, and what was the gain? (Rom. 6.20).[51]

One may also be enslaved to non-gods,[52] or to the powers of the universe: 'During our minority we were slaves to the elemental spirits of the universe' (Gal. 4.3).[53] Even the Jews are not exempt—their slavery is to the Law[54] as in the extended discussion of Sarah and Hagar.[55] Here, the traditional interpretation of Sarah and her slave[56] is inverted so that by identifying Hagar with Mt. Sinai, it becomes the Jews, not the Gentiles, who are the sons of slavery.

There is a close identification, too, between circumcision and slavery. The two are frequently grouped together as in 1 Cor. 7.21 (were you circumcised/a slave when you were called?). Those who wish to impose circumcision seek 'to bring us into bondage',[57] Christians are warned not to turn back to slavery (i.e. accept circumcision), and there

---

50. One for himself in Gal. 1.10; two for generic Christians in Rom. 14.18 and 16.18; one for named Christians in Col. 4.

51. See also Rom. 6.16 and Rom. 6. 6-7.

52. Gal. 4.8.

53. See also Eph. 2.2.

54. Col. 2.14-15.

55. Gal. 4.21-31.

56. On the background of the use of the Hagar/Sarah story in the Jewish tradition, see R.N. Longenecker, *Galatians* (WBC, 41; Waco, TX: Word Books, 1990), pp. 200-206.

57. Gal. 2.4.

is the implication that any who do so invalidate the freedom offered by Christ:

> For freedom Christ set us free. Stand fast therefore and do not let your-selves be burdened again by a yoke of slavery. I, Paul warn you that if you accept circumcision, Christ will be of no use to you (Gal. 5.1-2).

2. *Positive Slavery.* On the other hand, the slavery of the individual may be a slavery to Christ or to righteousness (he never uses the term 'slave of God'). The slavery may be explicitly stated, as Paul reminds his readers:

> You do not belong to yourselves; you were bought at a price (1 Cor. 6.20).

> He who thus shows himself to be a slave of Christ (ὁ γὰρ ἐν τούτῳ δουλεύων τῷ Χριστῷ) is acceptable to God... (Rom. 14.18).

> Emancipated from sin you have become slaves to righteousness... (Rom. 6.18).[58]

The slavery of the believer is also implied through Paul's image of Christ completely taking over the life of the believer in the same way that the slave's life is by his or her master:[59]

> For no one of us lives, and equally no one of us dies, for himself alone. If we live, we live for the Lord; and if we die, we die for the Lord. Whether, therefore, we live or die, we belong to the Lord (Rom. 14.7-8).

> His purpose in dying for all was that men, while still in life, should cease to live for themselves, and should live for him (2 Cor. 5.15).

3. *Freedom from Slavery.* There were, as has been discussed in earlier chapters, a number of procedures by which a slave might be granted freedom. Liberation through the payment of ransom, that is, redemp-tion, is, of course, a central theme in Paul's thought:

> We wait for the adoption as sons and the redemption (ἀπολύτρωσιν) of our bodies (Rom. 8.23).

> ...in (Christ) we are consecrated and redeemed (1 Cor. 1.30).

> Christ bought us freedom (Χριστὸς ἡμᾶς ἐξηγόρασεν) from the curse (Gal. 3.13).

---

58. See also Rom. 6.20.
59. See below, p. 87 n. 70.

As in Rom. 8.23, the individual may also be granted something better even than freedom—adoption by God:

> For all who are moved by the Spirit of God are sons of God. The Spirit you have received is not a spirit of slavery leading you back to a life of fear, but a spirit that makes us sons (Rom. 8.14-15).[60]

In Galatians there is a distinction made between the relatively similar positions of the slave and the young son:

> The heir as long as he is a child is no better than a slave, even though the whole estate is his; he is under guardians and trustees until the date fixed by his father. And so it was with us. During our minority we were slaves to the elemental spirits of the universe, but when the term was completed, God sent his own Son, born of a woman, born under the law, to purchase freedom for the subjects of the law, in order that we might attain the status of sons. To prove that you are sons, God has sent into our hearts the Spirit of his Son, crying 'Abba, father!' You are therefore no longer a slave but a son (Gal. 4.1-5, 7).

Garnsey points out that here Paul is making use of the technicalities of Roman law and doing so accurately.[61] In Rom. 8.15 (see above) Paul also makes the distinction between slavery and sonship.

We may note, however, that he does not speak of slaves of God becoming sons of God, preferring instead to talk of people who are slaves to things other than God coming directly to the state of 'sons of God' without any intermediate stage of being 'slaves of God'. In Paul's thought, therefore, unlike in that of some of his successors, we find no evidence of the *slave of 'non-god'* → *slave of God* → *son of God* form of the metaphor.

The new state of the believer is that of freedom and sonship. The sonship, as we have seen, is contrasted with slavery. However, he or she is also a slave of Christ.[62] In the world of the first-century Church, slavery and freedom were the fundamental divisions in human society.[63] It would seem impossible that a person could be at one and the

60. See also Rom. 8.21.

61. 'He has captured at once the ambiguity of the position of the son *qua* infant and the clarity of the son's position once he has received his inheritance, in both cases by comparing his condition to that of slave', Garnsey, *Ideas of Slavery*, pp. 181-82.

62. As found in Rom. 6.22, for example.

63. It was only after the third century CE that this slave/free demarcation began to give way to the *honestiores/humiliores* division. See Evans-Grubbs, *Law and the Family*, p. 6.

same time a slave and yet free. There is however, a tempting parallel to this state in the ancient world in the ceremony of sacral manumission, whereby slaves were granted freedom by means of a fictive sale to a deity, their rights and those of their ex-master gaining thereby the force of divine sanction.[64] In such a ceremony, the slaves would be 'purchased' by the god (usually with the slaves' own money). Following this purchase, the slaves would be free, having no obligations to the god and, except as laid out in the *paramone* contracts drawn up prior to the ceremony, few obligations to their ex-master.[65] However, this has long been discounted as an influence on Paul's thought. In the first place, it must be realized that the 'purchase' by the god is a legal fiction.[66] The slaves do not become the property of the god, and are left

64. For a detailed account of this procedure, see Hopkins, *Conquerors and Slaves*, pp. 133-71. For the procedure in the ancient Near East, see Mendelsohn, *Slavery in the Ancient Near East*, p. 83.

65. While this ceremony is not directly alluded to in the Pauline writings, the number of apparent parallels in his thought with this ceremony has led to an assertion on the part of many, notably Westermann, 'The Freedmen and the Slaves of God', pp. 55-64. See also A. Deissmann, *Light from the Ancient East* (trans L.R.M. Strachen; London: Hodder & Stoughton, 1927), pp. 228ff., who argues that it had a considerable influence on Paul's language. The association is certainly tempting given the common elements of purchase by the god, of entering the protection of the god and even, perhaps, the somewhat later Christian tendency to identify Christ with Apollo (the god in question in the Delphic sacral manumissions). The parallel seemed most attractive, however, in that it apparently solved the paradox that arises in describing the redeemed Christian as both slave and free, as, in the process of sacral manumission the slave, by being 'purchased' by the god, obtains freedom.

66. Contra Foucart, Deissmann, and Bömer, all cited by Bartchy, *Mallon Chresai*, p. 122, who describe this ceremony as a 'fictitious sale' whereby the slave became the property of the god who nevertheless did not assert his property rights, but afforded divine protection to the slave. Patterson, *Slavery*, also holds a similar view: 'The slave...merely acquired de facto freedom by virtue of the fact that the god did not exercise his property powers. This was a neat way of solving the problem created by the naturalistic theory of slavery...selling the slave to a god salvaged the idea of his slaveness and the permanence of his servile status', p. 68.

It is a legal rather than a religious matter, and a means of circumventing the slave's inability before the law to enter into contracts on his own behalf. See Bartchy, *Mallon Chresai*, who also cites H. Radle (*Untersuchungen zum griechischen Freilassungwesen* [Munich: Ludwig Maximilians Universität, 1969]) who 'agrees with the conclusion of the French legal scholars R. Dareste, B. Hausoullier and T. Reinach (*Recueil des inscriptions juridiques grecques* II (Paris,

with no obligations to the god, or to the temple.[67] This, of course, cannot be what Paul has in mind when he speaks of becoming the slave of Christ or righteousness. The obligations of the one purchased by Christ are, to Paul's mind, very real and ongoing.[68]

Although the god legally is a participant in the ceremony, the only truly religious aspect of the manumission is that the ceremony secures, by religious sanction, and through the setting up of an inscription describing the terms of the release, the rights of both parties: immunity from re-enslavement for the slaves and assurance to the master that the conditions of the *paramone* contract would be fulfilled.

It may further be seen that the ideas of divine purchase and redemption cannot really, as they might at first seem to do, parallel the Pauline ideas of the Christian redemption. After all, the funds for the slaves' release would have come from the slaves themselves, or from an interested third party. In no recorded case do they come from the temple, that is, from the god. Indeed it is more than likely that the temple would

1898), namely that the activity of the god was used in this form because the slave was not capable before the law', p. 123.

67. It should be pointed out that there is some disagreement on this point: 'After the complete manumission or after the *paramone*, the former slave is called ἱερος ...it seems that the name ἱερος was an official title used by the freedman in various kinds of public documents. We can say therefore that the sacral manumission through dedication or through sale went together with the consecration of the former slave to the divinity. The manumitted slave belongs to the god and is protected by him', F. Sokolowski, 'The Real Meaning of Sacral Manumission', *HTR* 47 (1954), pp. 173-81. In support of his argument, Sokolowski presents many cases suggesting that the dedication to the god did involve a real service to the temple. However, he also comments that 'it seems not unlikely that the first groups of Christians were composed in large part of slaves manumitted in the synagogues or in Christian places of worship. For this reason, perhaps, St. Paul in many of his letters plays on the comparison: a Christian is a freedman and slave of Christ in paramone.' This interpretation, however, cannot be accepted, since there is no evidence of any substantial number of slave manumissions within the Church in this period.

68. In contrast, the freedom granted from the previous master in sacral manumission was rarely immediate or complete, and in most cases, the slave would continue to be bound to his ex-master under the terms of a *paramone* contract of some kind. However, for the Christian there can be no question of having any obligations to the former masters '... you were the slaves of beings which in their nature are no gods. But now that you do acknowledge God—or rather, now that he has acknowledged you—how can you turn back to the mean and beggarly spirits of the elements? Why do you propose to enter their service all over again?' (Gal. 4.8-9).

actually have *received* some payment or commission for the ceremony. Such a situation bears no resemblance to Paul's concept of a god sacrificing himself as the price of purchase.[69] Thus, although the superficial aspects of sacral manumission might seem to parallel some aspects of Christian redemption, the nature and purpose of the ceremony is so far removed from the vital features of redemption that not only is it unlikely that any influence is at work here, but it is probable that Paul would probably even have discouraged any attempt to link them.[70]

4. *Death as Manumission.* A closer look at Paul's use of the images of manumission and slavery shows a strong correlation between these and the theme of death:

> We know that the man we once were has been crucified with Christ for the destruction of the sinful body, so that we may no longer be slaves of sin, since a dead man is no longer answerable for his sin (Rom. 6.6-7).

> His purpose in dying for all was that men, while still in life, should cease to live for themselves... (2 Cor. 5.15).

> Time was when you were dead in your sins and wickedness, when you followed the evil ways of the present age (Eph. 2.12).

This association is even more interesting if one considers it in terms of Patterson's definition of slavery as 'social death'. Slavery is not an alternative to death—it is effectively death with respect to the slave's

---

69. Westermann, 'The Freedmen and the Slaves of God', argues at length for the influence of sacral manumission on Paul's thought. He especially points to the *paramone* element of this form of manumission as providing a suitable metaphor for man's continuing relationship with God. I cannot agree with Westermann here. The *paramone* status, due to its limitation in time, cannot properly be compared to the eternal relationship between man and God. The *paramone* relationship is by nature one which is fixed to a certain term, which generally concludes with the demise of the ex-master. The relationship between the believer and God is, on the other hand, most emphatically asserted to have no such end. Furthermore, Paul does not make use of the idea of slaves of God becoming sons of God, as has already been pointed out.

70. Bömer, too, rejects completely the possibility that sacral manumission could have had any influence on Paul's thought (Bömer, *Untersuchungen über die Religion*, II, p. 138, cited by Bartchy, *Mallon Chresai*, pp. 123-25). In the same vein, see also *TDNT*, II, p. 275. See also Conzelmann, *Commentary on 1 Corinthians* (Philadelphia: Fortress Press, 1975), p. 113.

previous history and identity.[71] This has two implications: the first is that the slaves are free from slavery if they die[72] and the second is that in entering slavery, individuals 'die to the world', as their former identity is destroyed and their only life is that which is given by their master.[73] Both liberty and slavery are the direct consequences of death. It is death to one's own slavery which enables one to be alive in freedom; while at the same time death 'to the world' is an entry into the new slavery to Christ. Paul, as the prime example of this, has no life except that which Christ lives through him,

> For through the law I died to the law—to live for God. I have been crucified with Christ; the life I now live is not my life, but the life which Christ lives in me (Gal. 2.19-20).[74]

If Paul's use of the metaphor of slavery is therefore taken in the context of the crucifixion, the paradox of the individual as both slave and free ceases to be a problem. If slavery as death is the central metaphor, the consequence is that Paul can accommodate both the concept of the entire commitment of the slave of Christ and the freedom of the son or daughter of God in one image. The death of the believer in Christ, through baptism, leads to the surrender of the entire life and being of the individual to God. Equally, the believer through this death becomes entirely free from his or her previous master. Thirdly, as Patterson points out, the death of Christ replaces that death which the slave could have chosen instead of enslavement, and thereby cancels the slavery of the believer:

---

71. See also R. Blackburn, 'Defining Slavery: Its Special Features and Social Role', in L.J. Archer (ed.), *Slavery and other Forms of Unfree Labour* (History Workshop Series; New York: Routledge, 1988), pp. 263-79.

72. But note that there are slave epitaphs that seem to imply the continuation of the state of slavery even after death—e.g., Raffeiner no.7; σὸς ἐγώ δέσπορα, κῆν Ἀίδην (H. Raffeiner, *Sklaven und Freigelassene: Eine soziologische Studie auf der Grundlage des griechischen Grabepigrams* [Commentationes Aenipontanae, 23; Philologia und Epigraphik, 2; Innsbruck: Wagner, 1977].)

73. 'There was an almost perverse intimacy in the bond resulting from the power the master claimed over his slave, *the slave's only life was through and for his master*', Patterson, *Slavery*, p. 50. Hence also, the death symbolism in the rituals undergone, in many cultures, by the newly enslaved (Patterson, *Slavery*, pp. 51-62). Blackburn, 'Defining Slavery, pp. 263-79, describes slavery as a 'living death'.

74. See also Col. 2.20.

> The slave, it will be recalled, was someone who by choosing physical
> life had given up his freedom. Although he could, of course, have kept
> his freedom and died, man lacked the courage to make such a choice.
> Jesus, 'his saviour' by his death made this choice for him.[75]

Paul and other Christians are slaves of Christ. They are, therefore,
dead to the world and its priorities and are participants in the humiliation and crucifixion of Christ. Such a slavery cannot lead to honour in
the eyes of the world, as Paul reminds his readers:

> This doctrine of the cross is sheer folly to those on their way to ruin, but
> to us who are on the way to salvation it is the power of God... As God
> in his wisdom ordained, the world failed to find him by its wisdom, and
> he chose to save those who have faith by the folly of the Gospel. Jews
> call for miracles, Greeks look for wisdom; but we proclaim Christ—yes,
> Christ nailed to the cross; and though this is a stumbling block to Jews
> and a folly to Greeks, yet to those who have heard his call, Jews and
> Greeks alike, he is the power of God and the wisdom of God.
>
> Divine folly is wiser than the wisdom of man, and divine weakness
> stronger than man's strength...to shame the wise, God has chosen what
> the world counts folly, and to shame what is strong, God has chosen
> what the world counts weakness. He has chosen things low and con-
> temptible, mere nothings, to overthrow the existing order. And so there
> is no place for human pride in the presence of God. You are in Christ
> Jesus by God's act, for God has made him our wisdom; he is our righ-
> teousness; in him we are consecrated and redeemed (1 Cor. 1.18-31).

However slavery to Christ is not the only slavery to which the Christian is called.

5. *The Slave of All.* The believer is called not only to be a slave of
Christ, but to be a slave of all. Such a sentiment, which includes not
only the inversion of normal standards of honour but also the call to
mutual service has already been seen in the Gospel accounts. Paul
equally urges a mutual slavery of love[76] and points to his own actions
as a demonstration of such principles: 'although I am free, I have made
myself a slave of all'.

Martin argues that this claim of Paul goes even further and is
reflected in his 'slavish' self-support (in contrast to his right to be supported by others) and his claim to act under compulsion, giving up his

---

75. Patterson, *Slavery and Social Death*, p. 71.
76. Gal. 4.21-31.

needs in order to serve those of others.[77] Martin sees a definite political agenda in this. He identifies the 'weak' of Corinth, for whose sake Paul himself became 'weak', as those of a lower economic strata. In aligning himself with this group, the argument goes, Paul set himself up as a populist demagogue who lowers himself to the level of the people and leads from among them. While Martin has the support of Theissen and others in identifying the *weak* with low status rather than with weak faith, he omits to mention the parallel passage in Romans 14 which suggests that *weak* to Paul's mind is a matter of spiritual anxiety:[78]

> If a man is weak in faith you must accept him without attempting to settle doubtful points. For instance one man will have faith enough to eat all kinds of food, while a weaker man eats only vegetables. The man who eats must not hold in contempt the man who does not and he who does not eat must not pass judgement on one who does; for God has accepted him. Who are you to pass judgement on someone else's slave? (Rom. 14.1-4).

In 1 Corinthians, Paul has taken the part of those who do not eat; here he seems to take the part of those who do. Further,

> again, this man regards one day more highly than another…he who respects the day has the Lord in mind in doing so, and he who eats meat has the Lord in mind when he eats, since he gives thanks to God, and he who abstains has the Lord in mind no less, since he too gives thanks to God (Rom. 14. 5-6).

The parallels to the language of 1 Corinthians continue:

> For no one of us lives, and equally no one of us dies, for himself alone. If we live, we live for the Lord; if we die we die for the Lord. Whether therefore we live or die, we belong to the Lord… Let us therefore cease judging one another, but rather make this simple judgement; that no obstacle or stumbling-block be placed in a brother's way (Rom. 14.7, 13-14).

Granted, we are speaking of two different letters penned to two different congregations, but it seems unlikely that, even in these circumstances, Paul would have given such a different meaning to such similar words. There is a simpler explanation for the language of

---

77. See R.F. Hock, *The Social Context of Paul's Ministry: Tentmaking and Apostleship* (Philadelphia: Fortress Press, 1980), p. 61.

78. Theissen, *The Social Setting of Pauline Christianity*, pp. 128-39.

1 Corinthians than the argument that Paul is creating himself as a subversive demagogic leader and using these sentiments to urge a lowering of the upper classes according to his example. Rather, in recommending the virtues of a non-judgmental pattern of mutual service, Paul is simply following in the already established pattern of early Christian teaching on mutual service and humility. One needs only to look at the Gospels to see the importance of this pattern of discipleship in the Christian traditions. The occurrence of the command, 'Whoever would be first among you shall be your δοῦλος', in all four Synoptic Gospels[79] as well as the example of humble service given by Jesus in Jn 13.12-15 reflect the prominence of this theme in the teaching and traditions of the time.

c. Slavery as a Kenotic Pattern
There is no denying that Paul sees himself as a leader—and a leader with considerable authority who has the power to consign wrongdoers to Satan and to come upon his congregations 'with a rod' (1 Cor. 4.21). He is quite capable of exploiting the images of domestic management, agency and ambassadorship, all of which stem from his special relationship with Christ, and when he does so he makes use of appropriate vocabulary. I do not believe that δοῦλος, on the other hand, was specifically meant to convey such high status ideas, either by association with Old Testament leaders or by appeal to contemporary career structures. It is, rather, part of Paul's intense identification with the pattern of Christ:

> For the divine nature was his from the first; yet he did not think to snatch at equality with God, but made himself nothing, assuming the nature of a slave. Bearing human likeness, revealed in human shape, he humbled himself, and in obedience accepted even death—death on a cross (Phil. 2.7-9).[80]

Hengel sees here 'a direct connection between the "he emptied himself, taking the form of a slave" ...and the disputed end of the first strophe... Death on the cross was the penalty for slaves, as anyone

79. Mt. 20.27; Mk 10.44, Lk. 22.24-27.
80. 'Many scholars regard the Philippine hymn as non Pauline... Nevertheless, we might expect Paul to use his material in a Pauline way. And we find, when we examine the context, that this is in fact what he has done', M.D. Hooker, *From Adam to Christ: Essays on Paul* (Cambridge: Cambridge University Press, 1990), p. 20.

knew, and as such it symbolized extreme humiliation, shame and torture. Thus Θανάτου δε σταυροῦ is the last bitter consequence of μορφὴν δούλου λαβών.'[81] We can see from this passage how unlikely it is that Paul regarded δοῦλος as being a conventional title of dignity, for this is the sole instance of him using the term in reference to Christ and it is indissolubly linked with the humiliation of the cross.[82] Christ taking the form of a slave is an expression not only of his willing humiliation, but of his identification with man, whose nature here is synonymous with slavery, as we can see from the similar passage in Rom. 8.3: 'by sending his own Son in a form like that of our own sinful nature' (ἐν ὁμοιώματι σαρκὸς ἁμαρτίας). Paul's identification with the sufferings and the death of Christ is clear: 'All I care for is to know Christ, to experience the power of his resurrection, and to share his sufferings, if only I may finally arrive at the resurrection of the dead' (Phil. 3.10-11).

To be a slave of Christ is Paul's recommendation to every Christian, to be a slave to one another is, to him, the natural consequence of mutual love and he sets himself up as the pattern of this.[83] Of both forms of slavery discussed by Paul—the paradoxical abasement that is itself a glory and the mutual humility that proceeds from love—they are both patterned on Christ who found glory through lowering himself to the form of a slave and who became the servant (διάκονος) of the Jewish people for their salvation.[84] It is only in relation to this theology of the cross that Paul's metaphor of slavery makes sense. In the context of the crucified saviour, the leader can speak of himself in terms of the lowest ranks of society and claim that God has made him and his fellow apostles the last of all mankind.[85] This correlation between leadership and slavery is seen according to the pattern of the kenosis of Christ. It is a delicate balance and one that does not survive well in the centuries that follow.

81. M. Hengel, *The Cross of the Son of God* (London: SCM Press, 1986), p. 154.

82. R.P. Martin, *Philippians* (Leicester: InterVarsity Press, 1987), argues that the form of a slave here is not an indication of the humiliation of Christ, but an identification with the Suffering Servant and a title of dignity. This seems unlikely, as it would run counter to the entire kenotic thrust of the passage.

83. 'Agree together, my friends, to follow my example. You have us for a model: watch those whose way of life conforms to it' (Phil. 3.17).

84. Rom. 15.7.

85. 1 Cor. 4.9.

6. *Summary*

We have seen that slavery played an important role in the language and theology of the New Testament, and describes both the state of the unsaved and the new relationship with God brought about by Christ.

Nowhere in the New Testament (with the possible exception of Jn 8.30-35) is there any trace of the use of 'slave' as a label for the naturally inferior, the stupid or the vicious, as is so common in other forms of literature. The only time 'slave' or 'slavery' is used in a negative manner is in the context of slavery to sin, where it is frequently balanced by the exaltation implicit in slavery to righteousness.

In addition, although the abolition of slavery is never suggested in the New Testament, it is noticeable that slaves are not to be treated in any way as second-class Christians. With the proviso that they serve and obey their masters (for all secular authorities are to be obeyed), it is tacitly assumed that they will participate in the Christian life on an equal footing with the free, and no instructions are given to limit any aspect of their membership, nor to regulate their behaviour (as there are concerning women) within the context of worship.

Although the New Testament has often been criticized for its lack of interest in the abolition of slavery, it must be remembered that this completely consistent lack of prejudice against slaves and slavery, and emphasis on the equality of all people, already represents a significant departure from the conceptions of the time. While contemporary Stoics indeed denied the spiritual inferiority of the physically enslaved, they nevertheless regarded it as a state where, for sheer practical reasons, one is at a spiritual disadvantage and used it as a metaphor for spiritual or intellectual inferiority.

But let me return to and summarize the themes of slavery as they appear in the New Testament. As discussed earlier, a number of different uses of the metaphor can be found—often in combinations that give rise to some inconsistencies. First, and most importantly, there is the simple idea of the individual as the δοῦλος of Christ or God, a title which a number of writers use of themselves and others.

In a more complex version of the metaphor, we find the idea of the individual being in slavery to sin, or to the world. There are two paths out of slavery. In one case the slavery to sin is replaced by slavery to God or Christ, and in the other, the emphasis is on freedom and the individual moves out of slavery into freedom and adoption by God.

These transitions take place though death: Christ's death as a purchase price, the spiritual death of the believers to themselves as they become slaves to God or Christ, and the 'death' which cancels the old slavery and makes the believers free.

Another form of the metaphor, which we should note, does not play a large part in the New Testament, but will become important later. This is the version that sees the individual moving out of slavery to God into sonship to God. The individual who was once only capable of relating to God within the context of a slave/master relationship is now given the opportunity of entering a son/father relationship. The evidence for the use of this form in the New Testament is very limited, but it occurs, as we have seen, in the Gospel of John.

Running through all these themes is the basic conflict between the two perceptions of the status of the believer—that he or she is the slave of God or Christ and that he or she is the son or daughter of God. This conflict is given added force by the paradox inherent in the use of slave language at all, its associations with degradation and baseness being so much at odds with the exaltation and salvation of the believer.[86] This paradox is no error in judgment on the part of the users. On the contrary, it is perfectly in tune with the earliest Christian message, which is informed with the basic contradiction of the first as last and the glory of humiliation, summed up in the central message of the crucified saviour. In Dillistone's words:

> Here was the ultimate paradox, if not the ultimate contrary, Messiah, the encapsulation in a single world of the noblest memories and highest hopes of the Jewish people: estauromenos—crucified, the encapsulation in a single world of the lowest depths of human degradation imaginable in Hellenistic culture.[87]

It is no mistake, I believe, that Paul should therefore make use of so ambiguous a term as slavery to describe his own state and that of the believer in relationship to Christ. Such a metaphor, however, only makes real sense within the context of the New Testament emphasis on the paradox of crucifixion. It now remains to be seen how it survives when transplanted out of the world of the New Testament into a new set of contexts.

---

86. 'The devotees of the new religion expressed their relationship with their god in the most self debasing and self degrading term that society offered them', Bradley, *Slavery and Society*, p. 152.

87. F.W. Dillistone, *Traditional Symbols and the Contemporary World* (1968 Bampton Lectures; London: Epworth Press, 1978), p. 146.

Chapter 4

THE METAPHOR IN PATRISTIC DOCTRINE

In the previous chapter we have seen the various forms that the
metaphor of spiritual slavery took when it was first adopted into the
Christian context to describe the position of the believer in their relationship with God and with the world. These different forms of the
metaphor were continued and expanded in the subsequent texts, with
the result that although the metaphor of slavery was never the most
popular Christian metaphor (compared with, say, the metaphors of
fatherhood and adoption) it was certainly one of the most versatile, and
was readily put to use in a wide range of contexts.

Placing sources in categories is always dangerous; writers will not
have thought in terms of a division of their use of language into rigid
ranks, and there will always be exceptions and crossovers. Nevertheless, in order to make any sense of the material we are working with,
some structure must be imposed. We shall therefore look at the metaphor in terms of three broad categories:

Doctrine: This will be where the metaphor is used as a part of the
theological considerations of the writer, where it provides the vehicle
for particular perceptions of the human/divine relationship.

Liturgy: This will consist of those occasions where the metaphor is
used in a public sense, that is, either in the context of prayer or of
Church ceremonial, or in accounts and explanations of these. It is
where the metaphor is seen as functioning on the level of the general
believer in the context of worship or catechesis.

Exegesis: This will consist of examples of patristic exegesis of New
Testament texts that make use of the metaphor.

1. *The Metaphor in Doctrine*

The idea of slavery to God takes a number of different forms in this
period, and is expressed in a number of different ways. There are the

ideas of the slave of God, the slave of evil, the transition from one form of slavery to another and the transition from slavery to freedom. Each of these, moreover, has its own variations.

2. *The Slave of God*

a. *The Believer as δοῦλος*

The idea of the human/divine relationship as a master/slave relationship has many variations. One is the form of calling upon the experience of the hearer, as we have already found in the Gospels[1] such as in John Chrysostom's words:

> If you have a slave (οἰκέτην), and he, after suffering much evil from his fellow slaves, does not pay attention to any of the others but only considers how not to provoke his master; is he not able by this alone to avoid your anger? But what if his offences against you do not matter to him, while he considers only those against his fellow slaves; do you not give him the greater punishment? God does the same.[2]

In a more direct form, the formula may be used to describe a believer. The *Didascalia* (third century CE), for instance, speaks of believers as δοῦλοι καὶ υἱοὶ τοῦ Θεοῦ.[3] This title need not, however, necessarily indicate that the bearer is possessed of any special holiness: in the *Shepherd of Hermas* the δοῦλοι Θεοῦ are susceptible to temptation,[4] and wicked desire,[5] and in Clement of Alexandria (late second/early third century CE) we find that 'envying man the forgiveness of sins, (the Devil) offered causes of sin to the slaves of God'.[6] On this general level, it is frequently argued that all humans are the slaves of God in virtue of having been created by him. The natural and proper state of mankind and of creation is therefore one of obedient slavery. 'But now all know that he (the sun) is a servant, in his course the Lord is worshipped—all servants rejoice that as servants they are reckoned.'[7]

---

1.   Lk. 17.7-10.
2.   Chrysostom, *Homilies on I Corinthians* 8 (PG 61.74). See also *Homily 16 on Timothy* (PG 62.589-90).
3.   *Didascalia* 2.1.3.
4.   *Hermas* (GCS, 48, 48.4.2). See also *Didascalia*, 11.2.43.
5.   *Hermas* (GCS, 48.45.2.1-2).
6.   *Stromata* (GCS, 52, 2.13.56.2.4-5).
7.   Ephraim, *Hymn on the Nativity* 15.10. Also 12.17: 'The lord makes not himself strange to his slaves (or conceal) that he is lord of all' (NPNF 13).

The metaphor also finds its way—as a description of the common believer—into the Christian funerary inscriptions. A glance at the *CIG* yields an ample supply of these, attesting to a wide use of a δοῦλος Θεοῦ formula, most commonly in the areas of Egypt and Africa. Thus: Μνήσθητι κύριε, τῆς κοιμήσεως τῆς δούλης σου Νιλανθίον ('Remember, Lord, your sleeping slave Nilanthe') (*CIG*, 9110) and μνήσθητι ὅταν ἔλθῃς τῆς ψυχῆς τῆς δούλης σου ('Remember, when you come, the soul of your slave') (*CIG*, 9119).

The problem, however, lies in the dating of these epitaphs which, in many cases, cannot be ascertained in any satisfactory manner. In some of these cases, we might make some attempt to do this by looking at the theology that underlies the epitaph. As is so often the case in such things, we find that there are a number of formulaic epitaphs which may be found, with small variations, in a number of cases. One of these is the 'bosom of Abraham' formula: ὁ Θεός ἀνάπαυσον ψυχὴν τοῦ δούλου σου Σαμσὼν ἐν κόπις Ἀβραὰμ καὶ Ἰσαὰκ καὶ Ιακώβ ('Remember, when you come, the soul of your slave') (*CIG*, 9120). The idea of resting in Abraham's bosom, might guide us to a fairly early date for such monuments:

> At this period, when the theology of the last things was still rudimentary, Abraham's bosom was regarded as a provisional resting place for the souls of the just until the last judgement. Only the martyrs, it was thought, were allowed to see God before then.[8]

Horsley also agrees that such a formula indicates an earlier form of such theology:

> Whereas in the first couple of centuries the distinction remained between the pre-resurrection state of the Christian dead and the immediate bliss of the martyrs (cf. Rev. 6.9-11), gradually the situation enjoyed by the latter was widened in popular thinking to include the souls of all the faithful dead.[9]

Using this, we can cautiously date a number of the epitaphs to the early centuries of the Church, and in the standard formula seen above, we find *CIG*, 9113, 9116, 9120 dated around 489, 9121 all of which

8. A. Hamman (ed.), *Early Christian Prayers* (trans. W. Mitchell; London: Longmans, 1961), p. 289 n. 118.
9. *New Documents Illustrating Early Christianity: A Review of the Inscriptions and Papyri* (North Ryde, New South Wales: The Ancient History Documentary Research Centre, 1977–78), p. 107.

occur in the Egypt, Africa area. In the Sicilia/Melita area we find one case of this: Μνήσθητι ὁ Θεὸς τῆς δούλης σου Χρυσίδος καὶ δὸς αὐτῇ χώραν φωτινήν, τόπον ἀναψύξεως εἰς κόλφους 'Αβραάμ, 'Ισαὰκ καὶ 'Ιακώβ ('Remember, God, your slave Crysida and give her a shining place, a place of refreshment in the bosom of Abraham, Isaac and Jacob'), (*CIG*, 9533) which *CIG* dates to 373, 380 or 411. Given the content of their theology, I think we would be justified in therefore dating such inscriptions in the region of this date and earlier rather than later.

Apart from these, we may find an interesting range of variations and uses of the δοῦλος Θεοῦ theme. The use of the δοῦλος Θεοῦ + name formula is widespread and, in a number of cases, is used on the gravestone of a clergyman: *CIG* 9258 (presbyter), 9287 (priest), 9297 (priest), 9392 (deacon), 9396 (deacon). δοῦλος Χριστοῦ is very rare, occurring only twice in the *CIG* collection: Εὐφημίας δούλης Χριστοῦ ('Euphemia the slave of Christ') (*CIG*, 9250), and Γεώργιος μοναχὸς καὶ ἠψοίμενος δοῦλος Χριστοῦ ('George the monk and cherished slave of Christ') (*CIG*, 9420).

Horsley also gives an example: ἐνθάδε κῖται ἡ δούλη καὶ νύμφη τοῦ Χριστοῦ Σοφιά, ἡ διάκονος ('There lies the slave and bride of Christ, Sophia the deaconess'), and these examples suggests that the use of a δοῦλος Χριστοῦ formula is associated with holy orders.[10]

Interesting as these inscriptions are, however, the difficulties involved in dating them limit their use for our present study, except as an indication of the continuation of such use in the everyday world.

b. *The Saint as δοῦλος*

A more specialized form of the metaphor can be found in its use for saints. This would appear at first glance to be a direct continuation of the Pauline *Slave of Christ* formula—we find Cyril of Jerusalem[11] speaking of Peter and Paul as δοῦλοι Θεοῦ, and according to the *Gospel of Thomas* (c. 100), Jesus himself actually appears in the marketplace and sells the saint (my slave [δοῦλος] Judas) to Abbanes as a slave.[12] John in his apocryphal Acta is ὁ τοῦ Θεοῦ δοῦλος 'Ιωάννης.[13]

Various later figures are also spoken of in this way—Athanasius's

10. Horsley, *New Documents*, p. 239, item 122.
11. Cyril of Jerusalem, *Catechetical Lecture* 6.15.
12. *Acts of Thomas* 1.
13. *Acts of John* 47.7, and 4.3-4, 111.3-4.

(fourth century) *Life of Anthony*, for instance, refers to the saint as δοῦλος Θεοῦ and Χριστοῦ δοῦλος.[14]

c. *The Martyr as δοῦλος*
The metaphor is even more common in the context of the persecution of Christians, either by pagans or by heretics (in the latter case it denotes the orthodox Christians). God takes 'His chosen ones ἀπὸ τῶν ἰδίων δούλων'.[15] The use of the title δοῦλος or *servus* is an extension of a more general use of the formula to describe persecuted Christians in general. It may be used to describe individuals undergoing persecution—as Cyprian of Carthage (mid third century CE)[16] and Gregory of Nyssa (late fourth century CE) do, the latter speaking of 'Stephen, the slave of Christ'.[17] In the *Martyrdom of Polycarp*,[18] the martyr is referred to as φιλοδέσποτον, a common name for slaves.[19]

δοῦλος may also be claimed by martyrs themselves, again either by implication as in the case of Polycarp (who describes himself as having served Christ for 86 years, and compares rejecting him to a slave rejecting his master),[20] or by an explicit claim on the title. A good example of this may be found in the *Acta Justinini*, whose three recensions show an interesting variation in the language describing the trial of the martyrs.[21] In each case these martyrs are asked to identify themselves. In the shortest recension, the slave Euelpistos answers: κἀγὼ Χριστιανός εἰμι καὶ τῆς αὐτῆς ἐλπίδος μετέχων ('I too am a Christian and I partake in the same hope').[22] In the middle recension, this has become: Εὐέλπιστος δοῦλος Καίσαρος ἀπεκρίνατο Κἀγὼ Χριστιανός εἰμι, ἐλευθερωθεὶς ὑπὸ Χριστοῦ (Euelpistos the slave of Caesar replied, 'I

14. Athanasius, *Life of Anthony* 85; 52; 53.
15. *Martyrdom of Polycarp* 20.1, see also *2 Clement* 20.1.
16. E.g. *Epistle 8*, *Epistle 2*, 1; *Epistle 22*, 1, *inter alia*.
17. *Encomium in Sanctum Stephanum Protomartyrem* 2 (PG 46.725.28).
18. *Martyrdom of Polycarp* 2.2.a.
19. See also *1 Clement* 45, where the martyrs are said to serve God.
20. *Martyrdom of Polycarp* 9.3.
21. The *Acts of Justin* ('Acta Justini et Septem Sodalium', in H. Musurillo [ed.] *Acts of the Christian Martyrs* [Oxford: Clarendon Press, 1972], exists in three recensions. The shorter and middle length versions are considered to be the older, with the latter probably based on the former. The third and longest version is later and 'obviously reworked' (Musurillo, *Acts of the Christian Martyrs*, pp. xvii-xx).
22. Recensio A, 4.3 (Musurillo, *Acts of the Christian Martyrs*).

too am a Christian, having been set free by Christ').[23] The third version, however, reads: Δοῦλος, ἔφη, γέγονα Καίσαρος, νυνὶ δὲ Χριστοῦ, τῇ τούτου χάριτι τῆς ἐλευθερίας τυχών ('I am a slave,' he said, 'previously of Caesar but now of Christ, through whose grace I have received the gift of freedom.').[24] In this third recension, the other martyrs also call themselves slaves of Christ: Ναί, φησιν ὁ ἅγιος, καὶ Χριστοῦ δοῦλος (' "Indeed" said the saint, "and a slave of Christ" ').[25]

d. δοῦλος *as a Title for Clerics*
It is not long before the term δοῦλος Θεοῦ begins to take on almost technical connotations, and to be used as a kind of courtesy title for clerics or monks. In the *Apostolic Tradition,* the bishops and presbyters bear the title δοῦλοι, and this continues, especially in the case of bishops: οἱ δε γε ἐπίσκοποι, οἱ ἀληθῶς γνήσιοι δοῦλοι τοῦ κυρίου ('The bishops, the legitimate and orthodox slaves of the Lord').[26] Basil in directing the selection of a new bishop, requests that he only be a slave of God.[27] Athanasius, too, makes use of the δοῦλος Θεοῦ + *name* formula: τοῦ ἀληθῶς Θεοῦ δούλου Βασιλείου τοῦ ἐπισκόπου ('Basil the bishop, the true slave of God').[28] In this context the parallel with the title borne by members of the slaves of the Emperor holding posts in the Roman Imperial civil service cannot be ignored. Deissmann points out a parallel with the title *Christians*:

> The parallelism...obtains between the genitive Χριστου...and the simple genitive Καίσαρος 'belonging to the Emperor'. The latter, first revealed by the new texts goes back to the latin elliptic Caesaris and can be established for Egypt in several papyri of the reign of Augustus and by inscriptions of the reign of Hadrian. The analogy which has already been claimed on linguistic grounds between the oldest name for the followers of Christ Χριστιανός... and Καισαριανός, Caesar's Imperial (slave) receives in this connexion new and remarkable illustration.[29]

He is probably going too far here, but is on the right track as a truer parallel may be found in a comparison between the title δοῦλος

23. Recensio B, 4.3.2-3 (Musurillo, *Acts of the Christian Martyrs*).
24. Recensio C, 3.4.2-3 (Musurillo, *Acts of the Christian Martyrs*).
25. Recensio C, 3.1.2-3 (Musurillo, *Acts of the Christian Martyrs*).
26. Athanasius, *Epistle to the African Bishops* 3 (see also his *History of the Arians* 68.2, τοὺς δὲ τοῦ Χριστοῦ δούλους).
27. Basil, *Epistle* 190.1.18.
28. Athanasius, *Epistle* 62 to John and Antiochus.
29. Deissmann, *Light from the Ancient East*, p. 377.

Θεοῦ/Χριστοῦ as a 'professional' title and the title used for the Emperor's slaves. These slaves, members of the *Familia Caesaris*, were clearly of a higher social standing than other slaves and freedmen of the time,[30] and the names of this elite group included 'the distinctive mark of status "Caes(aris) ser(vus)" or "Aug(usti) vern(a)" or simply "Aug(usti)" or Caes(aris)"'.[31] This title, from the end of Hadrian's reign, appears in the Greek inscriptions as Καίσαρος δοῦλος.[32] Such slaves could hold the most responsible positions, controlling and limiting access to the emperor, and often receiving great respect and deference in virtue of their influential positions, much to the disgust of more traditionally minded members of the Roman aristocracy.

e. *δοῦλος as a Title for the Patriarchs and Old Testament Heroes*
It is clear that, in these texts, the New Testament prejudice against the use of δοῦλος in speaking of Old Testament figures of particular honour (such as Moses, David or Abraham) begins to lose some of its original force. The *Didascalia* speaks of David, Moses and the prophets as slaves of God.[33] We find Gregory of Nyssa and Gregory Nazianzus (late fourth century CE) calling David a δοῦλος of God,[34] and Chrysostom uses this term of Moses,[35] although θεράπων continues to be the most usual form of the metaphor in this context.

f. *διάκονος and παῖς*
We cannot, moreover, omit the classic case of the transformation of a servitude term into a Christian title: the case of the διάκονος. This is so quickly put to use, from the first centuries onward, as a title for a specific role in the Church, that it is hardly necessary to discuss its development in detail. Although it clearly becomes a title of some honour, it retains, in the early centuries at least, some of its associations with the δοῦλος metaphor, as may be seen in the tendency of some

30. Weaver, *Familia Caesaris*, p. 295 (However, he points out that 'this was not equally true for all its members nor for all periods').
31. Weaver, *Familia Caesaris*, p. 2.
32. Weaver, *Familia Caesaris*, pp. 52-54.
33. David: 2.1.8; Moses: 2.22.8; 6.15; the prophets: 2.22.10 and 6.2.
34. Gregory of Nyssa, *Homily on Song of Songs* 6.364.15; Gregory Nazianzus, *Oration* 2.117. Ephraim speaks of Isaac as a servant in *Hymn on the Nativity 6*.
35. Chrysostom, *Homily on Matthew* 56.3, for example.

earlier writers to use the term σύνδουλος when speaking of them.[36] However, διάκονος probably lacked the same degree of degradation implied by δοῦλος, since it is so readily used, in the New Testament for Jesus.[37]

It has already been noted that never in the New Testament, with the exception of Revelation, is Jesus referred to directly as δοῦλος. The closest any writer comes to this is to speak of him taking 'the form of a slave': μορφὴν δούλου.[38] Where the idea of servanthood is applied to Jesus it is in the form of the term παῖς which may be translated either as slave or child[39] and is the most usual translation of Isaiah's *ebed* in the Septuagint and in the New Testament. The custom of calling Jesus the παῖς Θεοῦ continues out of the New Testament into the earlier Christian texts, usually within the context of prayer.[40]

---

36. E.g. Ignatius *Eph.* 2.1, *Mag* 2.2, *Phil.* 4.1, *Smyr.* 12.2 and Polycarp, *Epistle to the Philippians* 1.133. 'If the inscriptions teach us anything it is that the original meaning of διακονεῖν ('to wait at table') persisted. In accordance with the saying and example of Jesus, early Christianity made this the symbol of all loving care for others. Here is the root of the living connexion between ethical reflection on service in the community and the actual diaconate', *TDNT*, II, p. 92. See also pp. 88-93

On the movement away from this understanding, see J.M. Barnett, *The Diaconate: A Full and Equal Order* (New York: Seabury Press, 1981), pp. 120-22.

37. For example: Mt. 20.26-28; Mk 10.43-45 and Lk. 22.24-27. For a fuller account of the use of διάκονος in New Testament, see Barnett, *The Diaconate*, pp. 17-18.

38. Phil. 2.7.

39. A more recent form of this kind of ambiguity may be found in the fact that the word 'boy' was commonly used in the slave-owning American south to refer to a black male slave of any age. The ambiguity between these two meanings persists even to this day to the extent that the word is still often used as a term of racial abuse.

40. As Hooker, *Jesus and the Servant*, points out: 'It has frequently been noted that the majority of these passages are of a liturgical character: those in I Clement, the Didache and the Martyrdom of Polycarp all appear in prayers, and those in the Epistle of Barnabas are quotations. Only the Epistle to Diognetus uses the term in a straightforward context. The meaning of the term παῖς in these books is by no means consistent; thus the context of the phrase in the Martyrdom of Polycarp and the Epistle to Diognetus and probably also in I Clement shows that the translation must be "child" or "son", while that in the Epistle of Barnabas necessitates "servant". The restricted use of the term παῖς Θεοῦ confirms not only that the title was an early one, but that it soon died out' (pp. 108-109).

This she attributes to 'the decrease of Jewish influence upon Christian thought

3. *The Slave of Sin*

Conversely, the metaphor may be adapted to describe an individual as the slave of sin, either in the more philosophical sense of one being enslaved by abstract forces such as fear or greed, or to Satan himself as in the *Peri Pascha* of Melito of Sardis which speaks of τῆς τοῦ διαβόλου δουλείας.[41] The *Epistle to Diognetus* (c. 150) states that Christians are not enslaved by false gods,[42] Gregory Nazianzus speaks of his father escaping the bondage of his own father's gods[43] and Ephraim uses the image of the worshippers of the sun becoming 'the servants of servants'.[44] The *Didascalia* warns of slavery to the Law.[45]

4. *Out of Slavery to Evil*

The second important form of the metaphor of slavery throughout patristic literature is that which describes the transition a believer must undergo upon conversion and as a part of spiritual growth. Slavery to evil is contrasted with a better slavery to God or freedom (sometimes in the form of the soul's marriage with or adoption by God). Conversion may be the purchase of the soul or its emancipation. Further, the believer may remain a slave of God or may progress on to sonship. In another variation, the pre-conversion state is seen as one of slavery to God which is then replaced by sonship.

a. *Slavery to Evil → Freedom in God*
This form of the metaphor can, as we have seen, be found in Paul's teaching concerning the nature of Christian salvation. It is a metaphor thoroughly bound up with ideas and metaphors of redemption and

---

before the ever growing influx of Hellenistic concepts' and to 'the use of a more considered christology which laid greater emphasis on the divinity of Christ' which would have thought that 'to speak of Jesus as the servant of God' would have been to use a disparaging term, while to call him a 'child of God' implied an element of subordination not found in the term υἱός which soon replaced it'.

41. Melito of Sardis, *On Easter* 67.
42. *Epistle to Diognetus* 2.
43. Gregory Nazianzaus, *Oration* 8.4.
44. Ephraim, *Hymn on the Nativity* 15.11.
45. *Didascalia* 6.16.

manumission. It can again be found in other Christian writings such as the *Epistle of Barnabas*, which speaks of the believer as having been enslaved to death, but who is now free, and 'without the yoke of necessity'.[46]

This release is sometimes described as a process of manumission—as in, for example, Macarius: 'and deigning to honour him with his voice, struck him like a slave and set him free'.[47] This may be compared to the Roman process of manumission, whereby the slave was struck on the head, in the presence of witnesses and declared free.[48] A similar reflection occurs in Ephraim's *Hymn on the Nativity*: 'He came down to set free his creatures—in this blessed month wherein are made releases to slaves—the lord underwent bondage to call the bond to freedom'.[49]

We thus find an emphasis on the nature of the freedom one enjoys in God, as in Ambrose (late fourth century CE) who places the emphasis on the friendship and the implications of such a relationship:

> What is more precious than friendship which is common to angels and to man?... God himself turns us from slaves to friends, as he himself says, 'You are my friends if you do whatever I command you'. He gave us a pattern of friendship to follow, that should fulfil the wishes of our friend, we should reveal to him whatever secrets we hold in our hearts and we should not disregard his confidences.[50]

and Cyril of Alexandria:

> what greater, what more magnificent thing can be thought of than to be and to be called a friend of God?[51]

and this emphasis leads to the point where Gregory of Nyssa asserts that God does not want believers to be slaves at all:

---

46. *Epistle of Barnabas* 2.B.

47. Macarius, *Hymns on the Nativity* 44.8 (also: 'I therefore brought back the body that was sold to you by the first Adam. I tore up the contract that enslaved mankind to you', 11.10. *Neue Homilien des Makarius* [TU 72; Berlin: Akademie Verlag, 1961]).

48. Buckland, *The Roman Law of Slavery*, p. 451: 'Some non-juristic texts speak of the master as taking the slave by a limb, slapping his cheek and then turning him around. This also Karlowa regards as part of the legal formality, the slap being a last indication of slavery, the turning round a sign of his changed position' (see references in Buckland, *The Roman Law of Slavery*, p. 451).

49. Ephraim, *Hymn on the Nativity* 15.5.

50. Ambrose, *Duties of the Clergy* 2.135.

51. Cyril of Alexandria, *On the Gospel of John* 10.

...the Divine Word does not wish even us to be slaves, our nature now having been changed for the better...in the life we hope for there will be neither disease, nor curse, nor sin, nor death so slavery also along with these will disappear, and that what I say is true, I call truth itself to witness, who says to his disciples, 'I call you no more slaves but friends'.[52]

The nature of the previous slavery tends to vary. It may be sin that the individual is escaping from, but the writers sometimes have other masters in mind. Eusebius of Emesa (mid-fourth century), for example, in relation to Gal. 1.1, speaks of the Church as coming out of slavery, not to evil or to the devil, but to the Law: 'He now calls God Father, because he wishes that the Church, coming into adoption should be free from slavery to the law',[53] and in such a vein, Chrysostom, commenting on Rom. 8.18, contrasts the freedom of the Christians and the slavery of the Jews: 'And so they (the Jews), even though they were called sons, were but as slaves; but we as having been made free, have received adoption, and are waiting for Heaven.'[54]

b. *Slavery to Evil → Slavery to God*
This variation of the metaphor is, again, one that we encounter in Paul, and is carried on into the patristic period, as in Origen: 'we were not slaves of God, but (slaves) of idols and demons, we are foreigners; yesterday or just now we have been acquired by God'.[55] It is not, however, often used by the Fathers in a directly transitional sense[56] and occurs more frequently in terms of a simple opposition between the state of slavery to evil and the state of slavery to God.

5. *Out of Slavery to God*

a. *Slavery to God → Sonship in God*
The idea of the believer passing through various stages in his relationship with God, moving from relating to God in a master/slave context to becoming his son, is one that becomes ever more popular over this period, and many writers distinguish between the believer whose faith has remained in the spirit of slavery and the believer who has

---

52. Gregory of Nyssa, *Against Eunomius*, 10.4.
53. Eusebius of Emesa, Frag. on Gal. 1.1.
54. Chrysostom, *Homily on Romans* 14.8.
55. Origen, *On Jeremiah* 4.5.54-55. See also Epiphanius, *Ancoratus* 24.5.7.
56. Except, as we shall see, in the liturgies of baptism.

progressed, sometimes via a state of 'faithful servanthood' to the status of a son.

The most interesting early use of this variation of the metaphor after the New Testament occurs in the parable, in the *Shepherd of Hermas*,[57] of the slave and the vineyard, where the believer is compared to a slave who goes beyond the letter of his master's command and as a reward is elevated to the position of a son.[58]

This parable makes use of the idea, which we come across in the Gospel of John, of the metaphor used in the sense of the 'slave to God' → 'son of God' progression, as opposed to the 'slave to sin' → 'slave/son of God' formula. It is important to note here that whereas the second of these usually describes the 'presaved' → 'saved' movement, the first describes a development within an already existing relationship with God. The idea of 'slave' in this sense describes the individual who is already a believer and is now perfecting his relationship with God.[59]

This may also take a more explicit form and speak of the spiritual life as being a progression out of a state of slavery and fear to one of son-ship, as in Origen (early/mid-third century CE):

> Those who do not strive in this way do not become children of God or belong to God, and because of this they do not hear his words or under-stand their meaning; they remain indeed in the age which precedes that of being children of God, a state of receiving only, as slaves of God, the spirit of slavery in fear and they are not eager to advance and progress so as to become capable also of that spirit of adoption, in which those who have it cry 'Abba'.[60]

He points out that some are called slaves of God, some are called his sons, and urges his readers to strive towards the latter state.[61] Athana-sius takes a similar line:

> From the beginning we are creatures by nature and God is our creator through the Word, but afterwards we are made sons and henceforth God our creator becomes God our father also.[62]

---

57. *Sim.* 5.2.

58. For a detailed discussion of the parable, see below, pp. 135-38.

59. This will be discussed in more detail later. See pp. 143-46.

60. Origen, *Commentary on the Gospel of John* 20.33.289-90.

61. Origen, *Commentary on the Gospel of John* 20.17.146. See also Origen, *On Prayer* 16.1.14-15: εἰσὶ γὰρ καὶ ἐν τῇ ψυχῇ μόνον τῷ καρδίας βλέποντι χαρακ-τῆρες φανεροῖς δούλων Θεοῦ καὶ υἱῶν αὐτοῦ.

62. Athanasius, *Against the Arians* 2.59 (PG 95.273b). Cited by P. Widdicombe

b. *Slavery to God → Freedom in God*
The movement from slavery, even slavery to God, is not, however, always necessarily linked directly to sonship and other metaphors, such as marriage, may be used to describe the freedom attained by the converted, as for instance, in Cyril of Jerusalem's words:

> Angels shall dance around you and say, 'Who is this who comes up in white array, leaning upon her beloved?' For the soul that was formerly a slave has now adopted her Master himself as her kinsman.[63]

and:

> ...it is not to his slaves, but to his friends that Jesus gives this commandment.[64]

> I posted the cherubim to guard you like slaves; now I make the cherubim worship you like God.[65]

In many cases, however, it is simply freedom which is promised as in Melito of Sardis' (late second century CE) assurance that Christ has delivered us ἐκ δουλείας εἰς ἐλευθερίαν.[66]

6. *Summary*

In the Early Church we find that the metaphor of slavery seems to retain its popularity long after the New Testament period.[67] The difficulty lies in establishing what the writers themselves thought it was to imply, and any single theory of this is bound to run into difficulty. It is true that, in some cases the formula is related to the idea of Christianity as the True Israel, but in others it is used in an entirely different form, and Jews are abused for remaining the slaves of God while Christians have progressed on to sonship. There is also a clear distinction between

(*The Fatherhood of God from Origen to Athanasius* [Oxford: Clarendon Press, 1994]), p. 251. See also Clement of Alexandria (*Strom.* 1.27.173) '(it is possible) by lending ear to wisdom, to be in the first place a slave of God (Θεοῦ δοῦλος) then to become a faithful servant (Θεράποντα) and if one ascend higher he is enrolled among the sons'.

63. Cyril of Jerusalem, *Lecture* 3.16.
64. Origen, *Exhortation to Martyrdom* 34.78.
65. Epiphanius, *Descent of Christ into Hell* (PG 43.463).
66. Melito of Sardis, *On Easter* 68.
67. K.H. Rengstorf, 'δοῦλος', *TDNT*, II, p. 274.

the sonship of Jesus and the slavehood of humanity, but this can hardly account for the increased use of δοῦλος Θεοῦ.

It is also clear that the idea of merit cannot be said always to play a role in this title. In many cases the δοῦλος Θεοῦ is described in very ordinary terms with little indication that this is meant to indicate a particularly serious believer. Indeed, it may be used to describe the very inadequacy of one's belief.

We have seen, thus, that the metaphor of slavery plays an important and varied role in patristic doctrine, expressing in different contexts the various aspects of the relationship between the human and the divine. We have seen it here in the context of a more literary and private use, we now turn to its use in the context of prayer and catechesis. It must be again stressed that there is no rigid division between the two and the texts would not have been produced with such distinctions in mind. We shall be considering, in the next section, the use of metaphor as part of liturgy but the sources on these must be, of course, occasionally doctrinal in nature. As far as is possible, the discussion will centre on the action of the liturgy—the way the ceremonial is formed by the metaphors of slavery and freedom.

Chapter 5

THE METAPHOR IN EARLY LITURGY

I turn therefore to the liturgy and prayer of the Patristic Church, the active response on the individual to their beliefs, in which the means of defining the relationship between God and the one who is praying is most vital. As we shall see, the metaphor appears in this context from the earliest days of the Church, both as an expression of service and devotion to God and, in a transitional context, as an expression of the freedom attained from the slavery to evil. It is in the liturgy of baptism, however, that the metaphor finds its most important role. It is almost completely absent from eucharistic liturgy, however, except insofar as this acts as the continuation of the baptismal ceremony, reminding the baptized believer of their new-found freedom.

1. *The Metaphor in Prayer*

The use of the metaphor of slavery in prayers is attested from as early as Acts, where in 4.25-30 we find: '...grant to your slaves (τοῖς δούλοις σου) to speak your word with all boldness', and as in the *Apostolic Tradition*,[1] the metaphor often appears in prayers of ordination and consecration. The *Apostolic Constitutions* makes use of the metaphor both directly in 8.6.10-13 and indirectly by a use of Lk. 2.29 in 7.48.1-4. The blessing of the people in the *Euchology* of Serapion of Thmuis (fourth century CE) speaks of the people as slaves: δεῖξον ἡμᾶς καὶ δούλους γνησίους καὶ καθαροὺς[2] ('Grant that we may be your true and genuine slaves') and the metaphor appears again in the blessing of the oil of the sick, the bread and the water.[3]

---

1. For the consecration of bishops, in 3.4, of presbyters, in 8.2 and of deacons in 9.11.
2. Serapion, *Euchology* 8.3b.27.5.
3. Serapion, *Euchology* 8.3b.29-30.

2. *The Metaphor in Baptism*

a. *Metaphors of Manumission*

The ritual of Christian baptism revolves around two basic elements, both of which have often been described in terms of slavery and freedom. The first of these is a turning away from, and a rejection of, the old way of life dominated by sin and the devil, and the second is a commitment to the new life in Christ. We find, however, that in the very earliest baptismal rites, the first of these tends to lack any formal expression. In general, it is sufficiently understood that the commitment to Christ must necessarily entail a rejection of sin, and this rejection therefore requires no expression as a separate ceremony. However, as the liturgy of baptism begins to develop into a more formal and established pattern,[4] the need to emphasize its thoroughgoing and irrevocable nature becomes more apparent. There appears, in most cases, during the process leading up to the immersion itself, a moment when the neophyte is called upon to verbally renounce 'Satan and all his pomp and his service (λατρεία)', and this renunciation is, in many case, described in terms of a rejection of slavery to Satan in preparation for entry into a new relationship with Christ. In order to discuss this fully, we should begin with a brief overview of the ritual of baptism itself.

The earliest detailed sources of information on Christian baptism after the period of the New Testament[5] are found in the *Didache* and in the *First Apology* of Justin Martyr (c. 155). These provide brief descriptions of a rite of baptism consisting of an unspecified period of preliminary instruction,[6] followed by the fasting of the catechumens (in which they may be accompanied by others).[7]

After this comes a washing in water 'in the name of God the Father

---

4.   When examining the rites of baptism one must, however, be wary of assuming that the sources give us a consistent set of practices. There was a great deal of variation in form and content from one area to another. See P.F. Bradshaw, *The Search for the Origins of Christian Worship: Sources and Methods for the Study of Early Liturgy* (London: SPCK, 1992), pp. 161-84.

5.   On the origins and New Testament doctrines of baptism, see also G. Lohfink, 'Der Ursprung der christlichen Taufe', *TQ* 1 (1976), pp. 35-54.

6.   *Didache* 7.1. Also Justin Martyr, 'Those who are persuaded that the things we say are true, and promise to live accordingly', *Apology* 1.61.

7.   *Didache* 7.4, (the baptizer and 'those who can'); Justin Martyr (the entire congregation).

and Master of all and of our saviour Jesus Christ and of the Holy Spirit'.[8] Justin goes on to describe the newly baptized as being led to the congregation, where prayers are offered for the congregation, the newly baptized and 'others everywhere'. The kiss of peace and the eucharist follow.

Baptism is described by Justin as an inward illumination and the means of remission of sins, as well as a rebirth and a regeneration that 'we should not remain children of necessity and ignorance, but of free choice and knowledge'.[9]

Our understanding of the rite of baptism in the third century derives, for the most part, from three main texts: the *Apostolic Tradition* of Hippolytus, the *Didascalia Apostolorum* and Tertullian's *De Baptismo*, all of which date from the first half of the century.[10] It is at this point that the originally simple ceremony of baptism 'suddenly appeared transformed into an elaborate ritual, the most striking new element of which was the diabolic dimension. The initiation ceremony was now a drama of resolute and sometimes fierce struggle against the devil, man's spiritual oppressor and the instigator of his sins'.[11] There appears in both the *Apostolic Tradition* and Tertullian[12] a formalized renunciation of Satan preceding the pre-baptismal anointing,[13] and metaphors of flight from bondage, in terms of the escape from Egypt through the Red Sea, a type of the waters of baptism, appear. In this spirit, the newly baptized are, in the eucharist following their baptism, given a taste of milk and honey, symbolizing the entry of the baptized into the promised land.[14]

8. See also *Didache* 7.1, 'The name of the Father and of the Son and of the Holy Ghost').

9. Justin Martyr, *Apology* 61.10.

10. For dating, see G. Dix, *The Treatise on the Apostolic Traditions of St Hippolytus* (London: SPCK, 1937), I, p. xi.; R.H. Connolly, *Didascalia Apostolorum* (trans. and accompanied by the Verona Latin fragment; Oxford: Clarendon Press, 1929), pp. lxxxvii-xci.

11. H.A. Kelly, *The Devil at Baptism* (Ithaca, NY: Cornell University Press, 1985), p. 10.

12. Tertullian, *The Crown* 3.

13. Hippolytus, *Apostolic Tradition* 2.21.9.

14. 'Tertullian says that this rite was practised by the Marcionites, so that it must go back to the middle of the second century at any rate', J.H. Bernard, *The Odes of Solomon* (Text and Studies; Cambridge, Cambridge University Press, 1916), p. 53 v. 10. See also J. Crehan, *Early Christian Baptism and the Creed*

By the fourth and fifth centuries, baptism, its meaning and its attendant mystery and ceremonial had become a subject of great interest to Christian writers. The long prebaptismal courses of instructions, including exhortations to the candidates before and after the ceremony, provide us with a number of collections of highly polished and sophisticated lectures discussing in details the spiritual and practical implications of the ceremony. Thus, in this genre, we have such texts as Basil's *On the Holy Spirit*, John Chrysostom's *Baptismal Homilies*, Cyril of Jerusalem's *Lectures on the Mysteries*, and Narsai's *Liturgical Homilies*. All have as a common theme the dramatic nature of the step the candidate is about to take.

The ceremony itself, which, as pointed out earlier is elaborate and complex, is clearly preceded by a long period of catechesis, a period which, E. Molland points out,[15] serves as a replacement for the prebaptismal scrutiny and inquiry as an effective means of screening out unsuitable candidates. Basil mentions the registration of candidates,[16] anointing[17] and the triple immersion.[18] The renunciation of Satan now forms a distinct element of the rite:[19] 'When they renounced the devil and his angels and uttered those life saving words'.[20]

Chrysostom also gives a detailed account of the ceremony, describing it as a receiving of the kingdom, a wedding, a mystic cleansing, regeneration, illumination, burial, circumcision and a spiritual combat.[21]

(London: Burns, Oates and Washbourne, 1950), pp. 171-75.

15. E. Molland, 'A Lost Scrutiny in the Early Baptismal Rite', *StudPat* (1962) 5.3, pp. 104-108.

16. Basil, *On the Holy Spirit* 8.26.

17. Basil, *On the Holy Spirit* 27.66.

18. Basil, *On the Holy Spirit* 15.35.

19. Basil, *On the Holy Spirit* 27.66.

20. Basil, *On the Holy Spirit* 11.27.5 and 27.66.

21. Chrysostom, *Baptismal Homily* 2.3 (SC 50). Reference to Chrysostom's baptismal homilies is complicated by the fact that the texts of these exist in three different collections: the Montfaucon series of two homilies, the Stavronikita series of eight homilies and the Papadoupoulos-Kerameus series of four. The Montfaucon series (Montf.) is published in PG, the Stavronikita series in SC 50 and the Papadoupoulos-Kerameus series (PK) was published in Varia Graeca Sacra by the University of St Petersburg in 1909 as *Catechesis ultima ad baptizandos*. For the complete series of the baptismal homilies (in translation) see P.W. Harkins, *St John Chrysostom, Baptismal Instructions* (New York: Ramsey Press, 1963).

The effects of baptism are described by him in exalted terms:

> ...you, the ones who before yesterday were captives, are now free and citizens of the Church; (you who were) lately in the shame of your sins, (are now) now in freedom (παρρησία) and justice. You are not only free (ἐλεύθεροι), but also holy; not only holy, but also just; not only just but, also sons; not only sons, but also heirs; not only heirs, but brothers of Christ...[22]

In the Syriac baptismal homilies of the fifth century Nestorian Narsai, we find a passionate and highly rhetorical description of baptism, drawing widely on all Christian symbolism connected with baptism. These homilies come in the form of two volumes, which, if Connolly is correct,[23] are designed to be complementary, with the first covering the prebaptismal rites and anointings and the second concerned entirely with the baptismal immersions.

In sum, whatever its variations over this period, the ceremony surrounding baptism itself breaks down into three basic elements: renunciation, commitment and sealing.

1. *The Renunciation of Satan.* The first explicit mention of the act of renunciation as a distinct element in the ritual occurs in the third century in Hippolytus[24] and in Tertullian.[25] It is impossible to conclude from this, of course, that it was not used any earlier. However, if it was, it was clearly not considered a vital enough element of the rite to be emphasized on its own account, 'Nevertheless, the concrete expression of this negative pole, the rejection of non belief, quickly took on various forms which coalesced into various ritual expressions just as its positive, more important counterpart, the confession of faith, quickly gained ritual form',[26] and by the fourth and fifth centuries, the baptismal liturgy invariably contains an expression of the renunciation of Satan and the acceptance of Christ, both of which naturally bring to mind ideas of slavery and freedom. This renunciation generally occurs as a variation of the statement: *I renounce Satan, his pomps and his service.*

---

22. Chrystotom, *Baptismal Homily* 3.5 (SC 50).

23. R.H. Connolly, *The Liturgical Homilies of Narsai* (Texts and Studies, 8.1; ed. J.A. Robinson; Cambridge: Cambridge University Press, 1909), pp. xlvi-xlvii.

24. Hippolytus, *Apostolic Tradition* and *Homily on the Theophania*.

25. Tertullian, *The Crown* 3.

26. H.M. Riley, *Christian Initiation* (Studies in Christian Antiquity, 17; Washington: Catholic University of America Press, 1974), p. 23.

From the point of view of finding slavery metaphors, these renuncia-
tions are surprisingly disappointing. Even where the term 'service' is
used it is as λατρεία rather than δουλεία. However, when we draw
back our focus to take in the context of the declaration, the situation
becomes more interesting.

In the detailed liturgy of the fourth and fifth centuries, we find that
the utterance of these words is meant to be accompanied by a number
of physical gestures—gestures which probably originally consisted of a
simple outstretching of the hand in rejection, but which soon extended
to various patterns of kneeling, rising and turning away. The candidates
described by Cyril of Jerusalem and Ambrose stand, facing the west,
stretch out their hand, pronounce the renunciation, and then, turning to
the east, declare their commitment to Christ. Cyril of Jerusalem, in his
first lecture on the Mysteries, describes how the catechumens enter the
baptistry and renounce Satan:

> You first entered into the vestibule of the Baptistry, and facing towards
> the West you listened and were commanded to put out your hand, and as
> if he were present, you renounced Satan.[27]

After this, turning from west to east: 'You were told to say "I believe in
the Father and in the Son and in the Holy Ghost and in the baptism of
repentance"'.[28]

At the beginning of the ceremony, as described by John Chrysostom
and Theodore of Mopsuestia, the catechumens are stripped naked. Then
they are commanded to kneel and to 'Stretch out your hands to
Heaven',[29] 'remain on your knees. To bend the knee is the mark of
those who acknowledge their servitude',[30] and to declare, 'I renounce
you, Satan, your pomps, your service and your works…and I join
myself to you, Christ'.[31]

> Ἀποτάσσομαι σοι, Σατανὰ καὶ τῇ πομπῇ σου καὶ τῇ λατρείᾳ σου καὶ
> τοῖς ἔργοις σου
>
> καὶ συντάσσομαί σοι, Χριστέ[32]

---

27. Cyril of Jerusalem, *Lectures on the Mysteries* 1.2.
28. Cyril of Jerusalem, *Lectures on the Mysteries* 1.9.
29. Chrysostom, *Baptismal Homilies* 2.18.
30. Chrysostom, *Baptismal Homilies* 2.22.
31. Chrysostom, *Baptismal Homilies* 2.20.
32. Chrysostom, *Baptismal Homilies* 2.21.

John Chrysostom gives the reason for this stance, telling his hearers that it illustrates the state of prebaptismal servitude:[33]

> In the same way as those who endure bodily captivity show even through their appearance their dejection at the misfortune which has come upon them, (so also) when those who have been made prisoner by the devil are about to be set free from his tyranny and to come under the yoke of goodness, they first, through their posture, remind themselves of their former condition.[34]

In the first of these, a great deal of interest is shown in the moment of the rejection of Satan:

> They first renounce the dominion of the Evil One who brought them to slavery; and then they confess the power of the Creator who has set them free.[35]

H.A. Kelly also describes this moment in the *Instructio ad Competentes* of Nicetas of Remesiana (fourth century) thus: 'When the candidate was freed from the works or pomps of the devil, he took the chains with which he had been bound and threw them behind his back as if into the enemy's face and then said the creed'.[36] One can only wonder what kind of physical gesture is indicated here!

33. This is also seen in a slightly different form—condensing the elements of Chrysostom, Cyril of Jersusalem and Ambrose—in the *Homilies* of Narsai, where the candidates first (standing and facing west) renounce Satan: 'They first renounce the dominion of the Evil One who brought them to slavery; and then they confess the power of the Creator who has set them free (trans. Connolly, *The Liturgical Homilies of Narsai*, p. 36). They then, stripped naked, kneel down and, with cast down eyes, beg to be received by God: '"I appeal to thee, O King", cries the captive to the King's servants, "approach the King and entreat for me that he may be reconciled to me. Enter and say to him, 'One of thy servants has returned from captivity, and lo, with love he beseeches to see thy face'. I have verily been made a captive by the slave that rebelled against thy Lordship; free my life from his slavery, that he may not deride me. I am thy servant, good Lord, and the son of thy handmaid, why should I serve a wicked slave who revolted from thee? Heretofore I have wickedly served the all wicked one; ransom me from him, that I may be thine, for thine I am"' (Connolly, *The Liturgical Homilies*, p. 38). Also, 'From his (Satan's) bitter slavery, the sinner has fled; and he has taken sanctuary with the good Lord whose love is sweet' (Connolly, *The Liturgical Homilies*, p. 39).
34. Chrysostom, *Baptismal Homilies* 2.14.
35. Connolly, *The Liturgical Homilies*, p. 36.
36. Kelly, *The Devil at Baptism*, p. 100 (Nicetas of Remesiana, *Instructio ad Competentes* 5.2.8; see also 5.3.2.

It is clear that these postures form part of the illustration of baptism as release from slavery. The kneeling of the candidate vividly evokes the degradation and enslavement caused by sin. Immediately after the rejection of Satan, however, this selfsame posture expresses the acknowledgment of the lordship of Christ uttered in the words of the commitment. This is, nevertheless, not a continuation in bondage, since, following this, the candidate will have to rise to his feet—a movement exploited to the full as representing the rising from the dejection of slavery to the exaltation of adoption.

The kneeling is not, however, absolutely necessary for a physical expression of such liberation. The turning from west to east described by Cyril of Jerusalem and Ambrose is also replete with the idea of the movement from slavery to freedom.[37]

It is in the verbal description of the spiritual effects of baptism that the idea of liberation is clearest: 'You who were a slave, a captive and a rebel have suddenly been raised to adoption as a son',[38] and, as in this passage from Basil this liberation from slavery is often equated with passing from death to life:

> but (for one) to become free from slavery (ἀπὸ δούλου) and to be called a son of God and to be brought alive from death, can be brought about by no other than the one who has through nature acquired kinship with us.[39]

2. *The Joining to Christ.* We come, thus, to the other aspect of the renunciation—the commitment to Christ and the acknowledgment of his lordship, which played a central role in baptism from 'the very earliest stages of Christian development'.[40] The commitment to Christ usually appears as the liturgical formula συντάσσομαί σοι, Χριστέ, which thus balances the formula of rejection, ἀποτάσσομαι σοι,

---

37. 'The image of turning from slavery δουλεία to freedom ἐλευθερία is well known in the cultural context of antiquity and is a familiar image to the fathers of the Church', Riley, *Christian Initiation*, p. 60.

38. Chrysostom, *Baptismal Homilies* 5.22.

39. Basil, *On the Holy Spirit* 8.29.

40. R.E.O. White, *The Biblical Doctrine of Initiation* (London: Hodder & Stoughton, 1960), p. 147.

Σατανά. συντάσσομαί σοι, Χριστέ is commonly rendered in translations as 'I enter your service, O Christ', but this is a misleading translation of the verb, which, in this context simply has the meaning of 'to join' or 'to swear allegiance to'.[41]

3. *The Seal.* From quite early in the history of the baptismal tradition we find mention of anointings having a place in the baptismal rite—sometimes before, sometimes after the immersion—anointing which were sometimes of just the head, sometimes of the whole body. Where the anointing is of the whole body, it is frequently described as the anointing of an athlete, that is, the preparing of the candidate for his struggle against Satan in the spiritual arena. Among these anointings there arises also an important idea, that of the imposition of a seal or σφραγίς.

Here the candidate has the sign of the cross traced with oil on his or her forehead by the priest, an event which immediately suggests the branding of the slave. Did such a concept play a part in the use of the seal? In the very early Church it would seem that it did. There is a possibility that this marking is even mentioned in the Apocalypse of John in the seal on the foreheads of the elect. However, early references to this seal must be handled with great care, as the term 'seal' is often used interchangeably to describe either baptism as a whole or just the anointing. It is also used sometimes to refer to confirmation. We must therefore confine ourselves as far as possible to those occasions where the seal is explicitly described as being the mark placed on the candidate by the priest.

As discussed earlier,[42] slaves, especially in the ancient Near East were occasionally marked with a brand or tattoo indicating ownership, often on the face but sometimes elsewhere.[43] It is quite probable that the earliest use of the baptismal signing was intended to evoke something of such a tattoo. Surprisingly, however, as soon as the marking becomes a clear part of the rite we find that, although it expresses ownership this is not the ownership, as we might expect, of a slave:

41. According to both the *LSJ* and the *Patristic Greek Lexicon*, neither of which acknowledge any implications of service in the verb.
42. See above, p. 38 n. 72, and p. 76 n. 31.
43. See also J. Ysebaert, *Greek Baptismal Terminology: Its Origins and Early Development* (Graecitas Christianorum Primaeva, 1; Nijmegen: 1962), p. 190.

> Absolutely fundamental in the Syrian tradition of the rushma (anointing)
> is the idea that it provides a mark of ownership, and by far the most
> frequent image is that of the newly baptized being branded as a sheep.[44]

and as we progress to the later writers, we find less and less evidence of
this signing being associated with slavery. Instead it points to an ownership by God which need not imply human bondage. We encounter,
thus, the image of the catechumen as a sheep of God's flock or the
increasingly popular idea of the candidate as a soldier marked with the
mark of the emperor, reflecting a custom of the Roman army:[45] 'The
great brand of the King of kings with which they are stamped that they
may serve (as soldiers) in the spiritual contest...'[46] evoking an image of
baptism as the spiritual battlefield against the forces of evil. Another
image which is also frequently used is that of the seal as a stamp which
imprints the image of God on the candidate who is compared to a coin
or a signet:[47]

> That you may be made the engraving of the signet...[48]

> In the case of the coin that was brought to him, the Lord did not say
> 'Whose property is it?' but 'Whose is the image and superscription?
> Caesar's' so that it should be given to him to whom it belongs. This is
> also the case for the faithful one: he has the name of God through Christ
> as a superscription, the Spirit as an image. And the dumb animals show
> through a seal whose property each is, and from the seal they are
> claimed. Thus also the faithful soul receives the seal of truth and carries
> the 'marks of Christ'.[49]

b. *Metaphors of Slavery*
The concept of entering via baptism into slavery to God forms another
theme in the baptismal ceremony and must not be ignored. Just as the

---

44. S.P. Brock, *The Holy Spirit in Syrian Baptismal Tradition* (Syrian Churches
Series, 9; Bronx, NY: John XXIII Centre, Fordham University, 1979), p. 96.

45. 'The military mark...is a mark of ownership which contains the name of
the emperor', Ysebaert, *Greek Baptismal Terminology*, p. 192.

46. Ysbaert, *Greek Baptismal Terminology*, p. 43.

47. See also Ysebaert, *Greek Baptismal Terminology*, p. 403, and Brock, *The
Holy Spirit in Syrian Baptismal Tradition*, p. 97.

48. Cyril, *Baptismal Lectures*, p. 47.

49. Clement of Alexandria, *Excerpta ex Theodoto* 4.86. 1-3. The idea of man as
a coin stamped with the image of God was also popular with Philo and the Rabbis.
J. Faur, *Golden Doves with Silver Dots: Semiotics and Textuality in the Rabbinic
Tradition* (Bloomington, IN: Indiana State University Press, 1986), p. 140.

candidate rejects slavery to evil, so, in some cases, this slavery is represented as being replaced by slavery to God:

> Like prudent servants (οἰκέται) prepared with much goodwill to obey your master (Δεσπότη) [you] have brought the neck of your soul with meekness and readiness beneath the bonds of Christ, and have received his easy yoke and taken his light burden.[50]

The writers speak of the contract sealed between God and the candidate at the moment of baptism, as in the following passage from Chrysostom:

> And just as when we buy slaves (οἰκέτας) we first ask those who are being sold if they are willing to serve us; so also does Christ. When he is about to receive you into slavery (δουλείαν) he first asks if you wish to leave that harsh and cruel tyrant and he receives covenants from you. For his mastership is not forced upon you. And see the love of God. For we, before we put down the price, ask those who are being sold, and when we have learned that they are willing, then we put down the price. But not so Christ, but he even puts down the price for us all, his precious blood. For, he says, you were bought with a price. Nevertheless, not even then does he force those who are unwilling to serve (δουλεῦσαι) him.
>
> …we would not have chosen to buy wicked slaves (οἰκέτας). But if we should have ever so chosen, we took them with a perverted choice, and put down a corresponding price for them. But Christ, buying ungrateful and lawless slaves (οἰκέτας) put down the price of a top quality slave (πρωτείου δούλου τιμήν).[51]

It is, however, emphatically denied that this can be seen as the same kind of bondage as was previously suffered:

> But be not gloomy when you hear the word 'captivity', for nothing is more blessed than this captivity. The captivity of men leads from freedom to slavery, but this captivity changes slavery into freedom. Furthermore, the captivity of men deprives one of his fatherland and leads him to foreign soil; this captivity leads you to the common mother of us all. That captivity separates you from kinsmen and fellow citizens, this one leads you to the citizens above.[52]
>
> If any here is a slave of sin, let him promptly prepare himself through faith for the new birth into freedom and adoption and having put off the

50. Chrysostom, *Baptismal Homilies* (Montf. & PK), 1.4.
51. Chrysostom, *Baptismal Homilies* (Montf.) 2.50-51.
52. Chrysostom, *Baptismal Homily* (PK) 2.15.

miserable bondage of his sins, and taken on him the most blessed bondage of the Lord, so that he may be counted worthy to inherit the kingdom of Heaven.[53]

3. *Summary*

The use of the metaphor in patristic liturgy is, as we have seen, important, if somewhat uneven. It is also here where its use is most apparently self-contradictory, for it is used both to describe the state of the believer and the state of the unconverted. In prayers, it is most often used as an affirmation of service and devotion, especially that of the clergy. The context of baptism, especially, provides a very fertile ground for both uses of the bondage terminology, so that it refers not only to a person's relationship with God but also to their relation with Satan, sin and the world, a relationship they must seek to shake off in order to attain freedom and adoption in God. In very many of these cases, however, there is also an emphasis on how such slavery actually implies freedom, and images of ownership which do not necessarily entail servitude are often used in preference to slavery. The more important emphasis is still that of the victory and freedom gained through baptism, the freedom from sin and the world that makes every believer, even if they are slaves on earth, free in God.

---

53. Cyril of Jerusalem, *Catechetical Oration* 1.2.

Chapter 6

The Metaphor of Slavery and Patristic Exegesis

My central concern in the previous chapters has been to discuss the use
made of the metaphor of slavery in the Early Church. But what conscious significance was attached to the use of such language? We now
turn to the understanding of these metaphors as an object in themselves
by the patristic writers. With Origen and the beginning of serious New
Testament exegesis,[1] the thoughts of the Fathers on the texts of the
New Testament which employ the metaphor become available and we
can examine the attempts they make to resolve the difficult issues that
the use of the metaphor raises.

Such a study is, of course, hindered by the lack of any fixed and clear
boundary between *use* of the metaphor and the *discussion* of the metaphor—the writer may use a metaphor and at the same time discuss it,
and there may thus be an overlapping of the categories in certain texts.
For the purpose of this section, therefore, I shall choose for the field
those passages where it is the metaphor of slavery itself which is the
main object of discussion and where the writer makes some attempt to
discuss the problem that the use of the language raises. I shall limit the
scope to the exegesis of a small selection of New Testament texts,
partly for reasons of space, and partly for reasons of practicality, for
since the Old Testament texts were available to Christian writers from
the earliest days of the Church, examples of Old Testament exegesis in

---

1.   For an overview of the history of patristic exegesis of the New Testament
and in particular, of the Pauline epistles, see M.F. Wiles, *The Divine Apostle: The
Interpretation of St Paul's Epistles to the Early Church* (Cambridge: Cambridge
University Press, 1967), pp. 3-13; P. Gorday, *Principles of Patristic Exegesis:
Romans 9–11 in Origen, John Chrysostom and Augustine* (Lewiston, NY: Edwin
Mellen Press, 1983), pp. 43-50 and pp. 103-35 and, on the Old and New Testament
interpretations, R.M. Grant, *A Short History of the Interpretation of the Bible*
(London: A. & C. Black, 1965), pp. 42-91.

Christian writings are widely spread over the period under consideration, whereas the quantity of New Testament exegesis in the same time-
span is more limited and concentrated. Further, Old Testament exegesis
is also heir to an enormous tradition of interpretation which could not
be practically considered here.

In order to discuss the nature of patristic exegesis of such texts we
will be considering the following selection, chosen as being representa-
tive of the major themes that the metaphor is used to express: slavery to
God as a title; spiritual freedom despite earthly slavery; transition from
slavery to sin to slavery to righteousness; transition from slavery to
God to freedom in God; slavery to God vs. slavery to others; slavery of
the earthly Christ, that is, Christ taking the form of a slave and Christ
performing the function of a slave. The specific texts I shall be considering, therefore, are:

1. Name + δοῦλος Χριστοῦ/Θεοῦ.[2]
2. No man can serve two masters (Mt. 6.24; Lk. 16.13).
3. Unloosing the shoes of Christ (Mt. 3.11; Mk 1.7; Lk. 3.16 and
    Jn 1.27).
4a. Christ taking the form of a slave (Phil. 2.5-9).
4b. Washing the feet of the disciples (Jn 13.5-14).

1. *Name + δοῦλος Χριστοῦ/Θεοῦ*

The 'name + δοῦλος Χριστοῦ' formula is used in the salutation of a
number of New Testament epistles,[3] as in the opening of the Epistle to
the Romans, and the time and thought devoted to it in patristic exegesis
bears witness to its importance and to the difficulties it raises. The
earliest expression of this may be found in Origen's commentary on
Rom. 1.1:

> We ask now why he calls himself a slave who elsewhere wrote *You did
> not receive a spirit of slavery leading again to fear, but you received the
> spirit of adoption in which we cry Abba, Father;* and again *Because,
> moreover, you are sons, God sent the spirit of his son into our hearts
> crying: Abba, Father.* Therefore you are now not a slave but a son. How
> therefore, when he called them this, he said even to those he was preach-
> ing to *now you are not a slave but a son,* does he declare himself to be a
> slave?[4]

2. Rom. 1.1; Tit. 1.1; Phil. 1.1; 2 Pet. 1.1; Jude 1.1 and Rev. 1.1.
3. See above, p. 77.
4. Origen, *Commentary on Paul's Epistle to the Romans* 1 (PG 14.857B).

The problem here as it appears to Origen is one of inconsistency—
how can Paul's emphasis on the sonship of those who believe and his
assertion that believers are set free from slavery be reconciled with his
use of the word 'slave' for himself? Origen's response to this dilemma
is to propose a number of possibilities. He suggests that it might be
seen as (a) a token of Paul's humility, or (b) as a participation, on
Paul's part, in the unfree status of those to whom he is writing, or (c) as
indicating that true freedom is not possible in this world. His final suggestion (d) which we shall discuss in more detail later, is that in using
'slave' Paul is actually talking about something entirely different, that
is, the issue of marriage and continence in the Christian life. Let us look
at these points in more detail.

a. *The Humility of Paul*

Origen's first suggestion is that Paul uses 'slave' as a demonstration of
his own humility: 'according to that humility, which the Lord taught:
learn from me for I am gentle and humble of heart'.[5]

Having made this association between 'slave' and humility, Origen
hastens to point out that this humility and slavery imply no loss of true
liberty: 'Nor indeed is the true liberty in Paul damaged. Indeed he says
himself: Although I am free from all, I have made myself a slave to
all',[6] and indeed that with such slavery is given the spirit of adoption:
'He therefore served Christ, not in a spirit of slavery but in a spirit of
adoption',[7] and that it is actually greater than freedom: 'slavery to
Christ is nobler than all liberty'.[8]

b. *Paul's Participation in the State of Others*

> Or perhaps he speaks as an imitator of him who said 'Behold I am in the
> midst of you, not as one who reclines at table but as one who serves';
> and him who emptied himself, taking the form of a slave, so that as for
> those who are under the law he made himself under the law, and to those
> who are without the law he made even himself without the law, so also if
> for those who are still slaves, and have not yet been led through the spirit
> of adoption into the freedom of sons, he was made a slave, this will not
> seem to be a contradiction.[9]

5.　Origen, *Commentary on Paul's Epistle to the Romans* 1 (PG 14.857B).
6.　Origen, *Commentary on Paul's Epistle to the Romans* 1 (PG 14.857B).
7.　Origen, *Commentary on Paul's Epistle to the Romans* 1 (PG 14.857C).
8.　Origen, *Commentary on Paul's Epistle to the Romans* 1 (PG 14.857B).
9,　Origen, *Commentary on Paul's Epistle to the Romans* 1 (PG 14.838B).

Thus, although Paul is not himself a slave, yet he takes on himself, in imitation of the kenosis of Christ, the status of a slave in order to participate in the condition of others. However, since, by implication, these same slaves are to be led into the freedom of sons, this slavery is only temporary.

c. *Marriage and Continence*

The last of Origen's suggestions is also the most unusual. In it he associates the issue with an exegesis of 1 Cor. 7.21-23 on marriage and continence:

> But this is how we understand Paul's meaning: that he who is bound by the condition of being yoked to a spouse is called a slave: for a wife has no power over her own body, but her husband has it; and a husband has no power over his own body, but his wife has it... He is therefore called a slave who in a state of marriage comes to Christ, to whom is said: Are you called as a slave? Do not worry: but if you can be free, use it rather; for in marriage the freedom of one in continence creates danger for the chastity of the other. They ought not to (abstain) except by mutual consent, to leave time for prayer, and immediately they should return to each other that Satan not catch them by their incontinency. He therefore who is called a slave through his marital condition is a freedman of the Lord...he is called a freedman of the Lord, in that he is free on account of the virtues of soul, and on account of conjugal necessity he is a slave. The true freeman is the one who comes to Christ without a wife, through the purity of continence, (and) who thus makes himself a slave of Christ, as long as he serves the virtues entirely. Paul, therefore, as some teach, was called with a wife; of whom he speaks to the Philippians writing: I beg you, true yokefellow, help these women:[10] because he was made free from her by mutual consent, he calls himself a slave of Christ.

As far as I have been able to ascertain, this particular analysis of the passage never gained any popularity.[11] Those points of his which do survive into the later writers are that slavery to God (1) is a special kind of slavery, and as such implies no loss of freedom, (2) is really given in a spirit of friendship and adoption, (3) is actually greater than any freedom and, (4) a point that will become important in the later Latin Fathers, is the only possible alternative to slavery to sin. People are inevitably the slaves of one or the other. I will now look at these points in the context of some later writers.

10. Phil. 4.3.
11. Although Origen is not the only one to see marriage as a kind of servitude and 1 Cor. 7 in this context. See, for example, Ambrose, *Concerning Widows* 69.

1. *Slavery to God as a Special Kind of Slavery.* The point made by Origen in his exegesis, that the particular form of slavery to God described by Paul implies no loss of freedom, is reflected in the moves by the later scholars to argue, in the exegesis of this passage, for the existence of different kinds of spiritual slavery. We find, therefore, Chrysostom asserting that:

> He calls himself the slave (δοῦλος) of Christ, but not just this, for there are many kinds of servitude. One is owing to Creation, according to which it is said 'for all are my slaves' and according to which it is said 'Nebuchadnezzar my slave' for the work is the slave of the maker. Another kind is that of faith, according to which it is said, 'But God be thanked that you were the slaves of sin, but obeyed from the heart that form of doctrine which was delivered to you, and being made free from sin, became the slaves of righteousness'. Another is that of a way of life (πολιτείας), according to which it is said 'Moses, my slave (θεράπων) is dead'; and indeed all the Jews were slaves (θεράποντες), but Moses especially, as shining most brightly in his way of life. Since then, in all these forms of servitude (δουλείας), Paul was a slave (δοῦλος), he puts this in the place of the greatest title of dignity, saying 'a slave of Jesus Christ'.[12]

Three roots of slavery are thus argued for here: creation, faith and way of life.

a. *Creation.* This comes from a very literal approach to the metaphor, taking the Old Testament example in the very Old Testament sense of a direct and literal ownership stemming, in this case, from God's status as the Maker. This kind of slavery implies nothing about the individual's personal merit or relationship with God, but simply acknowledges the absolute mastery of God over the world he has created.

b. *Faith.* The second of these forms of slavery is more conventional in the New Testament and patristic context—it is a slavery that stems from the individual's faith in and relationship with God and it contrasts with the slavery to sin to which the individual was previously subject.

c. *Way of Life.* The third category is where it results from the living of a life ordered by the commands of God. Here God exerts a personal and day to day authority over an individual or group, as a master exerts power over the day to day activities of his household. In this context, unlike the others which we shall see later, the slavery of the Jews to

---

12. *Homily on Romans* 1 (PG 40.395).

God is seen as a positive thing, a reflection of the proper order of their lives and of their special relationship with God.

It must be noted, however, that while Chrysostom begins by establishing a concept of there being different kinds of slavery, he concludes by applying all three to Paul, and does not here argue that Paul's particular slavery is less slavish than other kinds,[13] a step we find taken later in Jerome, where slavery leading into fear is distinguished from slavery leading into love:

> ...this slavery is not that of which the same apostle says, 'For you did not receive the spirit of slavery leading into fear, but you received the spirit of adoption in which we cry "abba, father"' but to the noble slavery of which David says to God 'I am your slave, the son of your handmaid' (Ps. 116.16). And the blessed Mary to the angel 'Behold the handmaiden of the Lord, let it be to me according to your word'. This slavery was the kind that Moses had, of which the Lord said to Joshua the son of Nun, 'Moses my slave is dead' (Josh. 1.2). Far be it from us indeed that we should believe that Moses and Mary had a spirit of slavery leading to fear and not to the love of God.[14]

2. *Slavery to God as an Honour.* Although, as we have just seen, Chrysostom did not take full advantage of the distinction in kinds of slavery, it is clear from his statements in other contexts that he held to the idea of slavery to God as an honour:

> Paul put down, as equal in merit, indeed much greater, incomparably greater that consulship or kingship or authority over the whole world, the title, 'Paul, the slave of Christ...'[15]

13. There are some other interesting gaps in Chrysostom's exegesis. No mention is made of what seems the most obvious implication of slavery, i.e., service. Paul is not defined as a slave on account of what he does or of his service to God. Neither is there any mention of the ideas of humility or self giving.

It should also be noted that the use of δοῦλος is not specifically important to Chrysostom here; he places it in conjunction with the servanthood of Moses which is generally expressed in both the Old Testament and the New Testament by the term θεράπων rather than δοῦλος. Neither does he seem to see here any distinction between the idea of *slave of God* and *slave of Christ,* although some writers do discuss the issue, as does Theodoret on *Titus* 1 (PG 82.85C), pointing out that Paul himself makes no distinction, 'He calls himself sometimes a slave of Christ, sometimes of God without distinguishing between the two. He knows that theirs is a common lordship.' Theodoret is, however, mistaken. Titus is deutero-Pauline.

14. Jerome, *Homily on Titus* (PL 26.555C-556A).

15. Chrysostom, *Homily on Ephesians* 8 (PG 62.67).

This most common and popular explanation we see, for example, in Theodoret of Cyrrhus (mid-fifth century CE): 'he places slavery to this one (Christ), before than any kingly authority'.[16]

Jerome (late fourth/early fifth century CE) makes a similar comparison of the use of the title 'apostle' with the human search after worldly honours:

> his words 'an apostle of Jesus Christ' seem equivalent to as if he had said 'a praetorian prefect of Augustus Caesar' commander of the army of Tiberius the emperor. As indeed the judges of this age, that they might seem more noble, from the kings which they serve, and from the dignity which they increase, seek titles, even so, claiming for himself the dignity of a great Apostle among the Christians, he put down the title of apostle of Christ, so that from this he should terrify the readers by the authority of the name, showing to all who believe that they should be subject to him.[17]

There are further uses of this passage. Ambrose uses a discussion of the 'slave of Jesus Christ' formula to make his own theological point:

> Paul, therefore, forbids me to serve the creature and reminds me that I must serve Christ.[18] Therefore Christ is not a created being. 'Paul', he says, 'slave of Jesus Christ'—and the good slave who recognizes the master, will himself forbid us to serve the creature. How therefore would he serve Christ himself if he thought him to be a creature?[19]

and a similar use of this to make such points is to be found in Ambrosiaster's (late fourth century CE) commentary on Romans:

> By calling himself a slave of Christ Jesus, he shows himself to be free from the Law. And for this reason he puts both down, that is, Jesus Christ: that he might indicate the person of God and of man: since that in each he is Lord, as Peter the Apostle himself attests, saying: He is, he says, Lord of all. On account of which, he is both Lord and God, as

---

16. Theodoret, *On Romans* (PG 82.47B).

17. Jerome, *On Titus* (PL 26.555-58). See also Didymus of Alexandria in his commentary on Jas 1.1: 'Just as men, desiring mortal glory, in their writings place first those dignities which they think they possess; even so the holy men in the epistles which they write to the churches, principally declare themselves slaves of our Lord Jesus Christ, considering this title to be better than rule of the whole world' (PG 39.1749A. See also 1481).

18. Rom. 2.25.

19. Ambrose, *On the Christian Faith* 16.104.

David says: For the Lord, he is God (Ps. 100.3) which the heretics deny.[20]

2. *No Man can Serve Two Masters*

As well as the points we have just discussed one must note also the emphasis on the distinction between slavery to God and slavery to anything else and on the idea of of the incompatibility of slavery to God with slavery to any other master, especially in connection with the Gospel assertion that 'no man can serve two masters'.[21] Of this text the so-called second Epistle of Clement asserts,

> 'No slave can serve two masters.' If we wish to serve both God and Mammon, it is not profitable to us... We consider that it is better to hate the things which are here, because they are trivial and shortlived and corruptible, and to love the things which are there, the good things which are incorruptible. For if we do Christ's will we shall gain rest; but if not, nothing shall rescue us from eternal punishment if we neglect his commandments.[22]

Comparing, however, the conflict between the two servitudes to what the equivalent would be in an earthly situation, Celsus, in Origen's account, objects that:

> In the sphere of human affairs, it would not be proper for a man who is serving one master to serve another man as well, as the other would be harmed by the service rendered to a different person; nor for someone who has already pledged himself to one person to also pledge himself to another because he would do the one harm. And it makes sense not to serve different heroes and demons of that kind at the same time. But where God is concerned whom neither harm nor grief can affect...it is irrational to guard against worshipping several gods, as one would in the case of men and heroes and suchlike demons.[23]

In reply, Origen points out the danger of taking the parallel too literally and lays the emphasis on the spiritual wellbeing of the believer rather than the possessiveness implied by a literal reading:

> It is not because God would be harmed, as a man would seem to be harmed by one who served another one besides him, that we avoid

20. Ambrosiaster, *On Romans* (PL 17.48).
21. Mt. 6.24.
22. *2 Clement* 6.1, cited by *B.Pat.*
23. Origen, *Against Celsus* 8.2.

serving any other than God (whom we serve) through the Word and
through truth, but that we may not harm ourselves by cutting ourselves
off from our share in God.[24]

Like Origen, Chrysostom emphasizes the fact that one falls away from
the service of God in serving Mammon and he is concerned about the
damage the individual does to him or herself. Service to Mammon
excludes the individual from the better service to God. The individual
is cast 'out of God's service whom, above all things it is indispensable
for you to serve'.[25] Didymus of Alexandria, however, discussing this
idea in another context, stresses the actual impossibility of service to
both: 'just as it is impossible to serve God and Mammon, so also is it
impossible to be at the same time a friend of God and a friend of the
world'.[26]

This passage is thus being taken to express the situation from the
point of view of the believer, stressing the importance of choosing the
better servitude and pointing out that it is logically impossible for one
to serve both these masters at once. A second line places the emphasis
on the activity of God who rejects those who try to serve Mammon at
the same time: 'See at least how every day he hears him saying "You
cannot serve God and Mammon" and threatening Hell and deadly pun-
ishments, and does not obey',[27] and Clement, in the same way, threatens the reader with eternal punishment.[28] Ambrose also emphasizes a
view of this as a command rather than a logical impossibility:

> The Lord Jesus refuses and rejects your service (*obsequium*), because
> you have served idols (*idolis obsecutus est*), for he has said to you 'you
> cannot serve two masters'.[29]

3. *Untying the Shoes of Christ*

There is one particular passage of the New Testament on which one
might have expected some detailed discussion of the activities of the
slave and its relation to the perception of an individual, and that is in
the Baptist's declaration that he is not worthy to unloose the shoes of

24. Origen, *Against Celsus* 8.6.
25. Chrysostom, *Homilies on Matthew* 21.1.
26. Didymus of Alexandria (PG 39.1754C).
27. Chrysostom, *Homily on Matthew* 28.5.
28. See also *2 Clement* above.
29. Ambrose, *Epistle* 17.14.

Jesus. Yet oddly enough, when the passage is discussed, the slavery aspect does not seem to be foremost in the writers' minds, as we see in Origen:

> Now it is a great thing to bear the shoes of Jesus, a great thing to stoop down to the bodily features of His mission, to that which took place in some lower region, so as to contemplate His image in the lower sphere, and to untie each difficulty connected with the mystery of His incarnation, such being as it were, His shoe-latchets.[30]

> If the passage about the shoe possesses a hidden meaning we ought not to pass over it. I think, therefore, that the incarnation, where the Son of God takes up flesh and bone, is one of his shoes; and the descent into the house of Hades, whoever Hades is, and the journey into prison with the Spirit is the other.

> Who then is able to stoop down and untie the latchet of such shoes, and having untied them, not to let them drop, but by the second faculty he has received to take them up and bear them by bearing the meaning of them in his memory?[31]

Ambrose uses the image as a symbol of the marriage of Christ and the Church:

> Moses was not the bridegroom: for to him it was said 'remove your shoe from your foot', that he might make way for his Lord. Nor was Joshua the son of Nun the bridegroom, for to him too it was said, 'remove your shoe', lest by the similarity of name he should be thought to be the bridegroom of the Church. No one else is the bridegroom but Christ alone, of whom John says, 'He who has the bride is the bridegroom'. They therefore remove their shoes, but his shoe cannot be removed, as John says, 'I am not worthy to loose the latchet of his shoe'.[32]

---

30. Origen, *Commentary on John* 6.34.

31. Origen, *Commentary on John* 6.35.

32. Ambrose, *On the Christian Faith* 3.10.71. This image almost certainly stems from the Jewish ceremony of Halizah or unloosening, by which, through a ceremonial removal of the shoe, a dead man's brother is released from the obligation of a levirite marriage (the obligation to marry his brother's widow if this brother has died childless, as laid down in Gen. 38.8). The widow in question ceremonially removes her brother-in-law's right shoe, before witnesses, and spits at him. Both parties are then free from the obligation and the widow may marry whom she pleases. For an account of the history of this ceremony, see *The Jewish Encyclopedia* (ed. I. Singer; London: Funk & Wagnall, 1944), pp. 170-74.

4. *Christ as Slave*

a. *Christ Taking the Form of a Slave (Philippians 2.5-9)*
In the above discussion of the use of the metaphor of slavery I have until now confined it to the use of the metaphor as a description of the human condition. While a detailed discussion of the use of the metaphor for Christ would be a whole separate study in itself, it would nevertheless be useful to glance briefly at the patristic exegesis of those texts that use the metaphor, or appear to use it, in such a context.

Any patristic discussion of the kenosis of Christ ventures, by its very nature, into dangerous waters. The problems with such discussions are numerous. In the first place, the patristic exegete must not only be wary of the dishonour that such a status implies and be careful to explain it properly to the reader, but must also stress that this 'becoming a slave' would not imply any permanent status of subordination to the Father or any forced obedience of the kind exacted from earthly slaves.

The humility and obedience that is implied in such statements as 'I am among you as one who serves' and in such actions as the washing of the feet of the disciples, is verbalized in this passage from Philippians, one of the only locations in the New Testament where Christ and 'slave' are equated. The potential dishonour of such a statement obviously requires defusing as in 'One hears "he became a slave" and counts it dishonour. I hear and wonder at his love for us',[33] or by emphasizing, as Ambrosiaster does, the willingness of his suffering: 'and to have accepted the form of a slave while he was humiliated like a sinner...'[34] This obedience which is demonstrated by Christ in his suffering is, he stresses, a willing one:

> Taking the form of a slave, while he was held and bound and tormented with beating, having been made obedient to the Father even to the cross, he did not defend his equality but submitted himself.[35]

It is such willing obedience that takes his action out of the realm of servility and subordination, preserving his equality and sonship, as Chrysostom insists:

33. Chrysostom, *Homilies on 1 Corinthians* 7.2.
34. Ambrosiaster (PL 17.409A).
35. Ambrosiaster (PL 17.409A).

> He became obedient willingly as a Son to his Father not thereby falling
> into a slavish state, but by this act above all guarding his wonderful
> sonship.[36]

This behaviour, in that it is willing and part of the greatness of Christ,
serves as an example for the believer to follow.

Moreover, by taking the form of a slave, he perfects it through willing obedience and love, so raising and redeeming the slave of God. The
slave whose form Christ takes and perfects is, of course, man—the
slave of God—and it is common to find the 'form of a slave' and the
'form of man' equated, as we see in Ambrose:

> 'He took upon him the form of a slave', that is, he took upon him all the
> perfections of humanity in their completeness, and obedience in its com-
> pleteness.[37]

b. *Washing the Feet of the Disciples*

This obedient taking on of the form of the slave further is actively illustrated by Christ when he washes the feet of the disciples, performing a
duty that was customarily reserved for slaves and Gentile ones at that.
The *Didascalia* takes this as an example of love, given for believers to
follow: 'Now this he did that he might show us an example of charity
and brotherly love'.[38] Chrysostom, on the other hand, takes it as an
example of humility:

> See how not only by washing their feet, but in other ways besides, he
> showed his humility, for it was not before reclining to eat, but after all
> had lain down, that he arose. Then not only did he wash (their feet), but
> he did so after laying aside his garment, and not satisfied with this he
> girded himself with a towel. Moreover, he was not content with this, but
> he filled the basin himself and did not order somebody else to fill it, but
> did everything himself, to show that we should not be perfunctory when
> we do well, but should do it with all enthusiasm.[39]

Yet this shows that the link between the activity and the status of slavery is not always made in this context. Only later in the discussion do
slavery metaphors enter, and even here they are not directly connected
with the activity in the main incident:

36. Chrysostom, *Homily on Philippians* 7 (PG 62.232).
37. *On the Christian Faith* 5.8.109.
38. *Didascalia* 16.3.13.
39. Chrysostom, *Homily on John* 70.2.

...where now are those who despise their fellow slaves? Where now are those who demand honours? Christ washed the feet of the traitor... And you give yourself airs and raise your eyebrows? ...and what great thing is it if it is the feet of slaves that we wash? For among us 'slave' or 'free man' is a distinction of names only, while in his case it is a matter of fact. He himself was lord by nature while we were slaves, yet he did not excuse himself from doing even this.[40]

However, in his argument against the Marcionites, he makes it clear that the action is regarded as a slavish one:

Is this (action) the form of a slave? It is not the form of a slave but the work of a slave.[41]

We find also in Origen the prayer: 'O Jesus, my feet are dirty. Come and slave for me; pour your water into your bowl and come and wash my feet'.[42] Jerome links this to the kenosis of Christ:

That which does not seem to have been taught by many words he showed by example. For putting on a towel he bent himself and filled the bowl with water and he washed the feet of the disciples. Nor is it impious to believe that he who took on the form of a slave should do this to those who are slaves, so that he might be said to serve the will of the Father, because he himself served his slaves. But this slavery is love, by which we are commanded to serve one another.[43]

Obviously concerned that it might be thought impious to suggest that Christ should perform such an action, he reminds the reader of Philippians, and goes on to use the formula of the 'different kinds of slavery'. In this case the slavery is love.

40. Chrysostom, *Homily on John* 71.1.
41. Chrysostom, *Homily on Philippians* 7 (PG 62.280).
42. Translation adapted from *Early Christian Prayers* (ed. A. Hamman; London: Longman, 1961), p. 63, Origen, *Hom.* 5.2 in Isaiah. There is a similar prayer in Ambrose, *On the Holy Spirit*: 'Come, then, Lord Jesus, lay aside the garments, which you put on for my sake; be stripped so that you may clothe us with your mercy. Gird yourself for our sake with a towel, that you may gird us with your gift of immortality. Pour water into the basin, wash not only the feet but also the head, and not only our body, but also the footprints of the mind... How great is that majesty! As a servant (*minister*) you wash the feet of your slaves (*famuli*)' (Ambrose, *On the Holy Spirit*, Prologue 13–14).
43. Jerome, *Homily on Titus* (PL 26.557B).

Chapter 7

SOME EXAMPLES OF THE METAPHOR IN PATRISTIC WRITINGS

In the preceding chapters, we have discussed the development of the
metaphor, its general use in the context of doctrine and liturgy and the
understanding of its implications demonstrated in patristic exegesis. It
now remains to discuss the function of this metaphor more specifically—to see the metaphor at work within the context of the theology
and interests of different writers, and to discuss the extent to which the
metaphor is moulded, by these writers, to fit into their own patterns of
thought. We have seen how the metaphor has been adapted to fit
general themes throughout this period: the commitment of the martyr,
the progress of the Christian, the struggle of conversion and so on. We
will now, by looking at a selection of different patristic texts, be seeking to answer this question: does the metaphor retain its vitality and
meaning over the period in question or does the multiplicity of forms
which we have seen indicate that the metaphor has died and degen-
erated into a meaningless cliché such that it can be used in any context
and for any purpose without regard for its meaning and connotations? It
would not be within the scope of a single book to give an exhaustive
analysis of the use of the slavery metaphor by each of these these writers or to give a comprehensive survey of the use over the period in
question. Rather, the intention will be to answer this question through
an examination of the emergence and development of some important
forms of the metaphor and the relationship of these to the interests and
priorities of the time.

1. *The Second Century*

In the immediate sub-Apostolic period, the metaphor of slavery as it
exists in the New Testament does not persist in its more complex theological form. Its appearance in this period takes more the form of a

simple image—that is to say, although we find no development of ideas of the transition from slavery to freedom, we do find an almost pictorial representation of the individual as the slave of God, and a direct comparison between the fact that a slave is under the authority of the master and the fact that the believer is under the authority of God.[1] Two texts of this period, the *Shepherd of Hermas*, and the *Epistles* of Ignatius of Antioch, illustrate this kind of use in different contexts.

a. *The Shepherd of Hermas: Slavery and Loyalty to God*
This is, of course, one of the more interesting writings of the period, from the point of view of this particular study, as its author seems to have been at some point a slave 'given the fact that the biographical note at the beginning serves no further purpose', and 'most urban slaves had a high expectation of manumission'.[2] By the time of the events described, however, he is a freedman.

Here we find repeated use of the metaphor in the form of 'slave of God' as a label for Christians. The representation is a simple one; it urges the believer to be faithful and obedient, since 'by doing these things you will be a pleasing slave of God and will live to him'.[3] There is a clear reference to the implications of slavehood which make the metaphor seem almost to have been intended as a literal representation of the relationship; the believer lives to God in the way that the slaves live to their master and the believer is alienated from his or her own place of birth, just as the slaves are alienated from theirs: 'you, the slaves of God, live in a foreign country, your own city is far from this city'.[4] A Christian should not apostasize from the faith for 'this is a wicked idea, that a slave should deny his own master'.[5] Moreover, 'If the heathen punish their slaves if one denies his master what do you

---

1. It is worth pointing out that the use of the metaphor is not particularly widespread in this period. It is entirely absent from the apologetic writings of this period, and from the *Didache*. Its use in the *Epistle of Barnabas* is limited to the reference to Moses as a servant (θεράπων) and to individuals being 'enslaved to death'. A similar use is found in *1 Clement*, where Moses is again a faithful θεράπων, and God's slaves appear twice.
2. Carolyn Osiek, 'Wealth and Poverty in the Shepherd of Hermas', *StudPat* 17.2 (1982), pp. 725-30.
3. *Mand.* 12.3.1.
4. *Sim.* 1.1.
5. *Sim.* 9.28.4.

think your master who has power over all will do to you?'[6] However, the picture is not entirely literalistic, for the writer has a fluid conception of who is being served. The believer is clearly the slave of God, but he is also urged to serve (δουλεύσῃ). Faith, Continence, Simplicity, Knowledge, Reverence and Love[7] is a theme that harkens back to the older philosophical use of this metaphor in recommending slavery to virtues and warning against slavery to vice.

The central theme of the *Shepherd* is the problem of post-baptismal sin and repentance, and this is reflected in the writer's use of the metaphor. Rather than speaking of a contrast between the good as being slaves of God and the bad as being slaves of sin, he speaks of all Christians, faithful or not, as slaves of God,[8] and therefore under the same inescapable commitment to loyalty as is any other slave. To these slaves, the Devil and his wiles pose an ever present threat, since those whose faith is incomplete are taken over by the Devil and become his slaves[9] and the slave who bears the names of envy and lust 'will see the kingdom of God but will not be allowed to enter in'. If the slaves fall away, they may be forgiven, 'but not too often, for there is only one repentance for the slaves of God'.[10] In some cases, the label also appears as a description of the persecuted Christian, and reference is made to those who 'hand over the slaves of God' presumably to persecution,[11] and he speaks of those who received τοὺς δούλους τοῦ Θεοῦ into their homes,[12] that is, have given sanctuary to persecuted Christians.

I have already mentioned the one exception to this simple use: the parable of the slave and the vineyard.[13] In this parable, a master gives a vineyard into the care of a slave, commanding him to fence it in, but not to do anything further with it until his (the master's) return, upon which the slave is to be released. The slave follows his master's orders but goes on, also, to weed the plot and till it, with the result that it becomes fruitful. The master, when he returns, is delighted at the

6. *Sim.* 9.28.8.
7. *Vis.* 3.28.8.
8. Although they may be 'kidnapped' by the Devil (see below).
9. *Mand.* 12.5.4.
10. *Mand.* 4.1.8.
11. *Sim.* 9.19.1.
12. *Sim.* 8.10.3 and *Sim.* 9.27.2.
13. *Sim.* 5.2.1-11.

faithfulness of the slave and thus decides not only to release him, but to make him a fellow heir with his own son. A feast is then held, from which the master sends the slave a quantity of food. The slave keeps only enough of this for his own needs, and gives the rest to his fellow slaves who are filled with gratitude and pray that he may find further favour with the master. Upon hearing this, the master, his son and his friends further rejoice at the conduct and character of the slave.

This parable is followed by a preliminary explanation,[14] revealing that it is intended to represent the proper manner of fasting—the fasting itself is good, but one ought to go beyond it by purifying one's heart from evil words and desires and, moreover, by calculating the difference between the cost of the bread and water consumed in the fast and the cost of the food one normally would have eaten and giving this to 'a widow, or an orphan, or to someone destitute', who will then pray for their benefactor. Thus:

master: God	slave: believer	fellow slaves: the destitute
vineyard: heart	weeds: sins	son of the master: Son of God
friends: angels	fence: fast	

As it stands, this parable takes us no further than a simple illustration, but it is interesting that the idea of the slave becoming a son is used in this context, and the parable may point towards the same conception on the writer's part of the use of the slavery → adoption perception of the Christian's spiritual journey.

However, when pressed, the *Shepherd* goes on to give another, more peculiar, exposition of the parable,[15] where the slave is the Son of God, and the cast of characters is as follows:

slave: Son of God	master: God	friends: angels
weeds: sins	fence: angels	vineyard: believers
food: commands	fellow slaves: people	son of the master?

Hermas seems to take objection to the identification of the Son of God with the slave, for he immediately questions it.[16] The Shepherd then explains that the Son of God is not really given the form of a slave 'but is given great power and lordship',[17] and that it was the flesh of the Son that served the pre-existent Son on earth and is thus elevated as

14. *Sim.* 5.3.1-9.
15. *Sim.* 5.5.1-3.
16. *Sim.* 5.5.5.
17. *Sim.* 5.6.1-8.

'companion to the Holy Spirit'. The son of the master is thus the Son of God as the pre-existent Holy Spirit, and the slave that becomes a son is the 'flesh that bore the spirit' (presumably the earthly Jesus) who is now elevated as the co-heir with the Holy Spirit.

This is a most strange interpretation. In the first place it makes explicit some of the obvious reluctance in earlier writings to associate slavery with Christ. The division of the earthly and spiritual Christ to explain this is ingenious but almost incomprehensible, but the adoption of the slave in this story and his elevation to co-heir may possibly be a reference to the bodily ascension of Christ, or even to the sanctification of the earthly nature that occurs in the incarnation, expressed more directly in Gregory of Nyssa.

b. *Ignatius: Slavery as Obedience to the Church*

The letters of Ignatius put a somewhat different slant on the metaphor. Here, instead of providing a pattern for the individual's relationship to God, it becomes part of the model of the Church as a well-run household with God as the master, and the deacons working together as σύνδουλοι[18] under the direction of the bishops who are the stewards in charge of the day to day running of the household and who possess, to their subordinates, all the authority of the master:

> For everyone whom the master of the household sends to order his household, we ought to receive as the one who sends him. It is therefore clear that the bishop ought to be looked on as the Lord.[19]

The motivation for such a use of the metaphor as an expression of commitment and subordination to authority is clear in Ignatius' repeated emphasis on the importance of this in the Church and his concept of rigidly hierarchical patterns of authority, and to such an extent can he take this that he asserts that anyone who acts without the knowledge of the bishop is serving the devil.[20] Thus the use of the metaphor of slavery in this corpus is very much directed towards an expression of the place of the Christian within the community of the Church rather than the direct, individual relationship to God. It does not express an individual relationship with and subordination to the divine will, but the

18. For example: *Mag.* 2; *Phil.* 4 and 12 among others.
19. *Eph.* 6. In his *Epistle to Polycarp,* he also urges the bishops to work together as stewards (οἰκονόμαι) *Epistle to Polycarp* 6.
20. ὁ λάθρα ἐπισκόπου τι τράσσων τῷ διαβόλῳ λατπεύει. *Smyr.* 9.

commitment to one's place within the structure of the Church. He only indirectly speaks of the individual as serving God, and even here he does not use terms that speak of a relationship between master and slave, but simply asserts that 'a Christian does not have authority over himself but devotes himself to God'.[21] Thus, the Christian is like the household slave whose time and being are entirely given up to and controlled by his master.

There is also one incidence, within his letters, of the slavery → freedom motif:

> I do not command you like Paul and Peter. They were apostles, I am a condemned man (κατάκριτος). They were free, I am even now a δοῦλος. But if I suffer I shall be a freedman of Jesus and I shall rise in him free.[22]

We should consider the implications of δοῦλος here. Is the word meant to indicate a physical (that is, in virtue of his earthly captivity) state or a spiritual one? Is he perhaps extending his spiritual hierarchy to the state of the apostles, in that he places himself on the level of the household slaves and them on the level of the free members of the household? We really have insufficient evidence to answer these questions. The 'slave'/'freedman of Christ' contrast might seem to suggest that the slavery is to Christ, were it not for the possible parallel with 1 Cor. 7.22, where it is asserted that whoever comes to Christ as a slave in the secular sense is, in the spiritual sense, Christ's freedman. There is no real way of knowing in this case, but a reference to physical slavery might seem more likely, given (1) the parallel given above, (2) the saint's repeated references, throughout the corpus of his letters, to his bonds and captivity and (3) the fact that it would be more logical for him to speak of himself as σύνδουλος, the word he uses for other clergymen. Nevertheless, if this is so, then the contrast with Peter and Paul is odd, given that they too were held captive. There is also the association of suffering with freedom, the implication that martyrdom confers freedom. This contrasts with the tendency, discussed in an earlier chapter, to speak of martyrs as slaves, using 'slave' as the title earned by their suffering. There is the possibility, of course, that he is thinking of the martyr as being a slave while he is on earth—and hence Peter and Paul were God's slaves; but as attaining, through his martyrdom, freedom in

21. *Epistle to Polycarp* 7.
22. *Epistle to the Romans* 4.

Christ—hence Peter and Paul are now free, and Ignatius will attain this freedom. But if this is so then there is no reason why he should not 'command' them 'like Paul and Peter'; seeing that they too were slaves.

2. *The Third Century*

The use of the metaphor in the immediate post-New Testament period is so sparse that it seems that it may well have ceased to be an important metaphor in Christian thought at all, were it not for the extensive use to which Origen puts it in the third century. The profile of the metaphor is, even in the case of the *Shepherd of Hermas* parable, illustrative rather than theological, and generally un-Pauline in character. There is no mention of the purchase and redemption of humanity or any real development of the implications of being a slave of God. The very structure of the metaphor is different, and the use of the un-Pauline δοῦλος Θεοῦ far outweighs that of the Pauline δοῦλος Χριστοῦ. This is accounted for in the character of the texts themselves, the fact that not much use is made of the Pauline Epistles in this period, and that the direction of the texts we have is not generally theological in character but rather practical, illustrative or apologetic. There is thus little scope for the use of the metaphor except in the texts we have discussed and in the Apocryphal Acts.

With Origen, however, the metaphor seems revived as a formula which need not only be used as a simple image, but can be adapted to fulfil a variety of roles in the expression of the complexity of human existence. The demographics of the Church are also different in this period, with the existence of second or even third generation Christians who had been brought up in the faith rather than being converted into it. Once the question of Christianity moves beyond a simple dualism between being a Christian and not being a Christian—of the kind that must predominate in an environment where the activity of the Church is primarily evangelistic and learning how to create and maintain churches—the metaphor of slavery takes on a more sophisticated role, and combined with metaphors of sonship and adoption becomes a vehicle for the expression of the steps in the spiritual journey.

Before turning to Origen, I will briefly consider the corpus of Apocryphal Acts, which are best discussed together and therefore, due to the variety of their dates, do not fit well into any particular period.

a. *Apocryphal Acts: Slavery as Witness*
While the Apocryphal Acts may not strictly fit into the discussion of patristic texts, they are a useful way of exploring the use of the metaphor at a more popular level and in a less theological setting. As we have seen earlier, it is commonplace to find the title as the title for the protagonist, as in the Acts of John: τοῦ Θεοῦ δοῦλος Ἰωάννης,[23] and others are often shown as addressing them as such, frequently in connection with the acknowledgment of the validity of their calling, and although they might seem to be imitations of the Pauline use of this, it is worth noting that the formula is more common as the un-Pauline δοῦλος Θεοῦ + name. Slavery is therefore extended to include other believers, although in not so general a sense as we encountered in *Shepherd of Hermas*. Thus, the saint may refer to his friends, co-workers and, sometimes, his audience as: 'Brothers and fellow slaves',[24] and potential believers.[25] In the *Acts of John*, God is called upon with the words, 'Arise master, save your slaves'.[26]

The implications of such a title are sometimes confused, and in the case of the *Acts of Thomas*, the image is taken so far as to become almost reality when, as we have seen earlier, Thomas is sold by Jesus, in the market, as a slave.[27]

Its use is especially important in the various Acts of the Martyrs. The martyrs speak of themselves as serving God. The deacon Papylus exclaims: Ἀπὸ νεότητος Θεῷ δουλεύω[28] and Eusebius's account of the letter of the martyrs of Lyons shows the writers describing themselves as δοῦλοι Χριστοῦ ('From childhood I have been a slave of God')[29] and accusing the devil of preparing his minions against τῶν δούλων τοῦ Θεοῦ.[30] Various other martyrs are spoken of as God's slaves—we have seen this earlier in the *Martyrdom of Justin and Companions* and we

23. *Acts of John* 111 and 51.
24. *Acts of John* 106.
25. *Acts of John* 45.3-4.
26, *Acts of John* 23.
27. *Acts of Thomas* 1.2, where Jesus sells Thomas to Abbanes for thirty pounds of silver and gives Abbanes a bill of sale declaring that 'I Jesus, son of Joseph...declare that I have sold my slave (δοῦλος) Judas to you Abbanes'.
28. *Martyrdom of Carpus, Papylus and Agathonice*, recension 1.34.
29. Eusebius, *Epistle of the Martyrs of Lyons* 1.3.
30. *Epistle of the Martyrs of Lyons* 1.5.

find this also in the *Martyrdoms* of Saint Conan,[31] of Montanus and Lucius[32] and of Agape, Irene and Chione at Saloniki,[33] but the metaphor is less common in later *Martyrdoms*.

b. *Cyprian of Carthage: Slavery as Community*

One of the central interests in Cyprian of Carthage's writings is the response of the Christian to persecution and the treatment by the Church of those who fall away through it. His interest is the problem of falling out of an established relationship with God, rather than the intricacies of conversion or of the development within one's Christian life, although he is, of course, intimately familiar with the experience of conversion.[34] This is reflected in his use of the metaphor of slavery: Christians in general are referred to as the slaves of God and are urged to behave in a corresponding manner, hence the Christian who acts in opposition to the bishop is behaving as an unruly slave (*inobsequens servus*)[35] since Christians should always be meek and humble 'as befits the slaves of God'.[36]

In a more important sense, however, this metaphor expresses the idea of the community under threat by the persecutor.[37] Here again, as in Ignatius, the Church is seen as a household of slaves, and Cyprian exclaims against an attack on this household,

> Does he now recognize who is the bishop of God, which is the Church and house of Christ, who are the slaves of God, now being molested by the devil, who are the Christians now being attacked by the Antichrist?[38]

Being, therefore, slaves of God, Christians are under an obligation not to be distracted into pagan behaviour or to fall away from their master, since 'The slave of God who has entangled himself in the

---

31. *Martyrdom of Saint Conan* 2.4.
32. *Martyrdom of Montanus and Lucius* 1.1, 2.2, 20.6—variations on *Dei servos*.
33. *Martyrdom of Agape, Irene and Chione* 20.
34. See his *To Donatus*.
35. Cyprian, *On the Unity of the Church* 17.20.
36. *Epistle* 4.2.
37. 'Warfare ranges abroad to defeat the slaves of God.' *On the Unity of the Church* 1.18. See also *On the Lapsed* 10.11.
38. *Epistle* 56.3.

snares of the devil will find himself unable to escape from the devil himself'.[39]

The slaves of God *par excellence* are the martyrs, who bear their title as a tribute to their devotion and suffering.[40] As Cyprian's interest in these texts is primarily directed towards the behaviour of Christians within this world, we have little evidence here of any use of the metaphor in terms of eschatological fulfillment, beyond the glory attained by the martyr. However, in the concluding words of *On the Unity of the Church*, we find once again an expression of the eventual movement of the Christian out of slavery into freedom and equality, when he assure his readers that in the end, '...from being watchful slaves we shall, with Christ as Lord, come to reign'.[41]

c. *Origen: Slavery and Progress*

Origen's use of the metaphor of slavery is very important and varied. His use of it as a label to describe believers has much in common with the New Testament conventions of using it to describe the believer's relationship with God as being in direct opposition with his relationship with evil, hence 'Being a slave of sin, he [Judas] was not a slave of the word of God';[42] 'We were not slaves of God but slaves of idols and demons'.[43] At the same time, he also continues with the simple labelling of certain individuals as slaves of God—he speaks of Paul as being a slave of Christ,[44] for instance, and of the clergy as being slaves of God.[45] He makes use of the Gospel convention of making comparisons between what his audience would take for granted in the case of a master and slave and what they must expect from God, thus,

> since Christ bought us with his own blood, we are his debtors, just as every slave (οἰκέτης) is a debtor for the money given for him by the one who bought him.[46]

---

39. *Epistle* 59.2. See also 56.14: 'the slave of God should not worship images'.
40. See, for example, the repeated use of the metaphor in *Epistle* 8.
41. *On the Unity of the Church* 27.16.
42. Origen, *Commentary on John* (GCS 3.32.14.149–150.1).
43. *Commentary on Jeremiah* (SC 232.4.5.54-55).
44. *Commentary on Proverbs* (PG 17.185.29).
45. 'Vidit et sedem puerorum eius. Ecclesiasticum puto ordinem dicit, qui in episcopatus vel presbyterii sedibus habetur', *Commentary on Song of Songs* 2.
46. *On Prayer* (GCS 2.28.3), see also (GCS 2.6.2).

The other and the most interesting aspect of Origen's use of the metaphor of slavery is, however, his very clearly-developed use of the three-part version of the metaphor which speaks of believers as progressing out of a state of slavery to God into one of sonship. As we have already seen, he provides some of the best early examples of the use of this form of the metaphor within the context of progressive salvation—a person's spiritual life may be charted in terms of progress from a state of slavery to sin on to slavery to God and thence to sonship. Thus, not all Christians may be described in the same way, as some will be further along the spiritual path than others. 'There are', he says, 'marks in the soul, visible only to him who looks upon the heart, which distinguish the slaves of God from his sons.'[47] In this vein we find in Origen a constant emphasis on the contrast between being a son or friend of God and being a slave of the same.[48] He uses the relationship between Jesus and his disciples as an illustration of this:

> ...and he said to them, 'I am ascending to my father and to your father and to my God and to your God', and immediately they were transformed from being slaves of Jesus; for the disciples were slaves before they became children, as is clear from 'You call me Teacher and Lord and you speak correctly, for I so am'.[49]

He also reminds his readers, 'that it is not to his slaves but to his friends that Jesus gives this commandment'.[50] Believers are urged to press on from one state to the other, with Origen urging his readers to

> give thanks to a God and a father and a lord, though in no sense a lord of slaves (δοῦλοι), for a father may properly be considered the lord of a son and he is lord of those who have become sons through him. Just as he is not God of the dead but of the living, so also he is not the lord of ignoble slaves, but of those who in the beginning were in fear through childishness but have been made noble and now serve more blessedly through love than they did through fear.[51]

This difference in the status of various believers means a corresponding variety in the message which must be preached to them:

---

47. *On Prayer* (GCS 2.16.1.15, 1-16).
48. *Commentary on John* (GCS 3.20.27.146.1).
49. *Commentary on John* (GCS 3.32.30.374).
50. *Exhortation to Martyrdom* (GCS 1.34.78).
51. *On First Principles* 16.1.

...if you can understand the differences of the Logos by which the fool-ishness of preaching is proclaimed to those who believe, and is spoken in wisdom to the perfect, you will see in what way the Logos has the form of a slave to those who are being introduced (to the subject), so that they say, 'we saw him and he had no form or beauty'.[52]

Indeed in the course of one's conversion one has to make some progress even to be worthy of becoming a slave of God:

...after someone has been set free from sin, he ought to serve first justice and equally all the virtues, and thence through his progress he will ascend to the point where he will be a slave of God...[53]

The emergence of this three-tier (sometimes more) form of the metaphor is a most important development. Origen has exploited the flexibility of slave language in this area to develop a form that sums up in itself his own progressive concept of salvation.[54] P. Widdicombe has argued that the roots of this lie in the Johannine themes of 'the father-hood of God, the children of God and the sharp distinction between those who know the Father and those who do not' and 'Paul's state-ment that through the spirit of adoption we may all call God Father'.[55] I do not think Widdicombe goes quite far enough. It would probably be more accurate to say that Origen has taken from Paul the contrast between the spirit of slavehood and the spirit of sonship,[56] and has combined it with the slave → friend motif of John. While we can see in Paul's contrast between the spirit of adoption and the spirit of sonship the beginning of a progressive view of spiritual growth, Paul's view of the nature of the mastership over the one who is still in slavery is vague—sometimes it is the Law, sometimes the powers of the cosmos. The addition of the point of view that appears in the Gospel of John, where the master is seen as being God himself, from whose slavery one has to strive to ascend to sonship, has the virtue of giving solidity to

---

52. *Commentary on Matthew* (GCS 10.12.30).

53. *Commentary on Romans* 6 (PG 14.1065D).

54. Widdicombe, *The Fatherhood of God*, pp. 37-38, shows the relationship between this concept of progress and the Platonic ascent.

55. Widdicombe, *The Fatherhood of God*, p. 116.

56. The emphasis on the contrast between slavery and sonship/friendship is repeatedly stressed: 'they were changed from being slaves of Jesus' (*Commentary on John* [GCS 10.30.374.1-2]); 'He gave this command not to his slaves but to his friends', *Exhortation to Martyrdom* 34.79.

Paul's words and the resulting metaphor of ascent through various levels of faith was to prove to be a popular one. After Origen we begin to see a definite revival in the use of slavery language, not only in this form, but also in its use as a title and an illustration.

3. *The Fourth Century*

In this period we begin to see a development of the descriptive side of the slavery metaphor as it flowers into detailed and elaborate images, competing, it is true, with an equal outburst in other metaphors. The metaphor particularly comes into its own, as we have seen earlier, as part of the language of baptismal instruction, but there are many other uses to which it is also put.

a. *Eusebius's* Life of Constantine: *Slavery as Honour*
This work demonstrates a very important use of slavery terminology, although in the form of a θεράπων Θεοῦ formula rather than a δοῦλος Θεοῦ one. This is used frequently to describe the emperor Constantine and appears both in descriptions of the emperor and in letters which he is reported as having written.[57] The term συνθεράπων is also shown as being used by the emperor to describe himself in relation to the bishops and the people of the Church.[58] This reiterated use of the 'slave of God' formula for the emperor—though admittedly in the milder form of θεράπων, rather than δοῦλος Θεοῦ—is strongly reminiscent of the use of such formulae in the apocryphal acts of saints and martyrs, and fits in well with what T.D. Barnes argues is the partly hagiographic nature of this treatise.[59] More important, however, is the relation of the formula to Moses, the archetypal θεράπων θεοῦ. The Mosaic overtones to the use of this form of the title affirm the status and role of Constantine as the leader, appointed by God, of his people. Constantine is presented by Eusebius, as A. Cameron points out, 'as having a role akin to Moses, if not to Christ himself'.[60] This is confirmed by the fact that Moses is

57. Eusebius, *Life of Constantine* 1.5; 1.6; 1.47; 1.50; 2.2; 2.29; 2.31; 2.55.
58. *Life of Constantine* 2.69; 3.12 and 3.17.
59. In his 'Panegyric, History and Hagiography in Eusebius' "Life of Constantine"', in R. Williams (ed.), *The Making of Orthodoxy: Essays in Honour of Henry Chadwick* (Cambridge: Cambridge University Press, 1989), pp. 94-123.
60. Cameron, *Christianity and the Rhetoric of Empire*, pp. 34-35. Although it is θεράπων that is always used for Constantine, there is one exception. He is reported

described as Constantine's συνθεράπων.⁶¹ Christian people are sometimes referred to with the θεράπων formula, as when Constantine—ὁ τῷ Θεῷ φίλος—grants access to his courts to the θεράποντας of God.⁶² There does, however, seem to be an interesting distinction here, for while Constantine and other Christians are referred to as θεράπων Θεοῦ, the title is slightly different for Christians who are being persecuted. They become ὑπηρέται... τοῦ Σωτῆρος,⁶³ and θεραπευταὶ τοῦ Χριστοῦ.

b. *Cyril of Jerusalem: Slavery as Relationship*
The catechetical writings of Cyril of Jerusalem make ample and vivid use of almost every imaginable Christian metaphor. In his *Protocatechesis*, he moves rapidly from metaphor to metaphor, building one image of baptism upon another: baptism is a marriage feast, and a promise of citizenship; Christ is a fisherman fishing for souls, and baptism is a killing, as a fish is killed; the catechumen is to make his mind a house for God; he is entering a contest and race, he is about to be married to the heavenly Bridegroom; at exorcism his soul is like gold being purified; he is receiving armour for spiritual combat; catechism is like the planting of trees and like building with the stones of knowledge; the candidates have become sons and daughters of one Mother and are like true metal whose rust is being rubbed away; and they are stars of the Church. Baptism is 'a ransom to captives, a remission of offences, a death of sin; a rebirth of the soul; a garment of light; a holy, indissoluble seal; a chariot to heaven; the delight of paradise; a welcome into heaven and a gift of adoption.⁶⁴ He speaks further of God planting them in the Church and enrolling them in his service (clearly this is military service, as this continues with 'and put on you the armour of righteousness').

His use of the metaphor of slavery is equally eclectic. In spite of the

---

to have once been excessively flattered by a priest and, responding to this in outrage, to have forbidden him to speak in such a way, urging rather that those present should pray that he might τῆς τοῦ Θεοῦ δουλείας ἄξιον φανῆναι, *Life of Constantine* 4.48. This is the only use in the entire work of δουλεία as a metaphor, save where it describes the suffering of populations under tyrants (*Life of Constantine* 1.35; 4.9).

61. *Life of Constantine* 1.12.
62. *Life of Constantine* 1.52; also 2.65; 2.62; 3.30.
63. *Life of Constantine* 2.46 and 3.1.
64. Cyril of Jerusalem, *Protocatechesis* 1; 5; 6; 9; 10; 13; 15 and 16.

idea of compulsory service, it is made to fit into Cyril's emphasis on the free will of the believer, for consent is an important part, both of slavery to God[65] and slavery to evil,[66] although in another sense one is inevitably a slave of God through one's creation:

> Nothing is withdrawn from the power of God, for the Scriptures say of him 'all things are your slaves'. All things indeed are his slaves, but one his only Son and one, his Holy Spirit are excepted from all these; and all things which are his slaves serve the master through his one Son in the Holy Spirit.[67]

Indeed it seems that he will call individuals slaves of God in spite of their behaviour being very far from what could be considered ideal, as when he describes

> ...the master (δεσπότης) judged by a council of slaves (δοῦλοι) and submitting to it...[68]

However, he also uses the title to describe the Christians as the new slaves of God, who are replacing the Jews as the chosen ones of God:

> But some will say that the name 'Christians' is new and was not in use previously. But the prophet made the point safe beforehand, saying 'My slaves (lit. those who serve [δουλεύω] me) shall be called by a new name, which shall be blessed upon the earth. Let us question the Jews. Do you serve (δουλεύω) the Lord or not? Then show your new name. For you were called Jews and Israelites in the time of Moses...and up to the present time. Where then is your new name? But we, since we serve the Lord, we have a new name.[69]

He describes Paul and Peter as slaves of God,[70] but he is very careful to distinguish the status of Christ from that of his followers:

> ...they (the prophets) were the slaves, but he the son of God.[71]

> The comparison is between the great slave (John) and his fellow slaves, but the preeminence and the grace of the Son is beyond comparison with slaves (οἰκέτας).[72]

65. *Catechetical Orations* 5.4.
66. *Catechetical Orations* 2.3.
67. *Catechetical Orations* 8.5.
68. *Catechetical Orations* 12.12. (This being a discussion of the trial and crucifixion of Jesus, the slaves in this case are the Jews).
69. *Catechetical Orations* 10.16, i.e., Christians.
70. *Catechetical Orations* 14.26; 10.19 and 6.15.
71. *Catechetical Orations* 14.26.
72. *Catechetical Orations* 3.6.

In doing so, he creates a picture of a hierarchy of slaves under the authority of the Son who is the master of all and not to be compared with his slaves.

c. *Basil: Slavery and Createdness*
Slave language is used with frequency by Basil to describe the positive commitment of individuals to God. Like many others, he uses θεράπων for Moses,[73] and he also uses the term for Gregory.[74] He is, however, also willing to speak of important Christians as δοῦλοι, and indeed quotes this as a prime requirement for one elected to the episcopacy— 'just let him be a δοῦλος Θεοῦ'.[75] Indeed, he makes an amusing, though perhaps unconscious, play on the fact that 'slave' in such a context can either be used as a sign of honour or of disgrace:

> And now the very title of bishop has been conferred on wretched and slavish men, for no slave (δοῦλος) of God would choose to come forward in opposition.[76]

He also makes an attack on the misuse of such metaphorical language:

> He (the Spirit), it is said, is neither a master nor a slave, but a freeman. The terrible insensitivity, the pitiful audacity of those that maintain this! Which should I lament, their ignorance or their blasphemy? They insult the dogmas concerning the divine nature by comparing them to human nature. They see differences of rank among men and then apply these to the ineffable nature of God, not understanding that even among men, no one is a slave by nature.[77]

This is especially interesting when considered in its context. This passage occurs in the middle of Basil's argument with those who claim that the Holy Spirit is a creature, an example of, as we shall see also in Gregory of Nyssa, the conviction that to call Christ or the Holy Spirit creatures would be to render them slaves. There is a strong association in this period between createdness and slavery, and thus all things are, in virtue of having been created, slaves of their creator:

> You say that the Holy Ghost is a creature. Every creature is a slave (δοῦλος) of the Creator 'for all things are your slaves'...tell me, how

73. See Basil, *Hexaemeron* 1.1, and *Epistle* 42.2.
74. *Epistle* 28.1.42.
75. *Epistle* 190.1.19.
76. *Epistle* 239.1.12.
77. *On the Holy Spirit* 20.51.

can you call him a slave who through baptism frees you from servitude?[78]

...the creature serves; but the Spirit sets free.[79]

The former of these is a common theme—appealing to the reader's baptism and asking how such a baptism could free the individual from slavery if administered in the name of one who is also a creature, and therefore a slave.

Although one is a slave in virtue of one's createdness, one may also be found to be a slave to evil, heresy, or to other people:[80]

...rather to serve the pleasures of the flesh than to serve God.[81]

...what we see is not a bodily slavery, but a carrying away of souls into captivity every day by the champion of heresy.[82]

Observance of the law is also spoken of as slavery: 'For we certainly must not, when we find anything which falls in with our pleasure subject ourselves to the yoke of slavery to the law'.[83] Since all are by nature slaves of God, those who do not obey and honour him are to be thought of as wicked and ungrateful slaves,[84] as one should seek to be worthy, through one's way of life, of this slavery: 'I cannot persuade myself that without love to others... I can be called a worthy servant of Jesus Christ'.[85]

The form of the slave that Christ takes is a way of speaking of the form of man that he took, as in *Epistle* 261.2 where it is asserted that 'the Lord assumed the "form of a slave" and not "the slave himself", and that he was made in the likeness "but that actual manhood was not assumed by him"'.

In spite of the fact that all are seen as being slaves to God and are encouraged to live up to obligations of service, there is a distinct emphasis, in Basil's work, on the liberation from slavery granted through baptism, as in speaking of Christ as, 'He who through baptism frees you from servitude'. Servitude to God is mentioned in the context

78. *Epistle* 8.6-8, 12-14.
79. *Epistle* 159.2.19.
80. *Epistle* 92.2.23-25.
81. *Epistle* 218.
82. *Epistle* 71.46-48.
83. *Epistle* 160.3.8-10.
84. *Epistle* 123.
85. *Epistle* 203.2.20-22. See also *Epistle* 165 and *Epistle* 138.2.36-38.

of baptism: 'by these we may recognize our Master (δεσπότην)' but this is secondary to the freedom attained through him:

> but (for one) to become free from slavery (ἀπὸ δούλου) and to be called a son of God and to be brought alive from death, can be brought about by no other than the one who has through nature acquired kinship with us.[86]

and there is no explicit expression of the idea of a slavery to God → sonship to God progression.

d. *Gregory Nazianzus: Slavery and Humanity*

Gregory Nazianzus makes use of the standard formulae of slavery, speaking of slavery to the world, to sin and to the law. He speaks of some as being δοῦλοι τῶν κάτω καὶ τοῦ κοσμοκράτος ('slaves of the world and of the ruler of the world'),[87] and of his father as having, in his conversion, 'escaped the bondage of his (own) fathers' gods'.[88] Some, equally, are slaves to the Jewish law.[89] Baptism and the redemption wrought by Christ are thus liberations from such wrongful slaveries,[90] although the proper state of all, whether they are willing or not, is one of slavery to God on account of the rightful ownership of the created by the creator, in which they are fellow slaves with all other creatures.[91]

While he does not employ the creation/slave argument against the createdness of any of the persons of the Trinity with quite the vigour of his contemporaries, he is concerned with the taking on of the form of a slave, associating it only indirectly with the form of man, and stressing that in doing so Christ elevates and restores the form of the slave to freedom.[92]

> Next is the fact of His being called slave (δοῦλος) and serving many well, and this too, that it is a great thing for him to be called a child of God (παῖς Θεοῦ). For in truth he was a slave to the flesh and to birth and to the things we suffer (experience) for our liberation, and for that of all those whom he has saved who were held under sin. What greater thing

86. *On the Holy Spirit* 13.29.
87. Gregory Nazianzus, *Oration* 1.4.
88. *Oration* 8.4.
89. *Oration* 31 (*Fifth Theological Oration*) 24.
90. *Oration* 30 (*Fourth Theological Oration*) 20.
91. Such as the stars, *Oration* 7.7 which they should therefore not worship.
92. *Oration* 1.5.

could come to man's humility than to be mingled with God, and to become God through this mingling, and that we should be visited by the Dayspring from on high, so that that Holy Thing that should be born should be called the Son of the Highest…and that every knee should bow to Him who was emptied for us, and who mingled the divine nature with the form of a slave and that all the House of Israel should know that God has made him both Lord and Christ?[93]

For as Logos he was neither obedient nor disobedient, for such expressions belong to those under authority and to inferiors… But as Slave (δοῦλος), he condescends to his fellow slaves (ὁμοδοῦλοι), indeed, to his slaves, and takes upon him a strange form, bearing all of me and mine in himself that in himself he may exhaust the bad.[94]

He shares in my flesh that he may both save the image and make the flesh immortal.[95]

He also places the title 'slave' in his list of the titles of Christ:

God, the Son, the Image, the Word, the Wisdom, the Truth, the Light, the Life, the Power, the Vapour, the Emanation, the Radiance, the Maker, the King, the Head, the Law, the Way, the Door, the Foundation, the Rock, the Pearl, the Peace, the Righteousness, the Sanctification, the Redemption, the Man, the Slave (δοῦλος), the Shepherd, the Lamb, the High Priest, the Victim, the Firstborn before Creation, the Firstborn from the Dead, the Resurrection.[96]

Here too we find some of the most explicit expressions of the slave → son progression:

For the fear of the Lord is the beginning of wisdom…but when wisdom goes beyond fear and rises up to love, it makes us friends and sons of God instead of slaves.[97]

There are three classes among the saved; the slaves, the hired servants, the sons. If you are a slave, fear the whip; if you are a hired servant, expect only your wages; if you are more than this, a son, honor him as a father, and do that which is good, because it is good to obey a father; and even though no reward might come of it, it is a reward in itself, that you should please your father.[98]

---

93. *Oration 30 (Fourth Theological Oration)* 3.
94. *Oration* 30.6.
95. *Oration* 38.8.
96. *Oration* 2.98.
97. *Oration* 21.6.
98. *Oration* 40.8.

He is, nevertheless, willing to use the 'slave' as a title of honour, and, speaking of David as God's δοῦλος,[99] recounts that his mother made his father into a 'good ὁμόδουλον rather than an unreasonable master'.[100] In *Oration 8*, however, he uses another term for Basil and addresses him as ἄνθρωπε τοῦ Θεοῦ, καὶ πιστὲ θεράπων, καὶ οἰκονόμε τοῦ Θεοῦ μυστηρίων ('Man of God, and faithful servant, and steward of the mysteries of God').[101]

He is also, like many of his contemporaries, concerned that the title of slavery should not be mistakenly applied to members of the Trinity:

> If he is God then He is neither a creature nor a thing made, nor a fellow slave (σύνδουλος) nor any of these humble things.[102]

> Can he who is baptized into a creature and a fellow slave (ὁμόδουλον, i.e. the Holy Spirit) honour Him (the Holy Spirit)?[103]

He contrasts earthly and spiritual slavery and emphasizes that the latter is no bar to spiritual equality between all people, pointing out that if Christ was humble enough to take on the form of a slave then they themselves should not be too proud to allow themselves to be baptized in the company of the poor or the lowborn or of their own slaves.[104]

e. *Gregory of Nyssa*, Against Eunomius: *Slavery and Createdness*
Gregory of Nyssa's *Against Eunomius* makes extensive use of the metaphor of slavery. The vast majority of these uses in the text fall into two contexts: the kenosis of Christ, and the arguments against the subordination of the Son, and in both cases the most important aspect of the metaphor is his association of slavery with createdness. To be a created thing is to be, by nature, a slave. This is again another example of the 'slavery in virtue of createdness' motif that we came across earlier, but argued this time with the aid of the 'all creation is in bondage' passage from Paul (Rom. 8.21).

99. *Oration* 2.117.
100. *Oration* 8.8.
101. *Oration* 17.1 (but see *Oration* 43.35]; 'Then, imitating the ministry (διακονία) of Christ, who, girded with a towel, did not disdain to wash the disciples' feet, using for this purpose the aid of his own slaves and also of his fellow slaves, he (Basil) attended to the bodies and souls of those who needed it)'.
102. *Oration* 31 (*Fifth Theological Oration*) 6.
103. *Oration* 33.17; see also *Oration* 34.8, arguing that the Son is not a σύνδουλος, and *Oration* 40.42, that there is nothing slavish in the Trinity.
104. *Oration* 40.28.

The use of the metaphor in this text thus has little to do with illustrating the details of the individual relationship to God and does not concern the actual interaction of the master and the slave. Rather, it focuses on the slave/master division and the slave/free division in order to illustrate the division between the status of man and that of Christ.

The main purpose of this association of slavery with createdness is the clarification of the nature of Christ who took on the form of man, that is, the form of a slave (Phil. 2.5-9).[105] Christ thus becomes Son of God and Son of Man, form of God and form of slave:

> (on the interpretation of Prov. 8.22)
> It is clear that 'possession' allegorically marks the slave who for our sakes 'took on him the form of a slave (δοῦλος)'. But if anyone should argue for the reading which prevails in the churches we do not reject even the expression 'created'. For this also in allegorical language is intended to indicate 'slave' (δοῦλος), since 'all creation is in slavery', as the Apostle says.[106]

The problem is then raised of whether the lordship of Christ might not be impaired through the taking on of such a form. This cannot be so, argues Gregory, and he asserts rather that it is the slave who is lifted up to Lordship and Christhood:

> For if the Logos, even if it is made flesh, remains Logos, and the light, even if it shines in the darkness, is not thereby weaker light and does not accept the fellowship of the opposite, and the Life, even if it is in death, preserves itself in itself, even so God, even if he receives the form of a slave (δοῦλος) does not himself become a slave, but raises that which is in subjection into lordship and kingship, making Lord and Christ that which was humble and human.[107]

In the other use of the metaphor, Gregory emphasizes the domination that is implied through slavery. His argument runs thus: all creation, as Paul tells us in, is in bondage, and therefore, if the Son is a created being, then he is part of this creation and therefore also a slave, which, he says, is absurd. Since humans are slaves they are to be carefully distinguished in status from the Son who, although in taking on the form

---

105. *Against Eunomius* 12.1. 'The bodily characteristics, that is the form of the δοῦλος in which God was'.

106. *Against Eunomius* 2.10. See also 5.2.

107. *Against Eunomius* 12.3.

of man took on the form of a slave, is not to be placed on the same
level as those who are slaves by nature, and to emphasize this he is
spoken of once as ὁ δεσπότης Χριστὸς.[108]

> For we recognize no other mark of a slavery (δουλεία) than to be under
> authority and controlled. The slave is altogether a slave, and that which
> is slave cannot by nature be Lord, even if he is improperly called one.
> And why should I bring forward the declarations of Paul in evidence of
> the lordship of the Lord? For Paul's Master (δεσπότης) himself says to
> his disciples that he is truly Lord, accepting the confession of those who
> call him Teacher and Lord. For he says, 'You call me Teacher and Lord;
> and you do well, for so I am', And in the same way he commanded them
> that the Father should be called Father by them, saying, 'call no man
> master (καθηγητής) upon earth: for you have one master, Christ: and do
> not call anyone father upon earth, for you have one Father, the one in
> Heaven' ... On one side the Lord himself and he who has the Christ
> speaking in him, tell us it is not proper to think of him as a slave, but to
> honour him even as the Father is honoured, and on the other side
> Eunomius brings his suit against the Lord, claiming Him as a slave,
> when he says that he who rules all is under domination.[109]

Man, of course is both created by and under the domination of
God—indeed, the very form of man is the form of a slave—so one
would expect to find a widespread use of the idea of man as the slave of
God in this text. However, Gregory seems to be more interested in
using slavery as a label for the wrong state of humanity, contrasting it
with liberty and sonship in God:

> For men, revolting from God, served those which were not by nature
> Gods, and although they were children of God, they went over to a
> wicked and false father.[110]

Furthermore, his association of slavery with the createdness of humanity is at odds with the importance he attaches to free will. Man, he
insists in the *Great Catechism,* was created having mastership over
himself, since,

> ...if necessity in any way ruled the life of man, the 'image' would have
> been falsified in that particular part, having been estranged owing to this
> unlikeness to its archetype. How then can that nature which is under a

108. *Against Eunomius* 12.2.
109. *Against Eunomius* 10.4.
110. *Against Eunomius* 2.8.

yoke and bondage to any kind of necessity be called an image of a master being?[111]

He rejects the idea of any sort of slavery for man, even slavery to God, claiming that the power to enslave mankind does not even belong to God himself and that the Divine Word 'does not wish even us to be slaves'.[112] Since each individual is possessed of a free will, however, it is possible for one to make oneself into a slave, like those who have sold spiritual freedom, making it necessary for Christ to pay a ransom for their freedom.[113] The duality of spiritual versus physical slavery takes on a third variation, therefore, in Gregory who must wrestle not only with the conflict between these kinds of slaveries but also with the idea of the freedom of the will, which is a separate matter from physical or even spiritual freedom. Hence,

> Who can buy a man, who can sell him, when he is made in the likeness of God, when he is ruler over the whole earth, when he has been given as his inheritance by God authority over all that is in the earth? Such power belongs to God alone, or rather it does not even belong to God himself. For as Scripture says 'The gifts of God are unrevocable'. Of his own free will God called us into freedom when we were slaves to sin. In that case he would hardly reduce human beings to slavery. But if God does not enslave what is free, who dares to put his own authority higher than God's?[114]

Since Gregory, in other places, clearly speaks of believers being slaves to God, it is unlikely that he is only contrasting spiritual freedom with earthly slavery. Rather he begins with the condemnation of the slavery of one person to another, then moves on to the assertion that God does not have the power to enslave the being that has been given authority over the whole world. This appeal to humankind's authority and rulership indicates that it is free will, that is, authority over oneself in virtue of being in the image of God and of being ruler of the world, that is the irrevocable gift of God. From there he moves onto more familiar ground with the contrast of slavery to sin and freedom in God. It is not, therefore, inconsistent that he should talk both of God being

111. *Great Catechism* 5.26.9.
112. See above, p. 105.
113. *Great Catechism* 23.
114. Gregory of Nyssa, *In Ecclesiasten* 4.

unable to enslave and of individuals being the slaves of God, for he is actually talking about two different kinds of enslavement[115]—the enslavement of service to God and the enslavement of the free will, which not even God, much less a fellow human being, can demand.

f. *Chrysostom: Slavery as Relationship*

It is Chrysostom who makes the most extensive and varied use of the metaphor of slavery in his writings, and a full enumeration of this theme would require a separate study in itself. His use of the metaphor is, in many ways, very similar to that of the New Testament in spirit. The most distinctive aspect of his use is his repetition of detailed illustrations, such as appear in the Gospels, drawing, sometimes at great length, on aspects of the slave/master relationship to describe and explain various aspects of the human/divine relationship. In his description of candidates awaiting baptism, for example, he dwells at great length on the image of the slave market, with prospective masters enquiring of the slaves whether they would be willing to serve if purchased,[116] while in another place he compares the care that is taken with preparing slaves for their house duties with the care that should be taken in preparing people to enter the Church.[117] He also points out that if some, despite being the slaves of men, have power and authority, this is even more true for those who are the slaves of God.[118]

As we have seen,[119] he makes particularly effective use of this metaphor in his descriptions of baptism. His distinctively detailed and vivid use of image and, sometimes almost fanciful, comparisons combine here with the metaphor of slavery to particularly happy effect. Here, as with so many of his other metaphors, he has observed the subject in detail and is able to find aspects of the institution to illustrate every nuance of the Christian life.

He shows great enthusiasm for the title 'slave of God', and

---

115. See M.M. Bergadá, 'La condemnation de l'esclavage dans l'Homélie IV', in *Gregory of Nyssa on Ecclesiastes: An English Version with Supporting Studies* (Proceedings of the Seventh International Colloquium on Gregory of Nyssa 1990 [Berlin: W. de Gruyter: 1993]), pp. 185-96.

116. See above, p. 119.

117. Chrysostom, *Homilies on I Timothy* 2 (PG 62.553).

118. *Homilies on Ephesians* 8 (PG 62.67).

119. See above, pp. 119-20.

frequently reminds his reader of the honour and glory inherent in being God's slave:

> He called them by the most delightful name, for he knew that in this way he flattered them most; for it was indeed that they might remain slaves of God, that they entered into the fire, for no other name could please them so. If he called them kings, if he called them lords of the world, yet would he not so have pleased them as when he said 'O slaves of the most high God'.[120]

He stresses that this service must be a free one, arguing that God 'will have no unwilling, no forced slave (οἰκέτης), but all of their own free will and choice and grateful to him for their service (δουλεία)'.[121]

In spite of the detail and sophistication of the images of slavery he draws on, the simple 'individual as the slave of God' is the only form of this metaphor he makes use of. Although his theology clearly sees the spiritual life in terms of a progression,

> Why then did he not give the whole at once? Because neither have we, on our part, done the whole of our work. We have believed. This is a beginning, and he too on his part has given an earnest. When we show our faith by works, then will he add the rest.[122]

Although he employs the slavery to sin → freedom in God theme within the context of the entry into a relationship with God, 'You were slaves and enemies and aliens—how have you received the right to call God Father?'[123] the slavery to God → sonship in God progression, except in a eucharistic prayer attributed to him ('raised us from the low estate of slaves and gave us the honour of heirs')[124] is conspicuous by its absence, perhaps because this would imply the inferiority of a state of spiritual slavery, something which he is frequently at pains to deny. Rather he repeatedly recommends the greatness of the state of obedient slavery to God, comparing those who reject it to ungrateful and worthless slaves.

An important aspect of Chrysostom's use of slavery is the great interest he shows in slavery as a reality. He emphasizes time and time again that those who are slaves are the spiritual equals of their masters:

---

120. *Homilies on Ephesians* 8 (PG 62.67).
121. *Homilies on John* 10.1 (PG 59.73).
122. *Homilies on Ephesians* 2.14 (PG 62.18-19).
123. *Homilies on Galatians* 1 (PG 62.617).
124. E. Renaudot, *Liturgiarum Orientalium collectio* (Frankfurt: J. Baer Bibliopolae, 1847), II, pp. 243-50.

> This one who before was a Greek or a Jew or a slave walks about with
> the form not of an angel or an archangel but of the master of all, showing
> forth Christ in himself.[125]

He seems deeply concerned about the well-being of slaves, both physically and spiritually. He urges mistresses only to strike their female
slaves if they are doing harm to their own souls and asks the unjust
mistress,

> ...has she not the same kind of soul as you? Has she not received the
> same privileges from God? Does she not partake of the same table? Does
> she not share with you the same high birth?[126]

Slavery is used to describe one's previous state, either in terms of
slavery to the law or as slavery to things other than God:

> It is thus that love grows cold, when we wish the praise of men, when
> we are slaves to the honour which is paid by the many, for it is not pos-
> sible for someone to be the slave (δοῦλος) of praise and also a true slave
> of God.[127]

> Nearly the whole human race has given itself over to him (the Devil) and
> all serve him willingly and of their own choice.[128]

4. Summary

A close look at the use of the metaphor of slavery in relation to its tex-
tual context brings out, more than anything else, the extraordinary
flexibility of the language of slavery in Christian writings. While there
are clearly some standard uses which are copied from the New Testament and form part of the tradition on which the writers draw,[129] there
is also wide scope for the language to be adapted to fit individual needs.
As we discussed earlier, the nature of slavery can vary, depending on
the relationship between master and slave. The possible variations on
slavery are widely exploited as a metaphoric source in the Christian
tradition, and thus metaphors of household slavery, houseborn slaves,
purchased slaves, captives and debt slaves, are all incorporated into the
patristic writings. The Church of God is like a well ordered household
of slaves; people are born into slavery to God in virtue of having been

---

125. *Homilies on Galatians* 3.28 (PG 61.656).
126. *Homilies on Ephesians* 15 (PG 62.110).
127. *Homilies on Philippians* 5.3 (PG 62.214).
128. *Homilies on Ephesians* 4.3 (PG 62.31).
129. The label of δοῦλος Χριστοῦ for Paul, for example.

created by him; slaves are purchased from the devil by Christ; those who have been taken captive by the devil are rescued and returned to their true city and those who through sin are being held as debtors are redeemed by the blood of Christ. Baptism is described in terms of manumission, of adoption and of the slave market. Among believers there may be a simple distinction between slaves and sons, or there may be a whole hierarchy of slaves, faithful servants and sons, as we find in Clement of Alexandria:

> by listening to wisdom (it is possible) to be in the first place a slave of God (Θεοῦ δοῦλον) then to become a faithful servant (θεράποντα) and if one ascend higher, he is enrolled among the sons.[130]

It is valuable, too, to consider the characteristics of these uses within a chronological framework, for, while taking care not to overgeneralize, we may note that each period seems to demonstrate a particular preference for certain uses of the metaphor. In Hermas and Ignatius, we find a very simple use of the metaphor. It is not discussed or elaborated by the writers, and one can only reach an understanding of the picture they wish to convey by understanding their use of the metaphor in relation to their own interests. A similar use of the language is also found in the Apocryphal Acts of this period, where the metaphor usually appears as a simple, unelaborated label for the saint or for the process of conversion.

The metaphor in its more complex form—where it is used to express transition and spiritual progress—finds its most important context within the writings of Origen, who uses it as a vehicle for explaining his own theology of progressive spiritual growth.[131] In the works of Cyril of Jerusalem and Chrysostom on the other hand, we find a resurgence of the use of the metaphor as image in a very elaborate and sophisticated way.

In the discussion of the metaphor in the New Testament, I noted the strong relationship between humility and slavery and the inversion of normal ideas of society that Paul's use of the metaphor suggests. This

130. Clement of Alexandria, *Stromata* 1.27.173.

131. A similar use is found in Clement of Alexandria's, *Excerpta ex Theodoto* 56.5–57.1: 'But Israel is an allegory, the spiritual man who will see God, the unlawful son of the faithful Abraham, he who was born of the free woman, not he who was according to the flesh the son of the Egyptian slavewoman. Therefore from the three species a formation of the spiritual element happens to one and a change of the psychic from slavery to freedom happens to the other.'

does not seem to have carried over into the earlier post-New Testament texts, an omission which is understandable considering the absence of Pauline themes in this period. There is no real question of radical humiliation in *Shepherd of Hermas*, and although humiliation as a theme plays an important role in the writings of Ignatius, this is not directly associated with slavery except in his assertion that Peter and Paul are free while he himself is a δοῦλος.

One of the very important themes we see developing in the metaphor over this period is that of creation in bondage, a view of all things being by nature slaves of God in virtue of having been created by him, although human beings have the choice as to whether or not they will acknowledge their obligation and serve God. This intimate connection between createdness and slavery plays a very important role in the understanding of the nature of the Son, and we find it being taken for granted that to say that the Son is a created being is as good as saying that he is a slave. There is also a very close connection between being human and being a slave, so that in this context *the form of a slave* is simply identical with *the form of a human being*, rather being than any particular indication of humility.

The extent to which the metaphor is worked out has varied from writer to writer, as we have seen. Some may use it in a very limited way, concentrating on particular characteristics of slavery, family organization in one case, domination in another. Others spin it out in great detail, as does Chrysostom, choosing various details from the master/ slave relationship to illustrate the point in question. Some are, of course, aware of the dangers of taking the metaphor too far or of thinking of it being literally true in the case of the human and the divine. Nevertheless, in such cases as the automatic association of createdness and slavery it seems that they may have sometimes disregarded their own warnings.

What is clear from what we have seen is that the metaphor has experienced over this period not a disintegration but an evolution. In each of the examples we have discussed, the metaphor has remained a lively and useful one. Even though it appears in a variety of contexts, sometimes far removed from the kind in which we first encountered it, it is very far from having become a meaningless cliché. Rather it has been adapted to to fit a very wide range of theological interests and needs. Our next question must be, therefore, how has this come about?

Chapter 8

CONCLUSION

1. *The Metaphor in the New Testament*

It has been shown earlier that in the New Testament, the metaphor of slavery, as used by Paul, exists in a state of tension between the idea of spiritual slavery and the reality of secular slavery and between the idea of slavery to Christ and freedom in God and Christ. We have also seen that the metaphor appears in a number of different ways. These may be summarized into four broad categories:

1. Slave of Christ as a title claimed by the apostle for himself and his colleagues.
2. Ordinary believers as slaves of Christ.
3. Salvation as a *slavery to sin → slavery to Christ* progression.
4. Salvation as a *slavery to sin → freedom in God* progression.

The enslavement of the believer to Christ is closely associated with images of death—the death of the individual that results in freedom from the old masters of sin and the Law, the death of the individual in Christ which leads to an entire dedication of that person's life to Christ and the death of Christ which annuls the slavery of the individual and sets him or her free for adoption by God. Paul, who has no life but that which Christ lives in him ('the life I now live is not my life, but the life which Christ lives in me...' [Gal. 2.20]), is the prime example and pattern of this slavery. It is part and parcel of his message of 'strength through weakness' and his emphasis on the crucified, humiliated saviour.

In this he is at one with the spirit of the earliest Church and its central figure of an unsettling and unexpected kind of saviour, a messiah who was executed by crucifixion—a degrading form of execution, usually associated with slavery—and who made himself thereby 'a stumbling block to the Jews and a folly to the Gentiles'.[1]

> Messiah anathema—Christos estauromenos—Rex crucifixus—in these
> amazing verbal contrasts the extremes of all human experience were
> brought together, the greatest antinomy of human history was momen-
> tarily resolved... the language of the paradox, the absurd, the contradic-
> tion was already at the heart of the Christian faith.[2]

'With its paradoxical contrast between the divine nature of the pre-
existent Son of God and his shameful death on the cross, the first
Christian proclamation shattered all analogies and parallels which
could be produced in the world of the time, whether from polytheism
or from monotheistic philosophy',[3] writes Hengel. Not only was this
contrast new and unprecedented, it was also a great burden for those
who had to proclaim it and had, as a result, to endure the outrage and
mockery of their audiences. We find the difficulties of this clearly
reflected in the early writers—Ignatius seems almost to wallow in the
idea of his own humiliation: 'My spirit is the offscouring (περίψημα)
of the cross which is a σκάνδαλον to unbelievers but is salvation and
life eternal to us'[4] and Justin Martyr put into the mouth of the Jew,
Trypho,[5] the words,

> This, your so-called Christ, is without honour and glory, so that he has
> even fallen into the uttermost curse that is in the law of God...

Even as late as Chrysostom, we find self-conscious references to the
possible misunderstanding of the cross:

> Indeed this matter (the cross) is thought to be a reproach, but only in the
> world and among unbelievers. And what is the boast of the cross? It is
> that Christ for my sake took the form of a slave and suffered for the sake
> of me, the slave, the enemy, the unfeeling one. If domestic slaves are
> pleased when they receive praise from their masters—who are only their
> fellow human beings—how can we not boast when the master who is
> very God is not ashamed of the cross which he suffered for us?[6]

It is not surprising therefore, that later writers should seek to rein-
terpret the cross in terms more acceptable to society in life and to play

1. 1 Cor. 1.23.
2. Dillistone, *Traditional Symbols*, p. 146.
3. Hengel, *The Cross of the Son of God*, p. 107.
4. *Eph.* 18.5.
5. *Dialogue with Trypho* 32.
6. Chrysostom, *Homily on Galatians* 6.14.

down its inherent humiliation and degradation.[7] A result of this was, Hengel points out, that 'the later interpretation of the cross which can be seen from Ignatius onwards, in symbolic-allegorical or cosmic terms, has little in common with Paul's λόγος τοῦ σταυροῦς.[8] At the same time there is a development and expansion in the Christian message of the theme of victory over death, slavery and the world:

> Both the experience (of the Easter ceremonies) and Irenaeus' explanation of it revolve around Christ's victory. And Irenaeus insists on defining that victory as the completion and climax of God's economium in creation and in the Old Testament. To be sure, when the Christian appropriated the victory, he found both a promise enabling a life of virtue and a demand requiring it. But the promise and demand of the victory bound the believer to the Christian community and were mediated to him in that setting. These themes remain consistent throughout the patristic period.[9]

A second important point about Paul's use of the metaphor of slavery is that it is a two-part metaphor. Where it occurs in the context of transition, it is used simply to describe the change wrought in conversion. While Paul does look forward to a future of freedom and adoption for all believers,[10] his main concern, when using the metaphor of slavery, is to stress the movement from one's previous life into a new one. The state which one must seek as a believer is the escape out of slavery to sin into a new state of slavery to God or freedom in God. This two-part metaphor is clearly reflective of the interests and emphasis of Paul's theology, expressing thereby an emphasis on conversion and the beginning of Christian life as a thorough escape from the baneful influences of the pagan world.

In the Gospel of John, however, we find the possible traces of a different and more complex version of the metaphor. Here it is the

7.   'Celsus and Julian the Apostate were not the only mockers at the crucified God. Can we blame those who were attacked in this way if they sought to retouch the image of the cross, to obviate the *scandalum crucis*?', A. Grillmeier, *Christ in Christian Tradition, from the Apostolic Age to Chalcedon (451)* (trans. J.S. Bowden; Oxford: Mowbrays, 1965), p. 84. Further on the paradox of the Cross and Christian suffering, see A.T. Hanson, *The Paradox of the Cross in the Thought of St Paul* (JSNTSup, 17; Sheffield: JSOT Press, 1987).

8.   Hengel, *The Cross of the Son of God*, pp. 109-10. See also p. 113.

9.   R.A. Greer, *Broken Lights and Mended Lives: Theology and Common Life in the Early Church* (Pennsylvania: Pennsylvania State University Press, 1986), p. 43.

10.   Rom. 8.18-25.

unbeliever or the imperfect believer who is as a slave in relationship
with God. This slave is, however, given the chance to be no longer a
slave but a son or daughter or friend. Thus the one who, through sin,
is a slave in relationship to God may be set free to relate to him as a
freeman and as a son or daughter. In this way, the disciples were
slaves in the early stages of their relationship with Christ, but they
then came to be his friends instead. In its most basic form, this use of
the metaphor is essentially a regression to its older use by philosophers, especially by the Stoics, in which the unenlightened and uninformed nature is seen as slave, and the wise and disciplined nature as
free.

2. *Patristic Use of the Metaphor*

Aspects of both the Pauline and the Johannine versions of the
metaphor continued to be used after the New Testament, and as time
went on, the metaphor began to emerge in the form of a three-part
formula, representing the spiritual journey not so much as a dramatic
change from slavery to freedom as a progression from one kind of
slavery to another, and through this into adoption and freedom. Thus,
two sets of variations emerge:

A.
1. The saint or martyr as slave of God.
2. Clergy as slaves of God.
3. Persecuted Christians in general as slaves of God.
4. Old Testament heroes (and sometimes Jesus) as slaves of
   God.
5. Conversion as a *slavery to sin → slavery to (or freedom in)
   God* progression.

B.
6. The unbeliever as, by nature, a slave of God.
7. Jews as slaves of God.
8. Humans in general as slaves of God, in virtue of having been
   created by him.
9. Conversion as a *slavery to God → freedom or sonship in
   God* progression.
10. Spiritual growth as *slavery to sin → slavery to God → son-
    ship in God*.

On one hand, thus, in category A, *slave* is used in recognition of Christian commitment. It describes the people of God who hold onto their faith in the face of persecution by pagans or heretics and is used for and by bishops, saints, martyrs and sometimes, even, emperors. On the other, in Category B,[11] it has become an expression of at best the beginning of one's journey, the bottom of the spiritual ladder, and at worst, of inadequacy and lack of faith, of a spiritual state to be avoided at all costs.

3. *The Problem of the Metaphor*

When the metaphor of slavery first appears in the Pauline writings, the paradox of the use of such language is clear and is used to great effect. When the metaphor is continued in the patristic age, this paradox ceases to have ongoing power and the use of this language simply becomes problematic, due to its inevitable associations with humiliation and degradation. Those who continue to use this language in the forms used in category A are therefore forced to develop explanations and justifications, both for their own use of the metaphor and for its use within the New Testament texts. There are several arguments that prove to be popular, the most common being to argue that slavery to God actually implies great glory and privilege, to deny that slavery to God is actually slavery at all in the proper sense of the word, or to argue that it is qualitatively different from any kind of slavery experienced in the secular sphere.

a. *That Slavery is an Honour*
We have seen that one solution to the problem is to argue that slavery to God is preferable to earthly honour. Let us consider the perception of honour that would lie behind such a statement. The statement that slavery to God is better than, or preferable to, earthly honour may be interpreted in one of two ways, either in terms of a scale or in terms of a paradox:

1. As a question of scale: the relationship with God may be seen as such a great good that even in its humblest form it exceeds the greatest human honour. Slavery lies at the bottom of the scale of relationship with God, but even here it exceeds the pinnacle of earthly greatness

---

11. With the exception of 8 (the idea of people in general as slaves of God), which is generally used in a relatively neutral manner.

and is valued by the bearer beyond any earthly status. This is a common enough formula in any context:

> I would rather be a doorkeeper in the house of my God than dwell in the tents of the wicked.[12]

> ... it is a better and greater thing to be in the lowest rank with God than to win the first place with an earthly king.[13]

This form, of course, leaves room for the extension of the metaphor to include potential growth up the scale from slave to son or friend. It does challenge human notions of greatness to an extent, but only by asserting that human greatness is inadequate and that there is a scale of greatness that far exceeds it.

2. The second interpretation is a direct challenge to the great-greater-greatest notion. Here the assertion of the preferability of slavery inverts the perceived human social values, discrediting the ideas of honour and precedence, asserting that 'If anyone wishes to be first, he must be the very last, and the διάκονος of all'.[14]

It is fairly clear that although the second of these is more consistent with the Gospel and New Testament background, the interest of the Fathers is much more in the former category. The concern is clearly to set slavery to God on the plane of earthly honour and to demand that its surpassing of all others be recognized. Paul, for instance, when he uses the term in the salutations of his letters, is seen as behaving in a way exactly parallel to those who hold earthly office—displaying his divine credentials in the same way as the 'judges of this age'[15] do theirs, and while the humility of the Apostle in reducing himself to the status of those around him is sometimes suggested as an explanation for his use of such humble terminology, the discussion of humiliation for its own sake, as a challenge to earthly values of status and superiority, is conspicuously absent from these writings.

12. Ps. 84.10.
13. Gregory Nazianzus, *Oration* 7.9.
14. Mk 9.35.
15. Jerome, *On Titus* (PL 36.555-58). See also Didymus of Alexandria in his commentary on Jas 1.1: 'Just as men, wishing for mortal glory, place first in their writings those dignities which they think they possess; in the same way, the holy men, in the epistles which they write to the churches, principally declare themselves slaves of our Lord Jesus Christ, considering this title to be better than rule of the whole world' (PG 39.1749 A; see also 1481).

b. *That Slavery to God is True Freedom*
The second solution is related to the first and lies in the assertion that slavery to God is not really slavery at all but freedom. This may be because it is given in the spirit of adoption and therefore leads to sonship, serving not under the constraint of fear, but out of love. It may also be so from the fact that the only real bondage is that which sin exerts over humanity, so that by becoming a slave of God one becomes free of sin—thus attaining the only true freedom.

An extension of this theme can be seen in the conviction that begins to emerge during this period but which will later be most fully argued by Augustine, that human beings are inescapably a slave of one or the other—they can be a slave to sin or a slave to God; there is no third choice.

c. *That Slavery to God is a Particular Kind of Slavery*
This approach to this problem lies in an analysis of the kind of slavery that is meant by 'slave of God'. A distinction is drawn between slavery to God and slavery to anything else, in order to emphasize that the implications of subservience and degradation which are part of other forms of slavery do not apply to slavery to God. A further distinction is drawn between the kinds of slavery to God that are possible, so that slavery leading to fear may be distinguished from slavery leading to love, even though both may be slaveries to God.

When we look, therefore, at the form of the metaphor of slavery in the patristic period we see that two things have happened to it. In the first place, the three-part metaphor has come into its own, becoming a complex structure that blends well with the increasing recognition of the complexity of Christian life and progress. Secondly, the emphasis on the humility is lost and replaced by an assurance of the glory, happiness and, indeed, freedom that such a state entails. As the emphasis on the latter grows, so does the emphasis on the glory that this implies. What we are left with, therefore, is a situation that might seem puzzling—an apparent contradiction where two seemingly incompatible metaphors are being used, that is, on the one hand it is a great thing to be a slave of God, and on the other it is a state of inadequacy to be only his slave.

4. *Metaphor and Society*

I began this study by discussing the relationship between the structure of secular society and that of religious language, and set out to discover the effect of the former upon the latter. If it be argued that it is the structure of society that controls the form of such metaphors, we should expect one of two things in the society in question, either that slavery would have changed to the point where the word *slave* had no contemporary context and could thus be used either positively or negatively, or that this contradiction reflected a contradiction in the perception of slaves in the society.

From the early Empire onwards there certainly begins to be a distinct change in the personal relationship between a master and his slave. In the first place the personal responsibility for the slave begins to weaken as the state takes an ever more active part in the slave's control and well-being.[16] The processes by which slaves could appeal against their master were also extended. Manumission, which originally was left entirely to the discretion of the master, was compassed round with various limitations. The Christianization of the Empire also saw the enactment of further legislation protecting, at least in theory, the physical and spiritual well-being of the slave. The boundaries between the slave and the free are also made more hazy as physical torture, once reserved for slaves alone, is extended, first to the *humiliores* and then through all ranks of society.[17] This, it must be stressed, indicates not only the loss of certain privileges or a growing brutality in the law, but a fundamental change in the idea of the person—a slave was originally the only human whose body was at the disposal of others for physical coercion, and the extension of torture out of this class shows a breaking of these barriers. Finally, as the

16. On the legal enactments that reflected this, see K.R. Bradley, *Slaves and Masters in the Roman Empire*, pp. 126-27; Westermann, *The Slave Systems in Greek and Roman Antiquity*, pp. 114-15; and Griffin, *Seneca*, pp. 268-69. 'It is beyond question that in the fourth century, men accused of crimes were liable to torture; only soldiers and persons of rank were exempt, and this exemption did not extend to charges of treason and (on occasion) of magic and forgery', P.A. Brunt, 'Evidence Given under Torture in the Principate', *ZRG* 97 (1980), pp. 256-65.

17. P.D. Garnsey and R. Saller, *Social Status and Legal Privilege in the Roman Empire* (Oxford: Clarendon Press, 1970), p. 152, and P.D. Garnsey and R. Saller, *The Roman Empire: Economy, Society and Culture* (London: Gerald Duckworth, 1987), p. 118. See also J. Evans-Grubbs, *Law and the Family*, p. 6.

empire moves into the fifth and sixth centuries, the emphasis on slaves as the main mode of production begins to wane and in its place comes the emerging colonate.

One glance at Chrysostom or Augustine however, is sufficient to show that, despite such changes, the institution of slavery, with all its old miseries still flourished. Out in the rural areas, slavery was beginning to give way to serfdom, but within the cities, the individual domination of the slave by the master in the domestic setting continued, probably in much the same way as ever, in spite of the legislative enactments that sought to improve the slave's lot.

In the forms of the metaphor we can, to some extent, find the occasional thread that appears to run parallel to the society at large. One might look to the other great change that would have affected our sources, the change of Christianity from being a persecuted minority religion to a recognized and wealthy state institution. It might be argued that the new respectability, status and wealth of the Church meant that its formulae which once expressed humility and abasement now took on new connotations consistent with power and honour. We might look to the ever greater emphasis on the kingship of Christ, the numerous writers and artists who depict him as an imperial ruler, surrounded by his court, his kingdom managed by an elite of imperial slaves for whom the title *slave of Christ*, like the title *slave of Caesar*, was an indication of status and power, expressing their membership of this elite and their proximity to the ruler which gave them the power of controlling access to him and of acting as intermediaries, receiving as his agents the honour due to the ruler.

All this would be well and good, if it were only necessary to explain why the idea of slavery to God has gone up the social scale—being changed from an expression of humiliation to one of glory. However, it is equally necessary to explain an equally important downward trend in the metaphor, in which it has changed from being an expression of humiliation (in which, nonetheless, one found one's proper relationship with God) to being an expression of a lack of faith and a personal inadequacy, a state which one is called to avoid or to strive to grow out of. The main feature of the metaphor of slavery in the patristic period is the contradiction in its use, a contradiction which cannot be satisfactorily explained by changes in society, but which indicates the power of theology in keeping language alive. The different forms of the metaphor continued to exist side by side in spite of their apparent contradiction because they were useful, because in their own contexts they were able to express aspects of the theology that the writer sought to articulate. In one, the image of a transition from slavery to sonship provided an excellent illustration for the progress of the believer in his spiritual life, and in another, the image of the slave of God was a useful label indicating the commitment and responsibility of the cleric and the saint. Because these were so effective they remained alive. While on one hand, those who rely on a social definition of slavery and its implications might be puzzled by the apparent contradiction in calling an inadequate believer 'only a slave of God' while praising a bishop as being 'a true slave of God', these uses make entire sense to the one who approaches the word by means of the theological context in which they are used, and the intentions of the individual users.

In this work, we have been looking at a metaphor which, although it originated from a particular social milieu, took on a life of its own and developed forms which in many ways seem at odds with the society in which it was used. It seems to have evolved independently of its social climate, being moulded more by the theology it sought to articulate than by the details of the society it might be thought to have been reflecting. What consequences does this have for religious language as a whole? It provides, I believe, a reason for the disentanglement of religious language from contemporary society, freeing it from the need to seek social relevance and understanding. Religious metaphors, as we have seen in this case, are dependent for their meaning on far more than their dictionary definition, and they cannot be understood simply by discovering what they would have meant to a person living in the time and social context of the writer. This should, however, also be a source of great liberation in religious language. Janet Soskice points out that

> It is a commonplace that in the twentieth century we have lost the living sense of the biblical metaphors which our forefathers had. Sometimes it is suggested that this is a consequence of urban life where few have any contact with shepherds and sheep, kings and vines. This simple view fails to see that the distinctively Christian reading of the metaphors of God as shepherd, or king or vinekeeper could never be had simply by knowing about sheep, kings, and vines...[18]

18. J.M. Soskice, *Metaphor and Religious Language* (Oxford: Clarendon Press, 1985), pp. 158-60.

Yet we may go even further and say that this 'living sense' is nothing more than peripheral to the meaning of the metaphor and that where a metaphor articulates theology efficiently, only the basic knowledge of the reality it draws on is needed. The advantages of this are obvious, for if religious writers may be set free from the notion that metaphors must be socially relevant for the time, then the great store of religious imagery laid up over the centuries becomes available to them. If it is the theology and spirit of a faith that gives life to the metaphors, then each stage of the unfolding of theology may give an opportunity for their resurrection. Perhaps the metaphor we have just been discussing is a case in point—in a theology of the humanity, humility and vulnerability of Christ and of his alignment with the poor and outcast, a language of slavery, even in a culture without the social context of such a metaphor, could enjoy a very valuable rebirth.

APPENDIX
INDICES TO USES OF THE δοῦλος TITLE

The following indices have been prepared from the *Thesaurus Linguae Grecae* using the *Ibycus* system. They show the occurrence, in selected Christian writers, of the following variations:

δοῦλος Θεοῦ	δοῦλος τοῦ Θεοῦ	Θεοῦ δοῦλος
δοῦλος Χριστοῦ	δοῦλος τοῦ Χριστοῦ	Χριστοῦ δοῦλος
δοῦλος Ἰησοῦ	δοῦλος τοῦ Ἰησοῦ	Ἰησοῦ δοῦλος
δοῦλος Κυρίου	δοῦλος τοῦ Κυρίου	Κυρίου δοῦλος

The full declensions of all these have also been applied, and the results have been collated into the following indices. Spurious and dubious works attributed to the various writers are not included. A similar New Testament index follows the patristic indices. It must be remembered that these indices concern the use of the specific phrases mentioned above and therefore do not include other forms of the metaphor of slavery.

The Shepherd of Hermas[1]

Μηδαμῶς ἐπὶ **τὸν δοῦλον τοῦ Θεοῦ** τὸ πρᾶγμα τοῦτο (2.4.1-2).

ἔστιν μὲν **τοῖς δούλοις τοῦ Θεοῦ** ἡ τοιαύτη βουλὴ ἁμαρτίαν ἐπιφέρουσα (2.4.3).

ἔδει γάρ σε ὡς **Θεοῦ δοῦλον** (28.4.2).

ἡ γὰρ ἐνθύμησις αὕτη **Θεοῦ δούλῳ** ἁμαρτία μεγάλη ἐστίν (29.2.3).

τοῖς γὰρ **δούλοις τοῦ Θεοῦ** μετάνοιά ἐστιν μία (29.8.4).

ὅτι ποιήσει τι κακὸν **τοῖς δούλοις τοῦ Θεοῦ** καὶ πονηρεύσεται εἰς αὐτούς (31.4.4).

καὶ πῶς **τοὺς δούλους τοῦ Θεοῦ** καταστρέφει τῇ ἑαυτῆς ἐνεργείᾳ...34.1.2

ταῦτα γὰρ πάντα μωρά ἐστι καὶ κενὰ καὶ ἄφρονα καὶ ἀσύμφορα **τοῖς δούλοις τοῦ Θεοῦ** (34.2.6–3.1).

---

1. *Der Hirt des Hermas, Die apostolichen Väter I* (ed. M. Whittaker; GCS, 48; Berlin: W. de Gruyter, 2nd edn, 1967).

καὶ τὰ ἔργα αὐτοῦ πονηρά καταστρέφοντα **τοὺς δούλους τοῦ Θεοῦ** (36.4.2-3).

ὅτι τὰ ἔργα αὐτοῦ πονηρά εἰσι καὶ ἀσύμφορα **τοῖς δούλοις τοῦ Θεοῦ** (36.6.2-3).

ἀπὸ τούτων οὖν τῶν ἔργων δεῖ ἐγκρατεύεσθαι **τὸν δοῦλον τοῦ Θεοῦ** (38.4.2).

καί γε πολλά, φησίν, ἔστιν ἀφ᾽ ὧν δεῖ **τὸν δοῦλον τοῦ Θεοῦ** ἐγκρατεύεσθαι (38.5.2).

καὶ λίαν πονηρά, φημί, **τοῖς δούλοις τοῦ Θεοῦ** (38.6.2).

ἐξ ἀναγκῶν λυτροῦσθαι **τοὺς δούλους τοῦ Θεοῦ** (38.10.3).

καὶ λίαν πονηρεύεται εἰς **τοὺς δούλους τοῦ Θεοῦ** (39.9.3).

ἡ λύπη πάντων τῶν πνευμάτων πονηροτέρα ἐστί καὶ δεινοτάτη **τοῖς δούλοις τοῦ Θεοῦ** (40.2.3-4).

καὶ ὁ καθήμενος ἐπὶ τὴν καθέδραν ψευδοπροφήτης ἐστίν ἀπολλύων τὴν διάνοιαν **τῶν δούλων τοῦ Θεοῦ** (43.1.4).

μάλιστα δὲ ἐὰν ἐμπέσῃ εἰς αὐτὴν **δοῦλος Θεοῦ** καὶ μὴ ἦ συνετός (44.2.2-3).

ἄκουε, φησίν, ἐν ποίοις ἔργοις θανατοῖ ἡ ἐπιθυμία ἡ πονηρὰ **τοὺς δούλους τοῦ Θεοῦ** (44.3.3-4).

πᾶσα γὰρ τρυφὴ μωρά ἐστι καὶ κενὴ **τοῖς δούλοις τοῦ Θεοῦ** (45.1.3–2.1).

αὗται οὖν αἱ ἐπιθυμίαι πονηραί εἰσι, θανατοῦσαι **τοὺς δούλους τοῦ Θεοῦ** (45.2.1-2).

ταῦτα ἐργαζόμενος εὐάρεστος ἔσῃ **δοῦλος τοῦ Θεοῦ** καὶ ζήσῃ αὐτῷ (46.1.4).

οὐ δύναται, φησί, καταδυναστεύειν **τῶν δούλων τοῦ Θεοῦ** τῶν ἐξ ὅλης καρδίας ἐλπιζόντων ἐπ᾽ αὐτόν (48.2.1-2).

ὁ διάβολος ἔρχεται ἐπὶ πάντας **τοὺς δούλους τοῦ Θεοῦ** ἐκπειράζων αὐτούς (48.4.2).

οἴδατε, φησίν, ὅτι ἐπὶ ξένης κατοικεῖτε ὑμεῖς **οἱ δοῦλοι τοῦ Θεοῦ** (50.1.1).

ἀσύμφορον γάρ ἐστιν ὑμῖν **τοῖς δούλοις τοῦ Θεοῦ** (50.10.3–11.1).

ταῦτα τὰ δύο δένδρα, φησίν, εἰς τύπον κεῖνται **τοῖς δούλοις τοῦ Θεοῦ** (51.2.2).

αὕτη οὖν ἡ παραβολὴ εἰς **τοὺς δούλους τοῦ Θεοῦ** κεῖται (51.4.5).

ὃς ἄν **δοῦλος** ἦν, φησίν, **τοῦ Θεοῦ** (57.3.1)

αἱ δὲ βοτάναι αἱ ἐκτετιλμέναι ἐκ τοῦ ἀμπελῶνος ἀνομίαι εἰσί **τῶν δούλων τοῦ Θεοῦ** (58.3.2-3).

οὗτος οὖν ἐκτρίβει τὰς ψυχὰς **τῶν δούλων τοῦ Θεοῦ** (62.1.2-3).

αὗται πᾶσαι τρυφαὶ βλαβεραί εἰσιν **τοῖς δούλοις τοῦ Θεοῦ** (65.6.1).

αὕτη οὖν ἡ τρυφὴ σύμφορός ἐστιν **τοῖς δούλοις τοῦ Θεοῦ** (65.7.2-3).

ἦσαν γὰρ ὑποκριταὶ καὶ διδαχὰς ἑτέρας εἰσφέροντες καὶ ἐκστρέφοντες **τοὺς δούλους τοῦ Θεοῦ** (72.5.2-3).

ἡδέως εἰς τοὺς οἴκους αὐτῶν ὑπεδέξαντο **τοὺς δούλους τοῦ Θεοῦ** (76.3.4).

οὖν τὰ πνεύματα ταῦτα ἐνεδυναμώθησαν καὶ ἦσαν μετὰ **τῶν δούλων τοῦ Θεοῦ** (90.7.3).

ταῦτα τὰ ὀνόματα ὁ φορῶν **τοῦ Θεοῦ δοῦλος** τὴν βασιλείαν μὲν ὄψεται τοῦ Θεοῦ, εἰς αὐτὴν δὲ οὐκ εἰσελεύσεται (92.3.5–4.1).

ἀποστάται καὶ βλάσφημοι εἰς τὸν κύριον καὶ προδόται **τῶν δούλων τοῦ Θεοῦ** (96.1.2).

ὅτι οὔκ ἐβλασφήμησαν τὸν κύριον αὐτῶν οὐδὲ ἐγένοντο προδόται **τῶν δούλων τοῦ Θεοῦ** (96.3.3-4).

οὐ κολλῶνται **τοῖς δούλοις τοῦ Θεοῦ** (97.2.2).

κολλῶνται **τοῖς δούλοις τοῦ Θεοῦ** (97.2.4).

ἀλλὰ πάντοτε ἀγαλλιώμενοι ἐπὶ **τοῖς δούλοις τοῦ Θεοῦ** (101.2.2-3).

μὴ κολλώμενοι **τοῖς δούλοις τοῦ Θεοῦ** (103.3.3).

οἵτινες ἡδέως εἰς τοὺς οἴκους ἑαυτῶν πάντοτε ὑπεδέξαντο **τοὺς δούλους τοῦ Θεοῦ** ἄτερ ὑποκρίσεως (104.2.2)

The Acts of John[2]
λέγει σοι **ὁ τοῦ Θεοῦ δοῦλος Ἰωάννης** ἀνάστα (47.7).

καὶ ἔστε πόρρω **τῶν δούλων τοῦ Θεοῦ** (60.11-12).

συνεῖδον τὸ γεγονὸς μακάριε **δοῦλε τοῦ Θεοῦ Ἰωάννη** (74.3-4).

τίς μὲν οὖν ἦν οὔκ ᾔδειν **δοῦλε τοῦ Θεοῦ** (76.20-21).

ὁ δὲ Βῆρος μὴ μελλήσας διεπράξατο ὁ ἐκελεύσθη ὑπὸ **τοῦ δούλου τοῦ Θεοῦ Ἰωάννου** (111.3-4).

ὅπως καὶ οἱ ἐκεῖ **δοῦλοι τοῦ Χριστοῦ** ἐπιστρέψουσι πρὸς αὐτόν (45.3-4).

ὁ δὲ **τοῦ κυρίου δοῦλος Ἰωάννης** (51.5-6).

Μηδαμῶς ἀπολλώμεθα **δοῦλε τοῦ θεοῦ** (Recensio[3] 42.8-9).

---

2. *Acta Joannis (Acta Apostolorum Apocrypha*; ed. R.A. Lipsius and M. Bonnet; Darmstadt: Georg Olms, 1891–98; repr. 1972).

3. *Acta Joannis: Recensio* (Lipsius and Bonnet [eds.], *Acta Apostolorum Apocrypha*).

Origen

εἰσὶ γὰρ καὶ ἐν τῇ ψυχῇ μόνῃ τῷ καρδίας βλέποντι χαρακτῆρες φανεροὶς **δούλων Θεοῦ** καὶ υἱῶν αὐτοῦ (*On Prayer*[4] 16.1.14-15).

τῇ πρὸ τῶν τέκνων τοῦ Θεοῦ καταστάσει τῶν πεπιστευκότων μόνον **δοῦλοι Θεοῦ** τῷ εἰληφέναι τὸ τῆς δουλείας εἰς φόβον πνεῦμα (*Commentary on John*[5] 20.33.289.4).

δοῦλος δὲ ὢν τῆς ἁμαρτίας, οὐκ ἦν **τοῦ λόγου τοῦ Θεοῦ δοῦλος** (*Commentary on John*[6] 32.13.149.1–150.1).

καὶ ἡμεῖς δὲ οὐκ ἦμεν **δοῦλοι τοῦ Θεοῦ**, ἀλλὰ εἰδώλων καὶ δαιμόνων (*On Jeremiah*[7] 4.5.54-55).

τινὰς μὲν τῶν πεπιστευκέναι νομιζομένων λέγεσθαι **δούλους τοῦ Θεοῦ** (*On Jeremiah*[8] 20.17.146.1-2).

καὶ τάχα ὥσπερ ἔστιν μεταβαλεῖν ἐκ **δούλου Ἰησοῦ** (*Commentary on John*[9] 30.374.1-2).

ὅτι οὐ **δούλοις τοῦ Ἰησοῦ** ἀλλὰ φίλοις αὐτοῦ δέδοται ἐντολὴ ἥδε (*Exhortation to Martyrdom*[10] 34.79).

εἰ Παῦλος ὁ ἀπόστολος **δοῦλος Χριστοῦ** (*Exposition on Proverbs*[11] 7.185.30).

τὸ ὑπ᾽ αὐτῶν ὁμολογούμενον περὶ αὐτῶν ὡς εἶναι **δοῦλοι τοῦ κυρίου** (*Scholia on the Apocalypse*[12] 1.2-3).

Scriptural Citations
Ἰούδας Ἰησοῦ Χριστοῦ δοῦλος, ἀδελφὸς δὲ Ἰακώβου (*Commentary on Matthew* 2[13] 10.17.42-43).

Χριστοῦ δοῦλον (*Commentary on Romans* 2[14] 2.27).

4. *On Prayer* (*Origenes' Werke*; ed. P. Koetschau; GCS, 3.2; Leipzig: Hinrichs, 1899).
5. *Commentary on John* (*Origenes' Werke*, ed. E. Preuschen; [lib.19,20,28,32], [GCS 10; Leipzig: Hinrichs, 1911).
6. *Commentary on John* (GCS, 10).
7. *On Jeremiah* (*Origene: Homilies sur Jérémie*, vol. 1 [hom.1–11]; ed. P. Nautin; SC, 232; Paris: Cerf, 1976).
8. *On Jeremiah* (SC, 232).
9. *Commentary on John* (GCS, 10).
10. *Exhortation to Martyrdom* (*Origenes' Werke*; vol. 1; ed. P. Kpetschau; GCS, 2; Leipzig: Hinrichs, 1899).
11. *Exposition on Proverbs* (PG 17).
12. *Scholia on the Apocalypse* (scholia 1.3-39) (*Der Scholien-Kommentar des Origenes zur Apocalypse Johannis*; ed. C. Diobouniotis and A. von Harnack; TU, 38.3; Leipzig: Hinrichs).
13. *Commentary on Matthew (110–11)* (*Origene; Commentarie sur l'évangile selon Matthieu*; vol. 1; ed. R. Girod; SC, 162; Paris: Cerf, 1970).
14. *Commentary on Romans* (ed. K. Staab, 'Neue Fragmente aus dem Kommentar des Origenes zum Romerbrief', *BZ* 18 [1928]).

...ἕως σφραγῖδας ἐπὶ τῶν μετώπων λάβωσιν οἱ τοῦ Θεοῦ δοῦλοι, ἐντέλλεται (*Scholia on the Apocalypse* 2[15] 31.3).

...ἄρχι σφραγίσωμεν τοὺς δούλους τοῦ Θεοῦ ἡμῶν (*Commentary on John*[16] 1.1.2.7; 4.6).

δοῦλος τοῦ Θεοῦ (*Commentary on John*[17] 1.32.228.6).

ἐτυφλώθησαν οἱ δοῦλοι τοῦ Θεοῦ (*Dialogue with Heraclides*[18] 17.16; *Commentary on Matthew*[19]16.3.113-15).

οὗτοι οἱ ἄνθρωποι δοῦλοι τοῦ Θεοῦ τοῦ ὑψίστου εἰσίν (*Commentary on John*[20] 28.16.130.5-6).

variations on Παῦλος δοῦλος Ἰησοῦ Χριστοῦ (*Commentary on Romans* 2[21] 1.4; 1.15; 1.20; 2.4; 2.6; *Commentary on Romans* 3[22] 1.1; *Philo*[23] 5.1.29; *Philo* 2[24] 35.1.28; *Commentary on John* 2[25] 19.5.31.2; *Commentary on Matthew*[26] 240.9).

...οἷον ὅτι βέλος ἐκλεκτὸς ἑαυτὸν καλεῖ καὶ δοῦλον τοῦ Θεοῦ (*Commentary on John*[27] 1.22.133.2).

Clement of Alexandria
καὶ παραθέντα τῇ σοφίᾳ τὴν ἀκοὴν νόμιμον εἶναι **Θεοῦ δοῦλον** μὲν τὰ πρῶτα (*Stromata*[28] 1.27.173.6.2-3).

15. *Scholia on the Apocalypse* (ed. C.H. Turner, 'Document: Origen, scholia in Apocalypsin', *JTS* 25 [1923], pp. 1-15).
16. *Commentary on John* (*Origene; Commentaire sur Saint Jean*; vol. 1; ed. C. Blanc; SC, 120; Paris: Cerf, 1966).
17. *Commentary on John* (SC 120).
18. *Dialogue with Heraclides* (*Entretien d' Origene avec Heraclide*; ed. J. Sherer; SC, 67; Paris: Cerf, 1976).
19. *Commentary on Matthew* (*Origenes Werke*; vol 10.1–10.2; ed. E. Klostermann; GCS 40.1–40.2; Leipzig: Teubner, 1935, 1937).
20. *Commentary on the Gospel of John* (GCS, 10).
21. *Commentary on Romans* (Staab).
22. *Commentary on Romans* (*Der Römerbrieftext des Origenes nach dem Codex von der Goltz*; ed. O. Baurenfeind; TUS 44.3; Leipzig: Hinrichs, 1923).
23. *Philocalia* (chs. 1–27; *The Philocalia of Origen*; ed. J.A. Robinson; Cambridge: Cambridge University Press, 1893).
24. *Philocalia* (chs. 23, 25, 27; *Origene; Philocalia 21–27. Sur le libre arbitre*; ed. E. Junod; SC, 226; Paris: Cerf, 1976).
25. *Commentary on the Gospel of John* (GCS, 10).
26. *Commentary on Matthew* (*Origenes Werke*; vol. 11; ed. E. Klostermann; GCS, 38.2; Leipzig: Teubner, 1933).
27. *Commentary on the Gospel of John* (GCS, 10).
28. *Stromata* (ed. O. Stahlin, L. Fruchtel and U. Treu; GCS, 52).

178 *The Metaphor of Slavery in the Writings of the Early Church*

ὡς ζηλώσας ἐπὶ τῇ ἀφέσει τῶν ἁμαρτιῶν τὸν ἄνθρωπον προστρίψεταί τινας αἰτίας τῶν ἁμαρτημάτων **τοῖς δούλοις τοῦ Θεοῦ** (*Stromata*[29] 2.13.56.2.4-5).

πᾶς ὁ λαὸς ὁ σῳζόμενος, **δοῦλος Θεοῦ** δι᾽ ὑπακοὴν ἐντολῆς κεκλημένος (*Eclogae Propheticae*[30] 61.1.2).

Αὐτίκα **δοῦλος Θεοῦ** ἅμα τῷ ἀνελθεῖν τοῦ βαπτίσματος (*Excerpta Theodoto*[31] 4.77.3.1).

καὶ εἶπεν πρὸς αὐτούς· **δοῦλος κυρίου** ἐγώ εἰμι (*Stromata*[32] 5.14.135.4.2).

Scriptural Citations
...μὴ ὡς ἐπικάλυμμα ἔκοντες τῆς κακίας τὴν ἐλευθερίαν, ἀλλ᾽ ὡς δοῦλοι Θεοῦ (*Stromata*[33] 3.11.75.2.3–3.10).

Athanasius
πολλὰ μὲν καὶ πολλάκις ἐτόλμησαν οἱ Ἀρειομανῖται κατὰ **τῶν δούλων τοῦ Θεοῦ** (*Arians*[34] 42.2.1).

ἀληθῶς εἶναι **τοῦτον δοῦλον τοῦ θεοῦ** (*Vit. Ant.*[35] 26.964.3).

τοῦ ἀληθῶς **Θεοῦ δούλου** Βασιλείου τοῦ ἐπισκόπου (*Epistle to John*[36] 26.1168.12-13).

συγκαλέσας **τοὺς τοῦ Θεοῦ δούλους** (*Epistle to Marcellus*[37] 27.33.56).

ὁ **τοῦ Θεοῦ δοῦλος** οὐκ ἀφίσταται τῶν δικαιωμάτων αὐτοῦ (*Expositions on the Psalms*[38] 27.484.38).

τὴν ἐλευθέριον ἡμέραν **τοῖς τοῦ Χριστοῦ δούλοις** πένθος πεποιήκασιν (*Encyclical Epistle*[39] 5.3.6).

τοὺς δὲ τοῦ Χριστοῦ δούλους οὐκ ἤφιει (*History of the Arians*[40] 68.2.5).

καὶ ὁ μὲν Ἀντώνιος μόνον ἑαυτὸν ἐσφράγισε, καὶ εἶπε· **Χριστοῦ δοῦλος** εἰμι (*Vit. Ant.*[41] 920.10-11).

29. *Stromata* (GCS, 52).
30. *Eclogae Propheticae* (ed. O. Stahlin, L. Fruchtel and U. Treu; GCS, 52; vol. 3).
31. *Excerpta ex Theodoto* (*Clément d'Alexandrie*; *Extraits de Théodoto*; ed. F. Sagnard; SCS 23; Paris: Cerf, 1948).
32. *Stromata* (GCS, 52).
33. *Stromata* (GCS, 52).
34. *Against the Arians* (*Athanasius Werke*; vol. 2.1; ed. H.G. Opitz; Berlin: W. de Gruyter, 1934).
35. *Life of Anthony* (PG 26).
36. *Epistle to John and the Priests of Antioch* (PG 26).
37. *Epistle to Marcellus on the Interpretation of the Psalms* (PG 27).
38. *Expositions on the Psalms* (PG 27).
39. *Encyclical Epistle* (Opitz).
40. *History of the Arians* (Opitz).
41. *Life of Anthony* (PG 26).

δοῦλοι μὲν αὐτοῦ οἱ ἅγιοι ἀπόστολοι, ὡς Παῦλος, **δοῦλος Ἰησοῦ Χριστοῦ** (*Expositions on the Psalms*[42] 27.313.34-35).

οἱ δέ γε ἐπίσκοποι, οἱ ἀληθῶς γνήσιοι **δοῦλοι τοῦ Κυρίου** (*Epistle to the African Bishops*[43] 1033.30-31).

Scriptural Citations
ἰδοὺ δὴ εὐλογεῖτε τὸν Κύριον, πάντες οἱ δοῦλοι Κυρίου (*Expositions on the Psalms*[44] 524.41).

εἰς τέλος τῷ δούλῳ Κυρίου τῷ Δαυίδ (*Expositions on the Psalms*[45] 173.22).

Παῦλος δοῦλος Ἰησοῦ Χριστοῦ, κλητὸς ἀπόστολος (*Expositions on the Psalms*[46] 476.12-13)

Eusebius
καὶ προγυμνάζων κατὰ **τῶν δούλων τοῦ Θεοῦ** (*Ecclesiastical History*[47] 5.1.5.4-5).

καὶ παραινῶν μὴ παρὰ φύσιν τολμᾶν κατὰ **τῶν τοῦ Θεοῦ δούλων** (*Martyrs of Palestine*[48] 5.3.10-11).

τῆς παρὰ τῷ Θεῷ γραφῆς καταξιωθήσονται καὶ · ἅγιοι κληθήσονται· **τοῦ Θεοῦ δοῦλοι** (*Martyrs of Palestine*[49] 2.3.77.11-12).

ὡς ἄρα οἱ τὸν τόπον μιάναντες μολλοὺς ἀνεῖλον ὁσίους ἄνδρας καὶ **Θεοῦ δούλους** (*Commentary on Psalms*[50] 941.35-36).

οὕτω καὶ πάντων τῶν ἀληθῶς **τοῦ Θεοῦ δούλων** (*Commentary on Psalms*[51] 988.41-42).

καὶ ὀνειδιζόντων **τοὺς δούλους τοῦ Θεοῦ** διὰ τὰ συμβεβηκότα (*Commentary on Psalms*[52] 1121.16-17).

κτημάτων δὲ καὶ αὐχημάτων τὸ μέγιστον χρηματίσαι **Θεοῦ δοῦλον** (*Commentary on Psalms*[53] 24.52.34-35).

42. *Expositions on the Psalms* (PG 27).
43. *Epistle to the African Bishops* (PG 26).
44. *Expositions on the Psalms* (PG 27).
45. *Expositions on the Psalms* (PG 27).
46. *Expositions on the Psalms* (PG 27).
47. *History of the Church Histoire ecclésiastique* (ed. G. Bardy; SC, 31, 41, 55; Paris: Cerf, 1952, 1955, 1958).
48. *The Martyrs of Palestine* (SC, 55).
49. *The Martyrs of Palestine* (SC, 55).
50. *Commentary on the Psalms* (PG 23).
51. *Commentary on the Psalms* (PG 23).
52. *Commentary on the Psalms* (PG 23).
53. *Commentary on the Psalms* (PG 23).

οἱ ἐν Βιέννῃ καὶ Λουγδούνῳ τῆς Γαλλίας παροικοῦντες **δοῦλοι Χριστοῦ** (*Ecclesiastical History*[54] 5.1.3.2-3).

οὐδὲν ἕτερον **ἢ Χριστοῦ δοῦλον** ἑαυτὸν ὡμολόγει (*Martyrs of Palestine*[55] 4.12.5).

λέλεκται δὲ ταῦτα **τῷ δούλῳ Κυρίου** τῷ Δαυῒδ (*Commentary on Psalms*[56] 317.5).

Basil of Caesarea

ὅσοι **δοῦλοι Θεοῦ**, ὥσπερ λάτρεις, ὑπέδραμον τοῖς γόνασί σου περιπλεκόμενοι (*Epistles*[57] 45.1.48-49).

μόνον ἐὰν ᾖ τις **δοῦλος Θεοῦ** (*Epistles*[58] 190.1.18).

ὅσοι **δοῦλοι Θεοῦ**, ὥσπερ λάτρεις, ὑπέδραμον τοῖς γόνασί σου περιπλεκόμενοι (*Sermons*[59] 1220.6-7).

ὅτι αἱ Θλίψεις αὗται οὐκ ἀργῶς **τοῖς δούλοις τοῦ Θεοῦ** παρὰ τοῦ ἐπισκοποῦντος ἡμᾶς Κυρίου γίνονται (*Epistles*[60] 101.1.19-21).

οὐδενὸς αἱρουμένου ἀντεισάγειν ἑαυτὸν **τῶν δούλων τοῦ Θεοῦ** ἢ τῶν ἀπεγνωσημένων (*Epistles*[61] 239.1.14).

ὁ δὲ οὐδὲ ἧς **οἱ δοῦλοι τοῦ Χριστοῦ** προσηγορίας μετέχουσιν (*Against Eunomius*[62] 613.1-3).

δύναμαι ἄξιος κληθῆναι **δοῦλος Ἰησοῦ Χριστοῦ** (*Epistles*[63] 203.1.22; *Sermons*[64] 1152.31).

Scriptural Citations

Παῦλος, **δοῦλος Ἰησοῦ Χριστοῦ** (*Rule*[65] 820.53).

ἀλλ᾽ ὡς **δοῦλοι Χριστοῦ**, ποιοῦντες τὸ θέλημα τοῦ Θεοῦ (*Rule*[66] 856.17)

ἐπείπερ **δοῦλον Κυρίου** οὐ δεῖ μάχεσθαι (*Asceticon*[67] 941.43).

---

54. *History of the Church.* (SC, 31, 41, 55).
55. *The Martyrs of Palestine* (SC, 55).
56. *Commentary on the Psalms* (PG 23).
57. *Epistles* (*Saint Basil, Lettres*; ed. T. Courtonne; Paris, 1957).
58. *Epistles* (Courtonne).
59. *Sermons* (PG 32).
60. *Epistles* (Courtonne).
61. *Epistles* (Courtonne).
62. *Against Eunomius* (book 5; PG 29).
63. *Epistles* (Courtonne).
64. *Sermons* (PG 32).
65. *Rule* (PG 31).
66. *Rule* (PG 31).
67. *The Asceticon* (PG 31).

Gregory of Nyssa

ἀληθῶς ἅγιοι οὗτοι καὶ **δοῦλοι Θεοῦ** (*Ephraim*[68] 836.13).

τῷ ἀδελφῷ **δούλῳ Θεοῦ Πέτρῳ** Γρηγόριος ἐπίσκοπος Νύσσης (*Making of Man*[69] 125.8).

ποῦ **δοῦλος Θεοῦ** ἐν τοῖς εἰρημένοις ὁ υἱὸς εἶναι διδάσκεται (*Against Eunomius*[70] 3.9.62.11-12).

ἀλλ' ὡς **Χριστοῦ δούλοις** (*Christian Institutions*[71] 87.17).

καθάπερ εὔνους καὶ ἁπλοῦς **δοῦλος τοῦ Χριστοῦ** (*Christian Institutions*[72] 67.13).

παρὰ **τοῦ δούλου τοῦ Χριστοῦ** μεμαθήκαμεν Παύλου (*Homilies*[73] 5.382.2).

ὁ δὲ **τοῦ Χριστοῦ δοῦλος Στέφανος** (*Stephen*[74] 725.28).

ἢ τῷ **δούλῳ κυρίου** ἢ τῷ Ἰδιθοὺμ ἢ τῷ Ἀιμὰν τῷ Ἰσραηλίτῃ (*Psalms*[75] 5.70.21).

καὶ τὸ λοιπὸν παύσασθαι κατὰ **τῶν δούλων τοῦ κυρίου** φονῶντας (*Against Eunomius*[76] 1.1.133.5).

καὶ Δαβίδ, ὁ **δοῦλος τοῦ κυρίου** (*Commentary on the Story of Songs*[77] 6.364.15).

Scriptural Citations

... δοῦλος Ἰησοῦ Χριστοῦ ὁ κλητὸς ἀπόστολος (*Apollinarius*[78] 3.1.191.3-4).

Παῦλος, δοῦλος Ἰησοῦ Χριστοῦ (*Against Eunomius*[79] 30.9).

Gregory of Nazianzus

Θέκλα μετὰ μικρόν, ἡ **τοῦ Θεοῦ δούλη** (*Epistles*[80] 222.5.2-3).

ὦ **δοῦλε Χριστοῦ**, καὶ φιλόθεε, καὶ φιλάνθρωπε (*Orations*[81] 893.37-38).

---

68. *On St. Ephraim* (PG 46).
69. *On the Making of Man* (*Gregorii Nysseni Opera*; Leiden: E.J. Brill, 1952–).
70. *Against Eunomius* (*Gregorii Nysseni Opera*, vol. 1.1 and 2.2).
71. *On the Christian Institutions* (*Gregorii Nysseni Opera*, vol. 8.1).
72. *On the Christian Institutions* (*Gregorii Nysseni Opera*, vol. 8.1).
73. *Ecclesiastical Homilies* (P. Alexander [ed.], *Gregorii Nysseni Opera*).
74. *On St Stephen* (PG 46).
75. *On the Psalms* (ed. J. McDonough).
76. *Against Eunomius* (*Gregorii Nysseni Opera*, vol. 2).
77. *Commentary on the Song of Songs* (*Gregorii Nysseni Opera*, vol. 6).
78. *Against Apollinarius* (*Gregorii Nysseni Opera*, vol. 3).
79. *Against Eunomius* (*Gregorii Nysseni Opera*, vol. 2).
80. *Epistles* (*Saint Gregorie de Nazianze, lettres*; ed. P. Gallay; GCS; Leipzig: Teubner, 1969).
81. *Orations* (PG 35).

δοῦλοι Χριστοῦ, καὶ ἀδελφοί (*Orations*[82] 909.26).

Scriptural Citations

εἰ ἔτι ἀνθρώποις ἤρεσκον, ὁ Παῦλος φησι, Χριστοῦ δοῦλος οὐκ ἂν ἤμην (*Orations*[83] 301.27-29; 420.7-9)

Chrysostom

ὁ γενόμενος **τοῦ Χριστοῦ δοῦλος** (*Homily on Matthew*[84] 183.41-42).

τῶν δὲ **δούλων τοῦ Χριστοῦ** καὶ τὰ σήματα λάμπρα (*Homily on Corinthians* 2[85] 581.54).

ὁ ἄρα τοιοῦτος οὐ δοῦλος τοῦ Χριστοῦ· ὁ δὲ **δοῦλος τοῦ Χριστοῦ**, οὐκ ἀνθρωπάρεσκος. τίς γὰρ **Θεοῦ δοῦλος** ὤν (*Homily on Ephesians*[86] 156.38-39).

ἐν τῷ νόμῳ Μωσέως **δούλου τοῦ Θεοῦ** (*Against Jews*[87] 892.30).

μεγάλη τῆς περὶ **τοὺς δούλους τοῦ θεοῦ** θεραπείας ἡ ἀνταπόδοσις (*Homily on the Gospel of John*[88] 389.20-21).

εἰ γὰρ ἵνα **δοῦλοι τοῦ Θεοῦ** μένωσιν (*Homily on Ephesians*[89] 67.39-40).

Scriptural Citations

...οἱ ἄνθρωποι δοῦλοι τοῦ Θεοῦ τοῦ ὑψίστου εἰσίν (*On Virginity*[90] 538.30; *Acts of the Apostles*[91] 253.36 [ὑψίστου]; 253.49 [οἱ ἄνθρωποι, λέγων, δοῦλοι τοῦ Θεοῦ τοῦ ὑψίστου εἰσίν]; 255.19 [ἐκεῖνος λέγει, ὅτι Δοῦλοι τοῦ Θεοῦ τοῦ ὑψίστου]; 292.40; *Diligentia*[92] 168.13-14; *Against Jews*[93] 913.59; *On Lazarus*[94] 983.45-46; *Homily on Corinthians*[95] 243.9-10; *Homily on Ephesians*[96] 76.40.41

...οἱ ἄνθρωποι δοῦλοι τοῦ Θεοῦ εἰσί τοῦ ὑψίστου (*Against Jews*[97] 913.45).

82. *Orations* (PG 35).
83. *Orations* (PG 36).
84. *Homily on Matthew* (PG 57).
85. *Homily on Corinthians* (PG 61).
86. *Homily on Ephesians* (PG 62).
87. *Against the Jews* (PG 48).
88. *Homily on the Gospel of John* (PG 59).
89. *Homily on Ephesians* (PG 62).
90. *On Virginity* (PG 48).
91. *On the Acts of the Apostles* (PG 60).
92. *Diligentia* (PG 51).
93. *Against the Jews* (PG 48).
94. *On Lazarus* (PG 48).
95. *Homily on Corinthians* (PG 61).
96. *Homily on Ephesians* (PG 62).
97. *Against Jews* (PG 48).

οἱ δοῦλοι τοῦ Θεοῦ τοῦ ὑψίστου, ἐξέλθετε καὶ δεῦτε, φησίν (*To the people of Antioch*[98] 87.54-55; 88.23-24; 88.38-39.[Σεδρὰχ, Μισὰχ, Ἀβδεναγώ, οἱ δοῦλοι τοῦ Θεοῦ τοῦ ὑψίστου, ἐξέλθετε καὶ δεῦτε]; *Homily on Ephesians*[99] 67.22-24; 42-51)

οἱ δοῦλοι τοῦ Θεοῦ τοῦ ὑψίστου (*On Genesis*[100] 456.7-8).

καὶ οὐκ εἶπε, τίς ἐγκαλέσει κατὰ τῶν δούλων τοῦ Θεοῦ, οὐδὲ, κατὰ τῶν πιστῶν τοῦ Θεοῦ, ἀλλὰ, κατὰ τῶν ἐκλεκτῶν τοῦ Θεοῦ (*Homily on Romans*[101] 543.23)

Παῦλος δοῦλος Θεοῦ, ἀπόστολος δὲ Ἰησοῦ Χριστοῦ (*Homily on Titus*[102] 663.22-23; 664.43-44).

Παῦλος δοῦλος Ἰησοῦ Χριστοῦ, κλητὸς ἀπόστολος (*Changing of Names*[103] 123.7; *Homily on Romans*[104] 395.1-2).

Παῦλος δοῦλος Ἰησοῦ Χριστοῦ (*Homily on Romans*[105] 395.25; *Homily on Philippians*[106] 182.50; *Homily on Titus*[107] 664.47)

Παῦλος καὶ Τιμόθεος δοῦλοι Ἰησοῦ Χριστοῦ (*Homily on Philippians*[108] 181.45)

δοῦλος Ἰησοῦ Χριστοῦ (*Homily on Romans*[109] 395.44).

ἀλλ᾽ ὡς δοῦλοι τοῦ Χριστοῦ, ποιοῦντες τὸ θέημα τοῦ Θεοῦ ἐκ ψυχῆς (*Homily on Ephesians*[110] 155.12-13; 156.14-15).

οἱ δοῦλοι Ἰησοῦ Χριστοῦ (*Homily on Colossians*[111] 301.40).

Ἐπαφρᾶ ὁ ἐξ ὑμῶμ δοῦλος Χριστοῦ (*Homily on Colossians*[112] 379.55-56; 382.20-21).

98. *To the People of Antioch* (PG 49).
99. *Homily on Ephesians* (PG 62).
100. *On Genesis* (PG 54).
101. *Homily on Romans* (PG 60).
102. *Homily on Titus* (PG 62).
103. *On the Changing of Names* (PG 51).
104. *Homily on Romans* (PG 60).
105. *Homily on Romans* (PG 60).
106. *Homily on Philippians* (PG 62).
107. *Homily on Titus* (PG 62).
108. *Homily on Philippians* (PG 62).
109. *Homily on Romans* (PG 60).
110. *Homily on Ephesians* (PG 62).
111. *Homily on Colossians* (PG 62).
112. *Homily on Colossians* (PG 62).

Use of the Title ΔΟΥΛΟΣ ΘΕΟΥ, ΔΟΥΛΟΣ ΧΡΙΣΤΟΥ in the New Testament

Title + Name

Παῦλος **δοῦλος Χριστοῦ Ἰησοῦ**
Rom. 1.1

Παῦλος καὶ Τιμόθεος **δοῦλοι Χριστοῦ Ἰησοῦ**
Phil. 1.1

Ἐπαφρᾶς ὁ ἐξ ὑμῶν, **δοῦλος Χριστοῦ**
Col. 4.12

Παῦλος **δοῦλος Θεοῦ**, ἀπόστολος δὲ Ἰησοῦ Χριστοῦ
Tit. 1.1

Ἰάκωβος Θεοῦ καὶ κυρίου **Ἰησοῦ Χριστοῦ δοῦλος**
Jas.1.1

Ἰούδας **Ἰησοῦ Χριστοῦ δοῦλος**
Jud. 1.1

Μωϋσέως τοῦ **δούλου τοῦ Θεοῦ**
Rev. 15.2

Other Forms

καὶ ἡμῖν ἔκραζεν λέγουσα, οὗτοι οἱ ἄνθρωποι **δοῦλοι τοῦ Θεοῦ** τοῦ ὑψίστου εἰσίν
Act.16.17

εἰ ἔτι ἀνθρώποις ἤρεσκον, **Χριστοῦ δοῦλος** οὐκ ἂν ἤμην
Gal. 1.10

μὴ κατ᾽ ὀφθαλμοδουλίαν ὡς ἀνθρωπάρεσκοι ἀλλ᾽ ὡς **δοῦλοι Χριστοῦ**
Eph. 6.6

μὴ ὡς ἐπικάλυμμα ἔχοντες τῆς κακίας τὴν ἐλευθερίαν, ἀλλ᾽ ὡς **Θεοῦ δοῦλοι**
1 Pet. 2.16

ἄρχι σφραγίσωμεν τοὺς **δούλους τοῦ Θεοῦ** ἡμῶν
Rev. 7.3

BIBLIOGRAPHY

Primary Sources

Old and New Testament translations are adapted from the *New English Bible*. *Loeb Classical Library* editions were used for all classical writers and for the Apostolic Fathers. Patristic editions are from *Corpus Christianorum Series Latina*, *Griechischen christlichen Schriftseller der ersten drei Jahrhunderte*, Migne's *Patrologia Graeca*, Migne's *Patrologia Latina*, *Sources chrétiennes*, or *Texte und Untersuchungen zur Geschichte der Altchristlichen Literatur* as specified in the footnotes, apart from the following:

Acts of the Christian Martyrs (ed. H. Musurillo; Oxford: Clarendon Press, 1972).

Acta apostolorum apocrypha (ed. R.A. Lipsius and M. Bonnet; vol. 2.1 and 2.2; Leipzig: G. Freytag, 1891–1903).

Athanasius, *Contra Gentes and De Incarnatione* (ed. R.W. Thomson; Oxford: Clarendon Press, 1971).

—*Athanasius Werke* (ed. H.G. Opitz; Berlin: W. de Gruyter, 1934).

Cyprian, *De Lapsis and De Ecclesiae Catholicae Unitate* (ed. M. Bévenot, *Early Christian Texts*; Oxford: Clarendon Press, 1971).

Didascalia Apostolorum (trans. and accompanied by the Verona Latin Fragments by R.H. Connolly; Oxford: Clarendon Press, 1929).

Ephraim of Syria, *Hymns on the Nativity* (trans. J.B. Morris, NPNF, 12; ed. J. Gwynn; Oxford: Oxford University Press, 1898).

Gregory of Nyssa, *The Catechetical Oration of Gregory of Nyssa* (ed. J.H. Srawley; Cambridge: Cambridge University Press, 1903).

—*Gregorii Nysseni Opera* (ed. W. Jaeger; Leiden: E.J. Brill, 1952–).

Melito of Sardis, *Peri Pascha* (ed. S.G. Hall; Oxford: Clarendon Press, 1979).

Narsai, *The Liturgical Homilies of Narsai* (ed. R.H. Connolly; Texts and Studies, 8 no. 1; ed. J.A. Robinson; Cambridge: Cambridge University Press, 1909).

Nicetas, *Nicetas Remesiana: Instructio ad Competentes* (ed. K. Gamber, Textus patristici et liturgici; Regensberg, 1964).

Origen, *Commentary on Romans* (ed. K. Staab, 'Neue Fragmente aus dem Kommentar des Origenes zum Römerbrief', *BZ* 18 [1928]).

—*Philocalia* (1–27) (ed. J.A. Robinson, *The Philocalia of Origen* [Cambridge: Cambridge University Press, 1893]).

—*Scholia on the Apocalypse* (ed. C.H. Turner, 'Document: Origen, scholia in Apocalypsin', *JTS* 25 [1923], pp. 1-15).

Socrates, *Socrates' Ecclesiastical History* (ed. W. Bright; Oxford: Clarendon Press, 2nd edn, 1893).

(Editions used by the *Thesaurus Linguae Grecae,* used by the *Ibycus* programme, are specified in the footnotes to the Indices).

Secondary Sources

Aland, K., 'The Relationship between Church and State in Early Times' *JTS*, NS 19 (1968), pp. 115-27.

—*A History of Christianity* (trans. J.L. Schaff; 2 vols.; Philadelphia: Fortress Press, 1985–86).

Alfödy, G. (ed.), *Antike Sklaverei: Widersprüche, Sonderforman, Grundstrukturen* (Bamberg: C.C. Buchners, 1988).

—*The Social History of Rome* (Totowa, NJ: Barnes & Noble, 1985).

Allard, P., *Les esclaves chrétiens depuis les premiers temps de l'église jusqu'à la fin de la domination romaine en Occident* ([first publ. Paris: 1876] New York: Georg Hildesheim, 1974).

Alexander, L., 'Paul and the Hellenistic Schools—the evidence of Galen', in Y. Egenberg-Pedersen (ed.) *Paul in his Hellenistic Context* (Minneapolis: Fortress Press, 1995), pp. 60-83.

Anderson, D., *St Basil the Great on the Holy Spirit* (Crestwood, NY: St Vladimir's Seminary Press, 1980).

Andrews, M.E., 'Paul, Philo and the Intellectuals', *JBL* 53 (1934), pp. 150-66.

Archer, L.J. (ed), *Slavery and other Forms of Unfree Labour* (History Workshop Series; New York: Routledge & Kegan Paul, 1988).

Arichea, D.A., and E.A. Nida, *A Translator's Handbook on Paul's Letter to the Romans* (Stuttgart: United Bible Societies, 1976).

Arnold, E.V., *Roman Stoicism* (Cambridge: Cambridge University Press, 1958).

Avila, C., *Ownership: Early Christian Teaching* (London & New York: Orbis, Sheed & Ward, 1983).

Baldry, H.C., *The Unity of Mankind in Greek Thought* (Cambridge: Cambridge University Press, 1967).

Balfour, I.L.S., 'The Relationship of Man to God from Conception to Conversion in the Writings of Tertullian' (PhD dissertation; Edinburgh, 1980).

Barclay, J.M.G., 'Paul, Philemon and the Dilemma of Christian Slave Ownership', *NTS* 37 (1991), pp. 161-86.

Barnard, L.W., *Justin Martyr: His Life and Thought* (Cambridge: Cambridge University Press, 1967 [New York, 1890]).

—'The Church in Rome in the First Two Centuries' & 'Early Syriac Christianity', in L.W. Barnard (ed.), *Studies in Church History and Patristics* (Thessaloniki: Patriarchal Institute for Patristic Studies,1978).

Barnes, J., M. Schofield and R. Sorabju (eds.), *Articles on Aristotle*, II (London: Gerald Duckworth, 1977).

Barnes, T.D., 'Panegyric, History and Hagiography in Eusebius' *Life of Constantine*', in R. Williams (ed.), *The Making of Orthodoxy* (Cambridge: Cambridge University Press, 1989), pp. 94-123.

Barnett, J.M., *The Diaconate: A Full and Equal Order* (New York: Seabury Press, 1981).

Barone-Adesi, G., 'Servi fugitivi in ecclesia: indirizzi Cristiani e legislazione imperiale', *Atti dell'accademia Romanistica Constantiana* 8 (1990), pp 696-741.

Barrett, C.K., *A Commentary on the First Epistle to the Corinthians* (London: A. & C. Black, 2nd edn, 1971).

—*The Gospel According to St John* (London: SPCK, 1978).

—*Freedom and Obligation: A Study of the Epistle to the Galatians* (Philadelphia: Westminster Press, 1985).

Bartchy, S.S., *Mallon Chresai: First Century Slavery and 1 Corinthians 7:21* (SBLDS, 11; Missoula, MT: SBL, 1973).

Barth, K., *The Epistle to the Philippians* (London: SCM Press, 1962).

—*The Epistle to the Romans* (trans. from the 6th edn by E.C. Hoskyns; London: Oxford University Press, 1968).

Baus, K., *The Imperial Church from Constantine to the Early Middle Ages* (trans. A. Biggs; London: Burns & Oates, 1980).

Beare, F.W., *A Commentary on the First Epistle to the Philippians* (London: A. & C. Black, 3rd rev. edn, 1988).

Beavis, M.A., 'Ancient Slavery as an Interpretive Context for the New Testament Servant Parables with Special Reference to the Unjust Steward, Luke 16.1-8', *JBL* 111 (1992), pp. 37-54.

Benoit, A., *Le bâpteme chrétien au second siécle* (Paris: Presses Universitaires de France, 1953).

Bergadá, M.M., 'La condemnation de l'esclavage dans l'Homélie IV', in G.S. Hall (ed.), *Gregory of Nyssa: Homilies on Ecclesiastes. An English Version with Supporting Studies* (Proceedings of the Seventh International Colloquium on Gregory of Nyssa, 1990; Berlin: W. de Gruyter, 1993), pp. 185-96.

Bernard, J.H., *The Odes of Solomon* (Texts and Studies; Cambridge: Cambridge University Press, 1916).

—*A Critical and Exegetical Commentary on the Gospel of St John* (International Critical Commentary, 1; Edinburgh: T. & T. Clark, 1928).

Beskow, P., *Rex Gloriae: The Kingship of Christ in the Early Church* (trans. E.J. Sharpe; Stockholm: Almqvist & Wiksell, 1962).

Betz, H.D., *Der Apostel Paulus und die sokratische Tradition* (Tübingen: J.C.B. Mohr [Paul Siebeck], 1972).

—*Galatians* (Philadelphia: Fortress Press, 1979).

Bigg, C., *The Doctrine of the Twelve Apostles* (rev. A.J. Maclean; London: SPCK, 1922).

Black, D.A., *Paul, Apostle of Weakness: Asthenia and its Cognates in the Pauline Literature* (New York: Peter Lang, 1984).

Blackburn, R., 'Defining Slavery: Its Special Features and Social Role', in L.J. Archer (ed.), *Slavery and Other Forms of Unfree Labour* (History Workshop Series; New York & London: Routledge & Kegan Paul, 1988), pp. 263-79.

Bömer, F., *Untersuchungen über die Religion der Sklaven in Griechenland und Rom* (4 vols.; Wiesbaden: F. Steiner, 1958–63).

Boylan, P., *St Paul's Epistle to the Romans* (Dublin: M.H. Gill & Son, 1934).

Bousett, W., *Kyrios Christos* (trans. J.E. Steely; Nashville: Abingdon Press, 1970).

Bradley, K.R., *The Unity of Mankind in Greek Thought* (Cambridge: Cambridge University Press, 1965).

—*Slaves and Masters in the Roman Empire: A Study in Social Control* (Collection Latomus, 185; New York: Oxford University Press, 1987).

—'Roman Slavery and Roman Law', *HR* 15 (1988), pp. 477-95.

—*Slavery and Society at Rome* (Cambridge: Cambridge University Press, 1994).

Bradshaw, P.F., *The Search for the Origins of Christian Worship: Sources and Methods for the Study of Early Liturgy* (London: SPCK, 1992).

Brent, A., 'The Relations between Ignatius and the Didascalia', *SecCent* 8 (1991), pp. 129-56.

—'The Ignatian Epistles and the Threefold Ecclasiastical Order', *JRH* 17 (1992), pp. 18-32.

Brock, S.P., *The Holy Spirit in Syrian Baptismal Tradition* (Syrian Churches Series, 9; Bronx, NY: John XXIII Centre, Fordham University, 1979).

Brockmeyer, N., *Antike Sklaverei* (Ertrage der Forschung, 2; Darmstadt: Wissenschaftliche Buchgesellschaft, 1979).

Brooks, B.A., 'The Babylonian Practice of Marking Slaves', *AJOS* 42 (1922), pp. 80-90.

Brown, P., 'Aspects of the Christianisation of the Roman Aristocracy', *JRS* 51 (1961), pp. 1-11.

—*Religion and Society in the Age of St Augustine* (London: Faber & Faber, 1972).

—*The Making of Late Antiquity* (Cambridge, MA: Harvard University Press, 1978).

—*Society and the Holy in Late Antiquity* (Berkeley: University of California Press, 1982).

—*The Body and Society: Men, Women and Sexual Renunciation in Early Christianity* (London: Faber & Faber, 1988).

Brunt, P.A., 'Evidence given under Torture in the Principate', *ZRG* 97 (1980), pp. 256-65.

—'Aristotle and Slavery', in *idem, Studies in Greek History and Thought* (Oxford: Clarendon Press, 1993), pp. 343-82.

—'Aspects of the Social Thought of Dio Chrysostom and of the Stoics', in *idem, Studies in Greek History and Thought*, pp. 210-43.

Buckland, W.W., *The Main Institutions of Roman Private Law,* (Cambridge: Cambridge University Press, 1925).

—*The Roman Law of Slavery: The Condition of the Slave in Private Law from Augustus to Justinian* (Cambridge: Cambridge University Press, 1970).

—*A Textbook of Roman Law from Augustus to Justinian* (rev. P. Stein; Cambridge: Cambridge University Press, 2nd edn, 1975).

Bultmann, R., *The Gospel of John: A Commentary* (trans. G.R. Beasley-Murray; Oxford: Basil Blackwell, 1971).

Cadoux, C.J., *The Early Church and the World* (Edinburgh: T. & T. Clark, 1925).

Caird, G.B., *The Language and Imagery of the Bible* (Philadelphia: Westminster Press; London: Gerald Duckworth, 1980).

—*New Testament Theology* (completed and ed. by L.D. Hurst; Oxford: Clarendon Press, 1994).

Cambiano, G., 'Aristotle and the Anonymous Opponents of Slavery', in M.I. Finley (ed.), *Slavery in Classical Antiquity* (Cambridge: W. Heffer & Sons, 1960).

Cameron, A., *Christianity and the Rhetoric of Empire* (Berkeley: University of California Press, 1991).

Carpenter, H.J., 'Creeds and Baptismal Rites in the Four First Centuries', *JTS* 44 (1943), pp. 1-11.

Carrington, P., *Christian Apologetics in the Second Century* (London: SPCK, 1921).

—'The Baptismal Pattern in the New Testament', *Theology* 29 (1934), pp. 162-64.

Cartledge, P., 'Rebels and Sambos in Classical Greece: A Comparative View', *HPT* 6 (1985), pp. 16-46.

—*The Greeks: A Portrait of Self and Others* (Oxford: Oxford University Press, 1993).

Casey, R.P., *The Excerpta ex Theodoto of Clement of Alexandria* (ed. Kirsopp Lake and Silva Lake; Studies and Documents; London: Christophers, 1934).

Chadwick, H., 'All Things to All Men', *NTS* 1 (1954–55), pp. 261-75.

—*Early Christian Thought and the Classical Tradition* (Oxford: Oxford University Press, 1966).

—*History and Thought of the Early Church* (London: Variorum Reprints, 1982).

Charlesworth, J.H., *The Odes of Solomon* (SBLTT; Pseudepigrapha Series; ed. R.A. Kraft; Missoula, MT: Scholars Press, 1977).

Chow, J.K., *Patronage and Power: A Study of Social Networks in Corinth* (JSNTSup, 75; Sheffield: JSOT Press, 1992).

Ciccotti, E., *Il tramonto della schiavitu nel mondo antico* (2 vols.; Udine: Edizione Accademica, 2nd edn, 1940).

Cochrane, C.N., *Christianity and Classical Culture* (London: Oxford University Press, 1968).

Coleman-Norton, P.R., 'The Apostle Paul and The Roman Law of Slavery', in P.R. Coleman-Norton, F.C. Bourne and J.V.A. Fine (eds.), *Studies in Roman Economic and Social History in Honour of Allan Chester Johnson* (Princeton, NJ: Princeton University Press, 1951), pp. 166-72.

—*Roman State and Christian Church: A Collection of Legal Documents to AD 535* (London: SPCK, 1966).

Collins, J.N., *Diakonia: Reinterpreting the Ancient Sources* (New York: Oxford University Press, 1990).

Combes, I.A.H., review of *Slavery as Salvation: The Metaphor of Slavery in Pauline Christianity* (New Haven, CT: Yale University Press, 1990), by D.B. Martin, in *JTS* 43 (1992), pp. 200-202.

—'Nursing Mother, Ancient Shepherd, Athletic Coach? Some Images of Christ in the Early Church', in S.E. Porter, M.A. Hayes and D. Tombs (eds.), *Images of Christ: Ancient and Modern* (Roehampton Institute London Papers, 2; Sheffield: Sheffield Academic Press, 1997), pp. 113-25.

Conzelmann, H., *Commentary on 1 Corinthians* (Philadelphia: Fortress Press, 1975).

Corcoran, G., 'Slavery in the New Testament', Parts 1 and 2, *MS* 5 (1980), pp. 1-40; 6 (1980), pp. 62-83.

—'The Christian Attitudes to Slavery in the Early Church I', *MS* 13 (1984), pp. 1-16.

—*Saint Augustine on Slavery* (Rome: Institutum Patristicum Augustinianum, 1985).

Cranfield, C.E.B., *A Critical and Exegetical Commentary on the Epistle to the Romans* (Edinburgh: T. & T. Clark, 1975).

Crehan, J., *Early Christian Baptism and the Creed* (London: Burns, Oates & Washbourne, 1950).

—'Ten Years Work on Baptism', *TS* 17 (1956), pp. 494-515.

Cross, F.L., *The Early Christian Fathers* (Studies in Theology; London: Gerald Duckworth, 1960).

Crossan, J.D., *Cliffs of Fall: Paradox and Polyvalence in the Parables of Jesus* (New York: Seabury Press, 1980).

Cuffel, V., 'The Classical Greek Concept of Slavery', *JHI* 27 (1966), pp. 323-42.

Cullmann, O., *Baptism in the New Testament* (London: SCM Press, 1950).

Cunliffe, B., *Greeks, Romans and Barbarians, Spheres of Interaction* (London: B.T. Batsford Ltd, 1988).

Cupitt, D., *The Long Legged Fly* (London: SCM Press, 1987).

Daly, L.W., *Aesop without Morals* (New York: Thomas Yoseloff, 1961).

Davidson, D., 'What Metaphors Mean', in A P. Martinich (ed.), *The Philosophy of Language* (Oxford: Oxford University Press, 1985), pp. 438-49.

Davis, D.B., *The Problem of Slavery in Western Culture* (Harmondsworth: Penguin Books, 1970).

—*Slavery and Human Progress* (Oxford: Oxford University Press, 1986).

Dawes, G.W., 'But If You Can Gain Your Freedom (1 Cor. 7.17-24)', *CBQ* 54 (1990), pp. 681-97.

Deissmann, A., *Light from the Ancient East: The New Testament Illustrated by Recently Discovered Texts of the Greco-Roman World* (trans. L.R.M. Strachan; London: Hodder & Stoughton, 1927).

Dennis, T.J., 'The Relationship between Gregory of Nyssa's Attack on Slavery in his Fourth Homily on Ecclesiastes and his Treatise *De Hominis Opificio*', *StudPat* 17.3 (1982), pp. 1065-72.

Dewey, A.J., 'A Matter of Honor: A Social-Historical Analysis of 2 Corinthians', *HTR* 78 (1985), pp. 211-17.

Dillistone, F.W., *Christianity and Symbolism* (London: SCM Press, 1955).

—*Christianity and Communication* (London: Collins, 1956).

—*The Christian Understanding of the Atonement* (London: James Nisbet, 1968).

—*Traditional Symbols and the Contemporary World* (1968 Bampton Lecture; London: Epworth Press, 1978).

Dix, G., *The Treatise on the Apostolic Traditions of St Hippolytus*, I (London: SPCK, 1937).

—'The Seal in the Second Century', *Theology* 51 (1948), pp. 7-12.

—*Jew and Greek: A Study in the Primitive Church* (Westminster: Dacre Press, 1967).

Dodd, C.H., *The Interpretation of the Fourth Gospel* (Cambridge: Cambridge University Press, 1953).

Dodds, E.R., *Pagans and Christians in an Age of Anxiety* (Cambridge: Cambridge University Press, 1965).

Dover, K.J., *Greek Popular Morality in the Time of Plato and Aristotle* (Oxford: Basil Blackwell, 1974).

Drane, J.W., *Paul: Libertine or Legalist?* (London: SPCK, 1975).

Driver, G.R., and J.C. Miles, *The Babylonian Laws: Ancient Codes and Laws of the Near East*. I. *Legal Commentary* (ed. with trans. and commentary; Oxford: Clarendon Press, 1952).

Duff, A.M., *Freedmen in the Early Roman Empire* (Cambridge: W. Heffer & Sons, 1958).

Eco, U., *A Theory of Semiotics* (Bloomington, IN: Indiana University Press, 1976).

Edsman, C.M., 'A Typology of Baptism in Hippolytus', *StudPat* 2.2 (1957), pp. 35-40.

Ehrenberg, V., *The People of Aristophanes*, (Oxford: Basil Blackwell, 1951).

Evans, P.W., 'Sealing as a Term for Baptism', *BQ* NS 16 (1955–56), pp. 171-75.

Evans-Grubbs, J., *Law and the Family in Late Antiquity: The Emperor Constantine's Marriage Legislation* (Oxford: Clarendon Press, 1995).

Faur, J., *Golden Doves with Silver Dots: Semiotics and Textuality in the Rabbinic Tradition* (Bloomington, IN: Indiana University Press, 1986).

Feltoe, C.L., *The Letters and Sermons of Leo the Great* (Oxford: James Parker, 1895).

Finegan, J., *Light from the Ancient Past: The Archaeological Background of Judaism and Christianity* (Princeton, NJ: University of Princeton Press, 1959).

Finley, M.I., 'Was Greek Civilization Based on Slave Labour?', in *idem* (ed.), *Slavery in Classical Antiquity*, pp. 53-72.

Finley, M.I. (ed.), *Slavery in Classical Antiquity: Views and Controversies* (Cambridge: W. Heffer & Sons, 1960).

—'Slavery', *International Encyclopedia of the Social Sciences*, 14 (New York: Macmillan and Free Press, 1968).

—*Ancient Slavery and Modern Ideology* (London: Chatto & Windus, 1980).

—*Classical Slavery* (London: Frank Cass, 1987).

Fisher, N.R.E., *Slavery in Classical Greece* (Classical World Series; ed. J.H. Betts; Bristol: Bristol Classical Press, 1995).

Flemington, W.F., *The New Testament Doctrine of Baptism,* (London: SPCK, 1948).

Fortenbaugh, W.W., *Aristotle on Emotion* (London: Gerald Duckworth, 1975).

—'Aristotle on Slaves and Women', in J. Barnes, M. Schofield and R. Sorabji (eds.), *Articles on Aristotle*. II. *Ethics and Politics* (London: Gerald Duckworth, 1977), pp. 135-39.

Fox, R.L., *Pagans and Christians* (New York: Viking, 1986).

Fragomichalos, C.E., 'The Question of the Existence of Slaves in Plato's Republic', *Platon* 36 (1984), pp. 77-96.

Frend, W.H.C., *Martyrdom and Persecution in the Early Church* (Oxford: Basil Blackwell, 1965).

—*The Rise of Christianity* (Philadelphia: Fortress Press, 1984).

Funk, R.W., *Language, Hermeneutic and the Word of God: The Problem of Language in the New Testament and Contemporary Theology* (New York: Harper & Row, 1966).

Gagarin M., and P. Woodruff, *Early Greek Political Thought from Homer to the Sophists* (Cambridge: Cambridge University Press, 1995).

Garcia y Garcia, A., *Historia del Derecho Canonico* (Salamanca: Instituto de Historia de la Teologia Española, 1967).

Garcia-Sanchez, C., *Pelagius and Christian Initiation: A Study in Historical Theology* (PhD dissertation; Catholic University of America, Washington, 1978).

Garlan, Y., *Slavery in Ancient Greece* (trans. J. Lloyd; Ithaca, NY: Cornell University Press, rev. and expanded edn, 1988).

Garnsey, P., *The Early Principate: Augustus to Trajan* (Oxford: Clarendon Press, 1982).

—*Ideas of Slavery from Aristotle to Augustine* (Cambridge: Cambridge University Press, 1996).

Garnsey, P., and R. Saller, *Social Status and Legal Privilege in the Roman Empire* (Oxford: Clarendon Press, 1970).

—*The Roman Empire: Economy, Society and Culture* (London: Gerald Duckworth, 1987).

Genovese, E.D., *Roll, Jordan, Roll: The World the Slaves Made* (New York: Vintage Books, 1976).

Goodspeed, E.J., 'Paul and Slavery', *JBR* 11 (1943), pp.169-70.

Gorday, P., *Principles of Patristic Exegesis: Romans 9–11 in Origen, John Chrysostom and Augustine* (Lewiston, NY: Edwin Mellen Press, 1983).

Gowan, D.E., *Bridge Between the Testaments: A Reappraisal of Judaism from the Exile to the Birth of Christianity* (Pennsylvania: Pickwick Press, 1982).

Grant, M., *Greeks and Romans: A Social History* (London: Weidenfeld & Nicolson, 1992).

—*A Social History of Greece and Rome* (New York: Charles Scribner's Sons, 1992).

Grant, R.M., *A Short History of the Interpretation of the Bible* (London: A. & C. Black, 1963).

Grayston, K., Review of *Diakonia Reinterpreting the Ancient Sources* (New York: Oxford University Press, 1990) by J.N. Collins, in *JTS* 43 (1992), pp. 198-200.

Greenidge, C.W.W., *Slavery* (London: Allen & Unwin, 1958).

Greer, R.A., *Origen Exhortation to Martyrdom, On Prayer, Selected Works* (Ancient Christian Writers; London: Longmans, Green & Co., 1972).

—*Broken Lights and Mended Lives: Theology and Common Life in the Early Church* (Pennsylvania: Pennsylvania State University Press, 1986).

Griffin, M.T., *Seneca: a Philosopher in Politics* (Oxford: Clarendon Press, 1976).

Grillmeier, A., *Christ in Christian Tradition, from the Apostolic Age to Chalcedon (451)* (trans. J.S. Bowden; London: Mowbrays, 1965).

Grosheide, F.W., *Commentary on the First Epistle to the Corinthians* (Grand Rapids: Eerdmans, 1953).

Gülzow, H., *Christentum und Sklaverei in der ersten drei Jahrhunderten* (Bonn: Rudolf Habelt, 1969).

Hamman, A., (ed.) *Early Christian Prayers* (trans. W. Mitchell; London: Longmans, 1961).

Hanke, L., *Aristotle and the American Indians: A Study of Race Prejudice in the Modern World* (Bloomington, IN: Indiana University Press, 1959).

Hanson, A.T., *The Paradox of the Cross in the Thought of St Paul* (JSNTSup, 17; Sheffield: JSOT Press, 1987).

Hargreaves, J., *A Guide to 1 Corinthians*, (London: SPCK, 1978).

Harries, J., and I. Wood (eds.), *The Theodosian Code: Studies in the Imperial Law of Late Antiquity* (London: Gerald Duckworth, 1993).

Harrill, J.A., Review of *Slavery as Salvation: The Metaphor of Slavery in Pauline Christianity* (New Haven, CT: Yale University Press, 1990) by D.B. Martin, in *JR* 72 (1992), pp. 426-27.

—'Ignatius *Ad Polycarp* 4.3 and the Corporate Manumission of Christian Slaves', *JECS* 1 (1993), pp. 107-42.

—*The Manumission of Slaves in Early Christianity* (Tübingen: J.C.B. Mohr [Paul Siebeck], 1995).

Harrison, A.R.W., *The Law of Athens: The Family and Property* (Oxford: Clarendon Press, 1968).

Hengel, M., *The Cross of the Son of God* (London: SCM Press, 1986).

—*The Pre-Christian Paul* (London: SCM Press, 1991).

Hock, R.F., *The Social Context of Paul's Ministry: Tentmaking and Apostleship* (Philadelphia: Fortress Press, 1980).

Hooker, M.D., *Jesus and the Servant* (London: SPCK, 1959).

—*From Adam to Christ: Essays on Paul* (Cambridge: Cambridge University Press, 1990).

Hopkins, K., *Conquerors and Slaves* (Cambridge: Cambridge University Press, 1980).

—*Death and Renewal* (Cambridge: Cambridge University Press, 1983).

Horsley, G.H.R., *New Documents Illustrating Early Christianity: A Review of the Inscriptions and Papyri* (North Ryde, New South Wales: The Ancient History Documentary Research Centre, 1977–78).

Inwood, B., *Ethics and Human Action in Early Stoicism* (Oxford: Clarendon Press, 1985).

Jackson, B.S., 'Biblical Laws of Slavery: A Comparative Approach, in L.J. Archer (ed.), *Slavery and Other Forms of Unfree Labour* (History Workshop Series; New York: Routledge & Kegan Paul, 1988), pp. 86-101.

Jaeger, W., *Paideia: The Ideals of Greek Culture* (trans. G. Highet; 3 vols.; Oxford: Basil Blackwell, 1939–45).

Jolowicz, H.F., *Historical Introduction to Roman Law* (Cambridge: Cambridge University Press, 1939).

Jones, A.H.M., *The Later Roman Empire 284–602: A Social, Economic and Administrative Survey* (Oxford: Basil Blackwell, 1986).

Jones, J.W., *The Law and Legal Theory of the Greeks* (Oxford: Clarendon Press, 1956).

Judge, E.A., *The Social Patterns of Christian Groups in the First Century* (London: Tyndale Press, 1960).

—'The Social Identity of the First Christians: A Question of Method in Religious History, *JRH* 11 (1980), pp. 201-17.

—*Rank and Status in the World of the Caesars and St. Paul* (Christchurch, New Zealand: University of Canterbury Publications, 1982).

Just, R., 'Freedom, Slavery and the Female Psyche', *HPT* 6 (1985), pp. 1-188.

Karayannopoulos, J., 'St. Basil's Social Activity, Principles and Praxis', in P.J. Fedwick (ed.), *Basil of Caesarea: Christian, Humanist, Ascetic* (Sixteenhundredth Anniversary Symposium; Toronto: Pontifical Institute of Mediaeval Studies, 1981).

Käsemann, E., *Commentary on Roman* (trans. and ed. G.W. Bromiley; London: SCM Press, 1980).

Kelly, H.A., *The Devil at Baptism* (Ithaca, NY: Cornell University Press, 1985).

Keyt, D., and F.D. Millar, Jr (eds.), *A Companion to Aristotle's Politics* (Oxford: Basil Blackwell, 1991).

Klein, R., 'Die Sklavenfrage bei Theodoret von Kyrrhos: "Die 7. Rede des Bischofs über die Vorsehung"', in G. Wirth (ed), *Romanitas-Christianitas: Untersuchungen zur*

Geschichte und Literatur der römischen Kaiserzeit, Johannes Straub zum 70 Geburt-stag am 18 Oktober 1982 gewidmet (Berlin: W. de Gruyter, 1982), pp. 586-633.

—*Die Sklaverei in der Sicht der Bischöfe Ambrosius und Augustinus* (Stuttgart: F. Steiner, 1988).

—Review of *The Manumission of Slaves in Early Christianity* (Tübingen: J.C.B. Mohr [Paul Siebeck], 1995) by J.A. Harrill, in *RQ* (1996), pp. 262-66.

Krestschmar, G., 'Recent Researches on Christian Initiation', *StudLit.* 12.2/3 (1977), pp. 87-106.

Kyrtatas, D.J., *The Social Structure of the Early Christian Communities* (New York: Verso, 1987).

—'Slavery as Progress: Pagan and Christian Views on Slavery as Moral Training', *IS* 10 (1995), pp. 219-34.

Lagrange, M.J., *Saint Paul, épitre aux Romains* (Paris: Libraire Lecoffre, 1931).

Lakoff, G., and M. Johnson, *Metaphors we Live by* (Chicago: Chicago University Press, 1980).

Lampe, G.W.H., 'The Seal of the Spirit: The Seal in the Second Century', *Theology* 51 (1948), pp. 7-12.

Lane Fox, R.L., *Pagans and Christians* (Harmondsworth: Viking, 1986).

Lash, N., *Theology on the Way to Emmaus* (London: SCM Press, 1986).

Laub, F., *Die Begegnung des frühen Christentums mit der antike Sklaverei* (Stuttgart: Verlag Katholisches Bibelwerk, 1982).

Leenhardt, F.J., *L'Epitre de Saint Paul aux Romains* (trans. H. Knight; London: Lutterworth Press, 1961).

Lenox-Conyingham, A., Review of *Die Sklaverei in der Sicht der Bischöfe Ambrosius und Augustinus* (Stuttgart: F. Steiner, 1988) by R. Klein, in *JTS* 43 (1992), pp. 255-58.

Lewis, J.P., 'Baptismal Practices of the 2nd and 3rd Century Church', *RestQ* 26 (1983), pp. 1-17.

Lightfoot, R.H., *St. John's Gospel: A Commentary* (ed. C.F. Evans; Oxford: Clarendon Press, 1956).

Lizzi, R., Review of *Die Sklaverei in der Sicht der Bischöfe Ambrosius und Augustinus* (Stuttgart: F. Steiner, 1988), by R. Klein, *JRS* 80 (1990), pp. 258-59.

Lohfink, G., 'Der Ursprung der christlichen Taufe', *TQ* 1 (1976), pp. 35-54.

Longenecker, R.N., *Galatians* (WBC, 41; Waco, TX: Word Books, 1990).

Lübermann, D., *Galatians: A Continental Commentary* (trans. O.C. Dean, Jr; Minneapolis: Fortress Press, 1992).

Lupton, J.M., *Tertullian: De Baptismo* (Cambridge: Cambridge University Press, 1908).

Lyall, F., 'Roman Law in the Writings of Paul: Adoption', *JBL* 88 (1969), pp. 458-66.

—'Roman Law in the Writings of Paul: The Slave and the Freedman', *NTS* 17 (1970–71), pp. 73-79.

—*Slaves, Citizens, Sons: Legal Metaphors in the Epistles,* (Grand Rapids: Zondervan, 1984).

MacDowell, D.M., *The Law of Classical Athens* (London: Thames & Hudson, 1978).

MacMullen, R., *Christianizing the Roman Empire AD 100–400* (New Haven: Yale University Press, 1984).

—'What Difference did Christianity Make?', *Historia: Zeitschrift für Alte Geschichte* 35 (1986), pp. 322-437.

—*Changes in the Roman Empire: Essays in the Ordinary* (Princeton, NJ: Princeton University Press, 1990).

Malherbe, A.J., *Social Aspects of Early Christianity* (Baton Rouge: Louisiana State University Press, 1977).

Manson, T.W., 'Entry into Membership of the Early Church', *JTS* 48 (1947), pp. 25-34.

—'Baptism in the Church', *SJT* 2 (1949), pp. 391-403.

—*The Servant Messiah* (Cambridge: Cambridge University Press, 1953).

Markus, R.A., *SAECULUM: History and Society in the Theology of St Augustine* (Cambridge: Cambridge University Press, 1970).

Marsh, H.G., *The Origin and Significance of New Testament Baptism* (Manchester: Manchester University Press, 1941).

Martin, D.B., *Slavery as Salvation: The Metaphor of Slavery in Pauline Christianity* (New Haven: Yale University Press, 1990).

Martin, R.P., *Carmen Christi: Philippians ii. 5-11 in Recent Interpretation and in the Setting of Early Christian Worship* (Cambridge: Cambridge University Press, 1967).

—*Philippians* (Leicester: InterVarsity Press, 1987).

McFague, S., *Metaphorical Theology: Models of God in Religious Language* (London: SCM Press, 1982).

Meeks, W.A., *The First Urban Christians: The Social World of the Apostle Paul* (Newhaven: Yale University Press, 1983).

Meggitt, J., *Economic Relationships in the Pauline Epistles: Poverty and Survival* (PhD dissertation; Cambridge, 1995).

Mendelsohn, I., 'The Conditional Sale into Slavery of Free-born Daughters in Nuzi, and the Law of Exodus 21:7-11', *AJOS* 55 (1935), pp. 190-95.

—*Slavery in the Ancient Near East: A Comparative Study of Slavery in Babylonian Assyria and Palestine from the Middle of the Third Millennium to the End of the First Millennium* (New York: Oxford University Press, 1949).

Miller, F.D., *Nature, Justice and Rights in Aristotle's Politics* (Oxford: Clarendon Press, 1995).

Molland, E., 'A Lost Scrutiny in the Early Baptismal Rite', *StudPat* 5.3 (1962), pp. 104-108.

Monxes, H., 'The Quest for Honor and the Unity of the Community in Romans 12 and the Orations of Dio Chrysostom', in T. Engberg-Pedersen (ed.), *Paul in his Hellenistic Context* (Minneapolis: Fortress Press, 1995), pp. 203-30.

Morris, L., *The Epistle to the Romans* (Leicester: InterVarsity Press, 1988).

Morrow, G.R., 'Plato and Greek Slavery', *Mind* 48 (1939), pp. 186-201.

—*Plato's Law of Slavery in its Relation to Greek Law* (Illinois Studies in Language and Literature; Illinois: University of Illinois Press,1939).

Murray, J., *The Epistle to the Romans* (The New London Commentary on the New Testament; London: Eerdmans, 1967).

Murray, R., 'Recent Studies in Early Symbolic Theology', *HJ* 6 (1965), pp. 412-33.

—*Symbols of Church and Kingdom* (Cambridge: Cambridge University Press, 1975).

Neusner, J., *Ancient Judaism: Debates and Disputes* (Chico, CA: Scholars Press, 1984).

Nicholls, D., *Deity and Domination: Images of God and the State in the Nineteenth and Twentieth Centuries* (London: Routledge & Kegan Paul, 1989).

Nineham, D.E., *The Use and Abuse of the Bible: A Study of the Bible in an Age of Rapid Cultural Change* (London: Macmillan, 1976).

Odeberg, H., *The Fourth Gospel*, part 1 (Stockholm: Uppsala, 1929).

Osiek, C., 'Wealth and Poverty in the Shepherd of Hermas', *StudPat* 17.2 (1982), pp. 725-30.

Oulton, J.E.L., 'Second Century Teaching on Holy Baptism', *Theology* 50 (1947), pp. 86-91.

Patterson, O., 'Slavery', *Annual Review of Sociology* 3 (1977), pp. 407-49.

—*Slavery and Social Death: A Comparative Study* (Harvard: Harvard University Press, 1982).

—*Freedom.* I. *Freedom in the Making of Western Culture* (London: I.B. Tauris & Co., 1991).

Perkins, J., *The Suffering Self: Pain and Narrative Representation in the Early Christian Era* (London: Routledge & Kegan Paul, 1995).

Peterlin, D., *Paul's Letter to the Philippians in the Light of the Disunity of the Church* (Leiden: E.J. Brill, 1995).

Petersen, N.R., *Rediscovering Paul: Philemon and the Sociology of Paul's Narrative World* (Philadelphia: Fortress Press, 1985).

Pharr, C., T.S. Davidson and M.B. Pharr, *The Theodosian Code: And Novels and Sirmondian Constitutions*, I (Princeton, NJ: Princeton University Press, 1952).

Phillips, W.D., Jr, *Slavery from Roman Times to the Early Transatlantic Trade* (Manchester: Manchester University Press, 1985).

Pietri, C., 'Christians and Slaves in the Early Days of the Church', *Concilium* 130 (1977), pp. 31-39.

Pleket, W.K., 'Religious History as the History of Mentality: The "Believer" as Servant of the Deity in the Greek World', in H.S. Versnel (ed.), *Faith, Hope and Worship: Aspects of Religious Mentality in the Ancient World* (Leiden: E.J. Brill, 1981), pp. 152-92.

Plank, K.A., *Paul and the Irony of Affliction* (Atlanta, GA: Scholars Press, 1987).

Porter, S.E., 'Problems in the Language of the Bible: Misunderstandings that Continue to Plague Biblical Interpretation', in S.E. Porter (ed.), *The Nature of Religious Language: A Colloquium* (Roehampton Institute London Papers, 1; Sheffield: Sheffield Academic Press, 1996), pp. 20-46.

Prior, D., *The Message of 1 Corinthians* (Leicester: InterVarsity Press, 1985).

Rabinowitz, J.J., 'Manumission of Slaves in Roman Law and Oriental Law', *JNES* 19 (1960), pp. 42-44.

Raffeiner, H., *Sklaven und Freigelassene: Eine soziologische Studie auf der Grundlage des griechischen Grabepigrams* (Commentationes Aenipontanae, 23; Philologia und Epigraphik, 2; Innsbruck: Wagner, 1977).

Rankin, H.D., *Sophists, Socratics and Cynics* (London: Croon Helm, 1983).

Rawson, B., *Roman Culture and Society* (Oxford: Oxford University Press, 1991).

Reicke, B., *The Disobedient Spirits and Christian Baptism* (Acta Semenarii Neotestamentici Upsaliensis; Copenhagen: Munksgaard, 1946).

Rengstorf, K.H., 'δοῦλος', *TDNT*, II, pp. 261-80.

Richardson, C.C., *The Christianity of Ignatius of Antioch* (New York: Columbia University Press, 1935).

Ricoeur, P., *The Rule of Metaphor* (London: Routledge & Kegan Paul, 1978).

Rikhof, H., *The Concept of Church: A Methodological Inquiry into the Use of Metaphors in Ecclesiology* (London: Sheed & Ward, 1981).

Riley, H.M., *Christian Initiation* (Studies in Christian Antiquity, 17; Washington: Catholic University of America Press, 1974).

Rist, J.M., *Stoic Philosophy* (Cambridge: Cambridge University Press, 1969).

—*Epicurus: An Introduction* (Cambridge: Cambridge University Press, 1972).

—*The Stoics* (Berkeley: University of California Press; London: SPCK, 1978).

Robinson, J.A., *Barnabas, Hermas and the Didache* (London: SPCK, 1920).

Roth, C.P., *St. John Chrysostom: On Wealth and Poverty* (New York: St Vladimir's Seminary, 1984).

Rousseau, P., *Basil of Caeserea* (Berkeley: University of California Press, 1994).

Rupprecht, A.W., 'Attitudes on Slavery among the Church Fathers', in R.N. Longenecker and M.C. Tenney (eds.), *New Dimensions in New Testament Study* (Grand Rapids, MI: Zondervan, 1974) pp. 261-77.

Russell, K.C., 'Slavery as Reality and Metaphor in the Pauline Letters' (PhD dissertation; Rome: Pontifical University of Rome, 1968).

Sandbach, *The Comic Theatres of Greece and Rome* (London: Chatto & Windus, 1977).

Sandmel, S., *Judaism and Christian Beginnings* (New York & Oxford: Oxford University Press, 1978).

Sass, G., 'Zur Bedeutung von δοῦλος bei Paulus', *ZNW* 40 (1941), pp. 24-32.

Schlaifer, R., 'Greek Theories of Slavery from Homer to Aristotle', in M.I. Finley (ed.), *Slavery in Classical Antiquity: Views and Controversies* (Cambridge: W. Heffer & Sons, 1960).

Schnackenburg, R., *The Gospel According to St John*, II (trans. C. Hastings; London: Burns & Oates, 1980).

Schoedel, W.R., *Ignatius of Antioch: A Commentary on the Letters of Ignatius of Antioch* (Philadelphia: Fortress Press, 1985).

Schütz, J.H., *Paul and the Anatomy of Apostolic Authority* (SNTSMS, 26; Cambridge: Cambridge University Press, 1975).

Shaw, G., *The Cost of Authority: Manipulation and Freedom in the New Testament*, (Philadelphia: SCM Press, 1983).

Sherwin-White, A.A., *Roman Society and Roman Law in the New Testament* (Oxford: Clarendon Press, 1963).

Singer, I. (ed.), *The Jewish Encyclopedia* (London: Funk & Wagnall, 1944).

Smith, N.D., 'Aristotle's Theory of Natural Slavery' in D. Keyt and F. D.Millar (eds.), *A Companion to Aristotle's Politics* (Oxford: Basil Blackwell, 1991), pp. 142-55.

Sokolowski, F., 'The Real Meaning of Sacral Manumission', *HTR* 47 (1954), pp. 173-81.

Soskice, J.M., *Metaphor and Religious Language* (Oxford: Clarendon Press, 1985).

Spence-Jones, H.D.H., *The Early Christians in Rome* (London: Methuen, 1910).

Stambaugh, J.E., and D.C. Balch, *The New Testament in its Social Environment* (Philadelphia: Fortress Press, 1986).

Stanley, D.M., 'The Theme of the Servant of Yahweh in Primitive Christian Soteriology and its Transposition by St Paul', *CBQ* 16 (1954), pp. 385-425.

Ste Croix, G.E.M. de, 'Early Christian Attitudes towards Property and Slavery', *Studies in Church History* 12 (1975), pp. 1-38.

—*The Class Struggle in the Ancient Greek World* (London: Gerald Duckworth, 1981).

—'Slavery and Other Forms of Unfree Labour', in L.J. Archer (ed.), *Slavery and Other Forms of Unfree Labour* (New York & London: Routledge & Kegan Paul, 1988).

Stevenson, J. (ed.), *Creeds, Councils and Controversies: Documents Illustrative of the History of the Church AD 337–461* (rev. with additional documents by W.H.C. Frend; London: SPCK, 1976).

Teja, R., 'San Basilio y la esclavitud: Teoria y praxis', in P.J. Fedwick (ed.), *Basil of Caesarea: Christian, Humanist, Ascetic* (Toronto: Pontifical Institute of Medieval Studies, 1981), pp. 393-403.

Theissen, G., *The Social Setting of Pauline Christianity* (ed. and trans. J. H. Schutz; Edinburgh: T. & T. Clark, 1982).

—*Social Reality and Early Christians: Theology, Ethics and the World of the New Testament* (trans. M. Kohl; Minneapolis: Fortress Press, 1992).

Toru, Y., and D. Masaoki (eds.), *Forms of Control and Subordination in Antiquity* (The Society for Studies on Resistance Movements in Antiquity; Leiden: E.J. Brill, 1988).

Tredennick, H., *The Last Days of Socrates* (Harmondsworth: Penguin Books, 1969).

Troeltsch, E. *The Social Teaching of the Christian Church* (trans. O. Wyon; London: Allen & Unwin, 1931).

Trümmer, P., 'Die Chance der Freiheit: Zur Interpretation des mallon Chresthai in 1 Kor 7.21', *Bib* 56 (1975), pp. 344-68.

Vogt, J. (ed.), *Ancient Slavery and the Ideal of Man* (trans. T. Wiedemann; Oxford: Basil Blackwell, 1974).

—*Bibliographie Zur Antiken Sklaverei* (Akademie der Wissenschaften und der Literatur, Mainz; Bochum: N. Brockmeyer, 1971).

Wainwright, G., *Christian Initiation* (London: Lutterworth Press, 1969).

Wallon, H., *Histoire de l'esclavage dans l'antiquité* (3 vols.; Hachette, 2nd edn, 1847).

Wand, J.W.C.; *A History of the Early Church to AD 500* (London: Routledge & Kegan Paul, 1963).

Ward, K., Review of *Metaphor and Religious Language* (Oxford: Clarendon Press, 1985) by J.M. Soskice, in *KTR* 10.1 (1987), pp. 34-35.

Warns, J., *Baptism : Studies in the Original Christian Baptism, its History and Conflicts, its Relation to a State or National Church, and its Significance for the Present Time* (trans. G.H. Lang; London: Paternoster Press, 1957).

Watson, A., *Roman Slave Law* (Baltimore: The Johns Hopkins University Press, 1987).

Watson, D.F., '1 Corinthians 10:23–11:1 in the Light of Graeco-Roman Rhetoric: The Role of Rhetorical Questions', *JBL* 108 (1989), pp. 301-18.

Weaver, P.R.C., *Familia Caesaris: A Social Study of the Emperor's Freedmen and Slaves* (Cambridge: Cambridge University Press, 1972).

—'Social Mobility in the Early Roman Empire: The Evidence of Imperial Freedman and Slaves', in M.I. Finley (ed.), *Studies in Ancient Society* (London: Routledge & Kegan Paul, 1974), pp. 121-40.

Weber, C.W., *Sklaverei im Altertum* (Düsseldorf: Econ, 1981).

Weiss, J., *Earliest Christianity: A History of the Period AD 30–150* (trans. F.C. Grant, *et al.*; New York: Harper, 1959).

Weiss, M., *The Bible from Within: The Method of Total Interpretation* (Jerusalem: Magnes Press, 1984).

Wells, C.B., 'Manumission and Adoption', *RIDA* (1949), pp. 507-20.

Westermann, W.L., 'Enslaved Persons who are Free', *AJP* 59 (1938) pp. 1-30.

—'The Freedmen and the Slaves of God', *Proceedings of the American Philosophical Society* 92 (1948), pp. 55-64.

—'The Paramone as General Service Contract', *JJP* 2 (1948), pp. 9-50.

—'Slavery and the Elements of Freedom in Ancient Greece', in M.I. Finley (ed.), *Slavery in Classical Antiquity: Views and Controversies* (Cambridge: W. Heffer & Sons, 1960), pp. 1-32.

—*The Slave Systems in Greek and Roman Antiquity* (Memoirs of the American Philosophical Society, 40; Philadelphia: American Philosophical Society, 1955).

Werblowsky, R.J.Z., 'On the Baptismal Rite According to St. Hippolytus', *StudPat* 2 (1957), pp. 93-105.

Wheelwright, P., 'The Semantic Approach to Myth', in T.A. Sebeok (ed.) *Myth: A Symposium* (Bloomington, IN: Indiana University Press, 1965).

White, R.E.O., *The Biblical Doctrine of Initiation* (London: Hodder & Stoughton, 1960).

Widdicombe, P., *The Fatherhood of God from Origen to Athanasius* (Oxford: Clarendon Press, 1994).

Wiedemann, T., *Greek and Roman Slavery* (London: Routledge & Kegan Paul, 1994).

Wiles, M.F., *The Divine Apostle: The Interpretation of St Paul's Epistles to the Early Church* (Cambridge: Cambridge University Press, 1967).

Williams, R., 'Pearls before Swine', review of *The Social Structure of Early Christian Communities* by D.J. Kyrtatas, in *The New Statesman,* 13 November 1987, p. 28.

Williams, R. (ed.), *The Making of Orthodoxy: Essays in Honour of Henry Chadwick* (Cambridge: Cambridge University Press, 1989).

Wood, E.M., and N. Wood, *Class Ideology and Ancient Political Theory: Socrates, Plato and Aristotle in Social Context* (Oxford: Basil Blackwell, 1978).

Yarnold, E., *The Awe Inspiring Rite of Initiation* (Slough: St Paul Publications, 1971).

Young, F., *From Nicaea to Chalcedon: A Guide to the Literature and the Background* (London: SCM Press, 1983).

—'The God of the Greeks and the Nature of Religious Language', in W.R. Schoedel and R. Wilken (eds.), *Early Christian Literature and the Classical Intellectual Tradition: In Honorem R. Grant* (Berkeley: Yale University Press, 1985).

—'The Rhetorical Schools and their Influence on Patristic Exegesis', in R. Williams (ed.), *The Making of Orthodoxy: Essays in Honour of Henry Chadwick* (Cambridge: Cambridge University Press, 1989), pp. 182-99.

Ysebaert, J., *Greek Baptismal Terminology: Its Origins and Early Development* (Graecitas Christianorum Primaeva, 1; Nijmegen, 1962).

Yuge, T., and M. Doi, *Forms of Control and Subordination in Antiquity* (Leiden: E.J. Brill, 1988).

Zeitlin, S., 'Slavery During the Second Commonwealth and the Tannaitic Period', in *Solomon Zeitlin's Studies in the Early History of Judaism. IV. History of Early Talmudic Law* (New York: Ktav, 1978), pp. 225-58.

INDEXES

INDEX OF REFERENCES

OLD TESTAMENT

NEW TESTAMENT

CLASSICAL AUTHORS

CHRISTIAN AUTHORS

OTHER ANCIENT REFERENCES

INDEX OF AUTHORS

JOURNAL FOR THE STUDY OF THE NEW TESTAMENT
SUPPLEMENT SERIES